Sailing Elysium

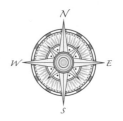

HELEN OLSON

Slater Creek Publishing
Florissant, Colorado 80816

Library of Congress Control Number: 2008901246

ISBN 978-0-615-19198-0

Printed in the United States of America

Cover and book design by Karen Dunne

*To all those people that sailed the oceans before us
and left inspiring words that led us to follow.*

Elysium is as far as to
The very nearest room,
If in that room a friend await
Felicity or doom.

What fortitude the soul contains,
That it can so endure
The accent of a coming foot,
The opening of a door!

– Emily Dickinson

Contents

Acknowledgments

Both Elmer and I are deeply grateful to Seinne Hemming for all of her diligent work editing and helping through the entire writing of the book. Other friends have read the manuscript and given their time to refine and correct the errors in the writing. Without their help I could not have accomplished a credible account of our experiences. We are grateful for their reorganization and gentle trimming of my ramblings. Without this dynamic editing, we would have been unable to produce a viable manuscript.

My husband Elmer collaborated with every word that was written. As I sat at the computer completely lost for words he always had the perfect phrase or description for me to use. He was very involved in the writing of the book; in fact, it was his deepest wish and only with his encouragement that it was written.

It is our wish that our experiences are helpful and insightful to the reader. We encourage any person looking for adventures to follow their dreams and find their joy.

Introduction

My husband, Elmer, and I spent six years building *Elysium*, each devoting time to the chores that needed to be accomplished for a successful voyage. When Elmer needed to work on the boat, our office manager, Lois, and I kept things going. Each of the men and women that worked for us were interested in the building of *Elysium* and did their part to make the completion possible. They took the responsibility of caring for the equipment and kept the business running knowing that Elmer was available when he was needed.

When we first started all of our evenings and weekends were spent working on the boat. When we were near completion, Elmer worked full-time to finish building *Elysium*. The men and women who worked for us were very competent and each person performed their job with knowledge and dedication. It took commitment to the vision we had of retiring and sailing the South Pacific to motivate us when things became difficult. We were able to sell our business after twelve years of ownership and retire when Elmer was forty-nine and I was forty-seven. Our plan was to live as inexpensively as possible and to save the equity in the business while living on the interest. Our accountant, Dean Janney, managed our affairs and sent us money in whatever country we were residing. We were also fortunate to meet our stockbroker, William Blount, who invested our income and kept us afloat. With these fine people supporting our needs, we were able to continue for ten years, visiting every place we had planned to see, twenty-five countries in all.

When we left Oregon we were uncertain about the length of our trip, but everything seemed to support our venture. We were able to sail *Elysium* for ten years and fulfill our desire to explore the various cultures in that part of the world.

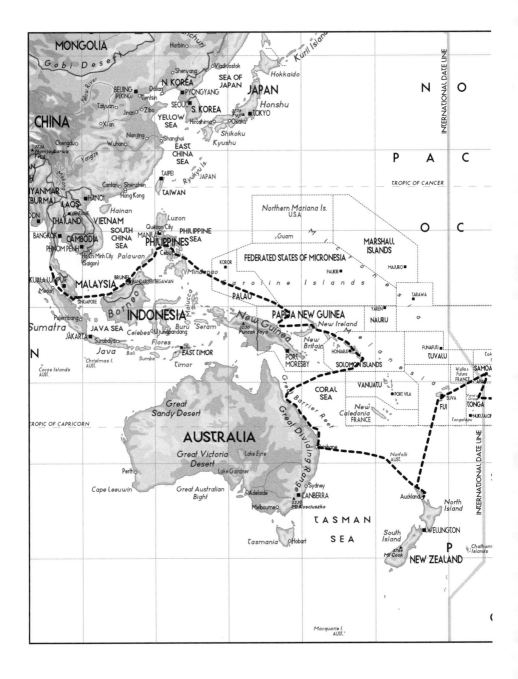

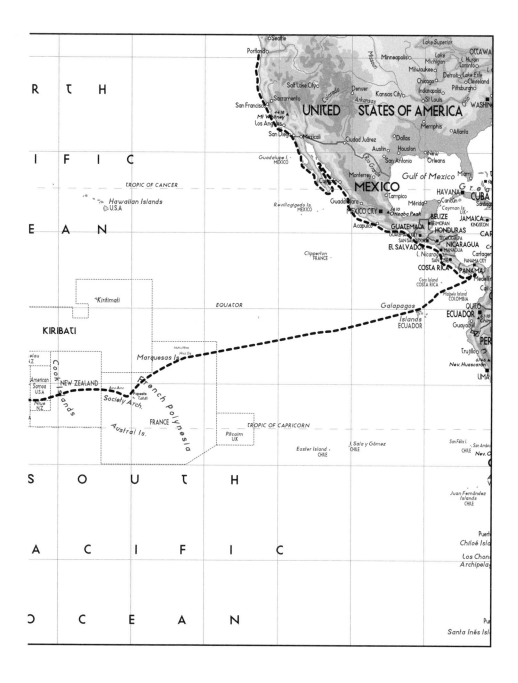

The Storm

Lord, my boat is so small, and the sea is so large.

– unknown

DAWN'S FIRST LIGHT peered through the angry-looking gray clouds and illuminated a menacing, dark, rusty-red sky. The extraordinary sunrise reminded us of the old adage "Red skies in the morning sailors take warning, red skies at night sailors delight," and this sky was definitely indicative of unsettled weather. Uneasily, we began the day aboard our yacht *Elysium* as it lay at anchor in Neiafu, Tonga. Elmer and I had sailed to this small island in the South Pacific several months before and were anchored off of the only small town in the Vava'u Group of the Tongan islands. Vava'u is the northern island of the island group and is situated north of New Zealand and west of the islands of Fiji. We had chosen to stop at this well-protected anchorage, a beautiful bay offering excellent shelter from wind and storms. People came from all over the world, chartering yachts to sail around the lush green landforms lined with coral reefs, and to dive in the crystal-clear water.

Later in the day, the weather was still making us nervous so we tuned in our radio to find a weather report for the South Pacific. Sixty knots of wind was forecast for the area. Sixty knots of wind! A hurricane could be coming! Despite the troubling forecast, we were comforted by the fact that we were in a safe anchorage. Tonga had not experienced a hurricane for twenty-one years, and life seemed to be continuing as normal on the small island. We noticed that several of the forty-to-fifty foot yachts that were anchored in the moorage were still bobbing around, and the people who had chartered them were sitting on deck enjoying their afternoon cocktails. We also saw the small Tongan fishing boats tied up inside the bay, suggesting to us that the local people, with their innate knowledge of the sea and its moods, were not concerned about the weather. Elmer and I believed that the locals would be the first to know about any impending danger and would have pulled their boats onshore for preparation.

Although most of our neighbors seemed to be unconcerned, Elmer and I were feeling very uneasy. We decided the boat would be more secure if we set out additional anchors. More anchors would provide greater holding power in case the wind did approach or exceed the forecast speed. In the back of my mind I had wondered how I would react if we were ever faced with a hurricane. How would I handle the extreme danger? Could I react adequately to the things that might be required of me? Or would I be paralyzed with fear?

Inside the one-mile wide bay there were sixteen visiting yachts at anchor. They were yachts running in lengths from thirty-two to seventy feet and had sailed here from various ports all over the world. We loaded two more anchors into the dingy and rowed out to set them in what we felt would be strategic areas to help us hold *Elysium* in a strong wind. While we were struggling with the anchors a large sailboat from Germany, anticipating a problem, began changing position in the bay. The owner and skipper of the fifty-eight foot sailing yacht, *Eisetta*, had also heard the weather forecast and was tying his stern to shore and setting out two anchors from the bow of the boat into the bay. Elmer and I realized that his choice of anchoring would put him directly in the lee of the wind. He had positioned himself so the full force of the wind would blow on the broadside of his yacht, a potentially dangerous situation.

As the wind increased throughout the day, the sea grew more and more agitated. There was an unusual roughness troubling it even though the wind was only blowing about thirty knots. We noticed that the relaxed mood in the bay was quickly changing to one of concern, as weather conditions grew more menacing. Skippers pulled up their anchors, and boats returning after a day of racing at sea all searched for a safe anchorage with more protection in case a hurricane did materialize. Afternoon faded and darkness brought progressively stronger winds. We watched our wind speed gauge rise. At forty knots, the anchorage began to feel rough and uncomfortable. At sixty knots, the wind was snatching the sea up into scary, sloppy chops and violently tossing the boat around. We watched with increasing apprehension as the needle of our wind-speed gauge indicated that the wind speeds had reached sixty-three knots. The sea was fierce, the waves were frighteningly large, and *Elysium* was tugging hard at her anchors. We were acutely aware of the danger we faced.

At sixty-three knots, the wind screamed furiously through the rigging and, impossibly, even seemed to be escalating. The night was pitch-black and all we could see out in the bay were the mast lights from other boats around us. I carefully made my way down to the cockpit below to look at the barometer. With my flashlight shining on the barometer, I saw to my dismay that it was down to nearly twenty-eight millabars. As I watched the needle, it visibly moved downward, a foreboding sight I had never before witnessed. I realized with horror that the worst was yet to come.

We turned on the VHF radio and to listen in on the conversation between the people aboard some of the other yachts. An inexperienced eighteen-year-old boy called from his father's yacht, *Leeway*. His desperate, young voice cried out to anyone who might be listening, "I'm all alone. I don't know what to do."

Red Hawk's skipper, Phil, replied calmly, reassuring the terrified boy, "These are some very heavy winds. Just hold on the best you can and you'll come through this all right." Phil was a paid skipper with lots of experience, and I think we all felt somewhat reassured by his calm, quiet voice.

The wind was still increasing with an alarming speed. We could see the mast lights moving around in the bay, indicating that several yachts were dragging anchor. This was a threatening and disquieting sight. *Eisetta*, the repositioned German yacht, was struggling against the full force of the wind right on her beam. We watched, horrified and fascinated, as the brightly lit yacht dragged anchor past the stern of *Elysium*, like a bizarre carnival appearing in the dark night. *Eisetta* was so close we could easily see into the boat where Wolfgang, the skipper, was standing helplessly at the wheel. Then, with the extremely strong force of the wind pushing her along, *Eisetta* heaved and shuddered as it rammed up onto a coral bank and lay over very close to where we were riding out the storm.

The radio came to life again with the young man from *Leeway* yelling frantically, "I'm dragging. I can't hold her into the wind. I'm using all my motor power and I don't know what to do." Elmer and I listened helplessly as he continued, "It's so dark out here. I can't see anything and I have no idea where I am." Suddenly he was silent. We held our breaths through the ominous silence waiting to hear more. We called to him several times and received no reply. I checked our wind gauge and realized, to my horror, that the winds were raging at ninety knots, or maybe more, for that was the highest wind speed our gauge could record. We finally heard the weak and shaky voice of the boy calling over the radio from *Leeway*. "The wind smashed the boat onto the bulkhead in town. Water's coming in fast so I'm going to jump for it while I can…good luck everybody." Appalled, I jumped down the companionway ladder into the pilothouse for another look at the barometer. My stomach turned over with a nauseous feeling as I watched the needle ominously moving down, indicating even lower pressure. It was a sight I knew was possible only in the height of an extremely strong hurricane.

We received more panicked radio transmissions from our friends, calling out frantically saying that their boats were being smashed against the shore. Will and Judy on *Adagio* called to say they had heard a terrible smash against the hull of their fiberglass boat and they were now sinking. Judy was six months pregnant, so Will tied a mattress and a float around her and waited for their home to sink into the inky-black swirl of ocean below.

I made my way on up on deck where Elmer had the motor going full throttle, trying desperately to ease the surge of the wave on the anchor. Using all of our horsepower to keep *Elysium* steady, Elmer valiantly struggled against the wind. The screeching wind made it nearly impossible to hear anything else, but I yelled into Elmer's ear that I had seen the barometer needle visibly moving lower. The radio was eerily silent as everyone wrestled with their tillers, hoping just to hold on to their anchorage until the storm might subside. Helplessly, I prayed.

Suddenly we heard a terrible crashing sound from below. I scaled the ladder into our main cabin just in time to see the rudderpost slashing through the stern of the boat. I ran into the back of the cabin and grabbed my guitar just as the rudderpost came crashing through the second time, mutilating the entire stern area. Water spewed up through the hole like a geyser, soaking the walls and the bookshelves on both sides of the stern cabin. Elmer had come down behind me and grabbed my arm. "Come on! We have to let the anchors go or we'll sink here in this deep water!" Elmer yelled as he bolted back up the ladder.

Once we reached the deck we crawled on our bellies toward the anchor windless. A giant, ten-foot wave raced across the one-mile fetch between the shore and where we were anchored. The trough of the wave brought the rudder down and slammed it with terrific force onto a big coral head. One of the charter yachts had dragged by and released the anchor that was holding us off shore. Their rudder caught the marker buoy that we had attached to the anchor line. I was shouting at Elmer, but the ear-splitting sound of the wind prevented Elmer from hearing me until my lips touched his ear. We released the other two anchors to prevent her from sinking. In the time it took for us to draw our breath, *Elysium* was high up on the coral beach laying full over on her side. Everything aboard *Elysium* was askew and eerily still.

After enduring the endless, enormous waves for so many hours, we actually felt an immense relief to finally be motionless. We stumbled and slid down the slanted deck, exhausted. The crooked, slippery ladder to the cabin was difficult to maneuver and when we finally reached the bottom, we found the entire starboard side of the boat soaked with seawater. Our bunk was heavily slanted, but dry, so we climbed in and slid down against the wall. We must have looked like acrobats in a fun house climbing into our crooked bunk, but we didn't care. We were just relieved to be alive and on solid ground.

The wind continued to screech above, but we could finally relax and sleep until the storm ceased. Just as we were sleeping peacefully, we heard a terrible bang, then an awful crunch and then a repeated smashing noise that made the whole boat shudder. Whatever was making the sound was pounding *Elysium* on her port side. As if that was not trouble enough, we smelled gas! Our propane tanks were on the port side, and because we had been cooking when the storm started, the propane valve had been left turned on. We knew there was a danger of a devastating explosion if the propane leaked and a spark occurred. Each time we were pounded, the danger increased.

We both leaped out of the bunk, leaving our warm, secure place, and struggled up the slanted ladder onto the deck. We could barely make out a broken mast that was wrapped around our stanchion. The broken mast was slamming across the deck with each heave of the sea and a large yacht was crashing rhythmically against *Elysium's* hull. We turned on our flashlights and in the eerie light of the heavy rain, we could just make out the shadowy forms of a man and woman standing near the side of their now wrecked yacht. The big hulk rose and fell as it crunched and splintered against *Elysium's* side. We were making our way over to where they were standing when the woman tried to jump onboard. Instead she disappeared into the yawning crack between the two yachts and down into the dark black cavern of the sea beneath the hull of the boat. The man jumped aboard *Elysium* still yelling to his wife down in the surf. He was screaming as he ran across the deck to the down side of *Elysium*. "Do something. My wife's down there," he yelled at Elmer.

Elmer jumped ashore and ran down into the water below where the boats were still crashing together. Even with a powerful flashlight my eyes strained to follow his path down into the dark, ferocious water. It seemed like an eternity before I could make out his form emerging from the turmoil. Elmer was barely visible through the rain and foaming surf along the shoreline beside the boat. I could see that he was half carrying and half dragging the woman up out of the water. He gently laid her down on a flat space behind a tree area and I could see him heaving a sigh of relief. It was a miracle that he had avoided being caught between the rolling boats. I was so relieved to see him safely on shore with the woman that it took a bit of time for me to come to my senses and rush over to help. The woman was moaning and in tremendous pain. She had taken a crushing blow to her pelvic area when she fell between the boats.

We had brought morphine in our medical kits, so I climbed back up into the boat and made my way along the steep corridor to the back head where it was kept. I also grabbed our blood-pressure gauge in case we had to determine if her blood pressure was sufficient for the use of morphine. Once back at her side I took her blood-pressure and found it to be extremely low, an unsafe situation in which to administer morphine. We had to get her to a more stable place. Her position on the uphill side of the tree kept her from rolling downhill, so we felt she would be safe there with her husband while we went to find help.

The bank above us was very steep, covered with slippery, wet mud and tangled roots and brush. Snarled roots and vines gave a bit of a foothold, though many had washed loose in the terrific downpour of rain that came with the hurricane. We searched for good footing on the steep incline wondering the best way to bring the woman up this slope to a safer place. I couldn't imagine having to scale the mud slide cascading down the embankment with a hurt woman in tow. At the last moment I thought of our valuables on the boat and I rushed back and grabbed my address book, one thousand five hundred dollars in American money and our passports. Elmer had made a dry-bag of thick yellow plastic with a Velcro closure to use when we needed to keep anything completely dry. I shoved the articles inside and rolled it up securely. Then I hurried back to where Elmer was waiting for me.

I clutched the bag in one hand and we started up the very steep and dark jungle-filled embankment. We climbed along side our mast, now resting against the brush and to our relief we found it was in one piece, undamaged. Getting up the slippery, wet jungle slope was frustratingly slow. Our thongs were immediately sucked off of our feet into the thick, slick mud. Now with no shoes, we were even more cautious about finding secure footholds. We climbed about seventy-five feet and it seemed to take forever for us to get to the top. Although I fell many times, I was able to hold onto our important yellow bag with an iron grip.

When we got to the top of the bank we found chaos. Corrugated roofing was slicing the air above our heads and electrical wires lassoed menacingly at us. Palm fronds flew past our heads like missiles making a loud swishing sound. We stumbled up to the first little native house that we found across the road. We pounded on the door and they immediately opened it, pulling us inside so that I hardly knew what was happening. The Tongan lady took the yellow bag out of my hand and told us to come in and sit down. Breathlessly, we told them about the terrible accident and the woman at the bottom of the bank who needed help. In Tonga, English is not the primary language so we used some Tongan words and sign language to tell them about the accident and the woman who was injured. We pleaded with them to go with us out into the storm to help bring the injured woman back up to the top of the bank. They listened to us as things crashed loudly into their little house. "No, no cannot go out," they said over and over again. We told them that we had to go; they sighed and gave us their thongs to put on our bare, muddy feet. When they opened the door again we jumped out quickly so their door would not be torn from its hinges. I remember very well the look on their faces when we left, "They will not make it," they thought.

Pushing against the strong rain and wind we set out for the building housing the yacht-charter headquarters. The couple that had crashed into our boat had chartered their yacht from Don and Robin, who owned the chartering business. When we reached the building, we found Robert, the young man from *Leeway*, and a very strong Tongan man named Paul, huddled inside with Don. We told them that the woman from their chartered yacht had been injured between our boat and their leased yacht. We asked all of them to come out and help us. Don immediately said that he could not go with us because he had twisted his knee. We told them we had to have help or the woman might die from her injuries. We pleaded, "If you would come with us you can stay at the top; just release the rope for us so we can go back down to the place where she is lying."

Elmer rummaged around in the building for something to wrap the woman in that could be used to haul her up the bank. He found a large sail bag and some oars to use as a stretcher. There was also a very large coil of rope, which could be used to pull her up through the jungle to the top of the bank. With this equipment and the three men to lend their hands, we went to Don's house to fetch his wife Robin who was a nurse. We needed all the assistance we could find.

Together with our crew, we went back to the area where our boat was aground on the coral reef. Don stayed on top and I stayed a quarter of the way down the bank. Robin went half way down and Paul, three quarters of the way. Robert went with Elmer to help place the woman in the sail bag stretcher. They enclosed her with the bag and protective padding and tied the rope around her using oars inside the bag to maintain the shape of the stretcher. With our passenger wrapped up like a papoose and securely bound, we were all prepared to help. Elmer shouted up along the line of people, station to station, to start pulling. The relay of voices came up to us and we started pulling as hard as we could. Our shouts were carried away by the overpowering voice of the hurricane so it was almost impossible to hear each other. We would finally hear, "PULL," and we all would relay that to the top. By the time we were all pulling the bundle would become ensnared in the jungle vines and we would hear, "STOP". With the stop and go, backing up and going forward, we laboriously raised her to the top. It took almost an hour before we were all finally able to fight our way to the top of the bank.

On the road, we decided to carry our precious bundle to Robin's house about a half a mile away. We carried the injured woman by holding onto the oars of our makeshift structure but the slippery material made it difficult to maintain a grip. We had to set the large woman down on the ground while we rested. Each time we laid her down it caused her a great deal of pain, and she would moan, but at least we knew that she was still alive and conscious! It was a tremendous relief to finally see Robin and Don's house and it gave us strength to move faster so we could find a place safe for all of us to shelter away from the fierce storm and flying debris. When we entered the house we were surprised to find that most of the roof had blown off. To our relief there was a small portion left that offered shelter. After relegating the responsibility to Robin, Elmer and I crawled over to the sidewall and curled up together. We were exhausted and shaking all over, feeling the weight of the danger and pressure we had experienced together. We wrapped up in each other's arms and stayed there until daylight. By daylight the storm was beginning to subside.

Elmer and I were preoccupied with thoughts of our *Elysium*. I just sobbed, "I know she is gone. What will we do now?" If salvage was necessary, anything that was not ruined could be packed up and sent back to the United States. All of our plans and the time spent building and preparing for the trip came into our minds. It was extremely hard to believe that it was all over and we had not even visited Australia. Our experience of three years of sailing nine thousand miles seemed like an anticlimax. We were just becoming seasoned sailors and this was only a portion of what we expected to accomplish.

Building *Elysium*

You do not have to know where you are going
as long as you are on your way.
— unknown

ELMER AND I had both planned to sail beyond the confines of the Oregon coast one day, to visit the island shores and continents of the Pacific Islands. Each of us had experienced the joy of sailing small boats during our youth. Elmer had grown up in the small town of Spirit Lake in northern Idaho. When he was out on the lake as a small boy he would tie a sheet up onto his small raft and wait for the wind to push him along over the water. My summer days were spent on Laurel Lake near the Oregon coast, where we had a summer cabin. George Chaney, our next-door neighbor at Laurel Lake, was a real sailing enthusiast. His hobby was building and sailing small boats, which I was free to use. There was always an afternoon wind because Laurel Lake was only a mile in from the coast. This made our sailing experiences wild and reckless. George loved to take ladies out sailing knowing that the wind would come and give them a terrifying ride. Many times they were swimming as he brought the boat in.

Elmer built a beautiful fifteen-foot sailboat for us, painted bright red.

Every summer, with anticipation, *Little Red* traveled to Laurel Lake for our vacation. One vacation she was pulled all the way to Spirit Lake in Idaho where Elmer had grown up. This was a very different sailing experience for me, as the lake was much larger and the winds less dependable. We spent several hours adrift with no wind. Elmer pointed out the landmarks that he remembered from his childhood. These wonderful vacations were spent with our children, reliving our experiences and imparting the love of sailing to them.

As we hiked along the waters edge the horizon beckoned to us. It was time to begin our building project. The maritime docks were interesting, with the smells of the salt soaked fishing boats and the beauty of the sailboats bobbing lazily in the water. To decide on our cruising vision, we interviewed many sailboat owners and gathered very valuable information.

We owned a small business of our own, building pre-cast concrete products. I had resigned from my job as a high school teacher to join Elmer in this new venture. There was no money in our budget to buy a sailboat, but the dream was now a force to be followed. All of our energy that was not used to build our new business was focused on our vision of sailing.

Elmer was an excellent carpenter and was able build anything, from fine furniture to custom-built homes, so we searched for an affordable sailboat hull we could build ourselves. As we searched, one of our cement salesmen told us that there was an interesting concept of building sailboats from concrete! It was called the Ferro-cement process (steel and concrete). As we thought back, we remembered seeing a barge that had been made from concrete used during the First World War, still being used in New Jersey at Cape May as a part of a jetty. It looked to be in very good shape, still strong after so many years. Warren persevered and found some books that displayed beautiful boat plans built from the Ferro-cement concept.

He knew of a Ferro-cement fishing boat being built on the Oregon coast and invited us to go with him to see it. "Just come with me to look at this boat and don't expect too much in the way of beauty," he said. The builder had chosen to build a very large fishing boat, working when he had time to spare. The giant hulk had the wirework done and was being plastered when he was able to find some spare time. It was definitely not beautiful. The boat was thick and rough, with the big lumps that were cold joints showing where he had plastered a bit; let it set, and started plastering again. This big monster, which he called the *Endurance*, became a strong and able boat. We saw it many years later still handling the very heavy work of fishing off the Oregon coast.

We learned of a group of engineers building Ferro-cement boats in Seattle. They had been laid off from Boeing during a slump and shared our vision of sailing the seas, each in his own boat. Here we observed both ways of building concrete boats. The abilities and temperaments of builders also were obvious in the amount of work they chose to do to build their hull. The builders that wanted to do the job quickly and without a lot of work were forming the steel rod and mesh on an inverted wooden frame and stapling it on. The builders using the longer and more difficult method that required more skill and patience were building theirs upright. This method was a freestanding form without a mold. They had to bend half-inch water pipe to shape and form the hull and further attach the quarter-inch reinforcing rod, and tie the wire mesh inside and outside. This method was tedious and extremely time consuming.

This carnival of boat building became the place to visit when we had any bit of spare time. Watching each wire sculpture manifest into a sailing hull was a wonder to us and we decided that this was a viable process to investigate. The Ferro process would be an inexpensive way to start our building process and would only require labor and spare time, which we had. We were finding more and more information about Ferro-cement boats. A book published in New Zealand was filled with pictures of racing sailboats made from concrete. They had names like "*Slippery Sidewalk*" and "*Rocky Racer*" reflecting the building product as one of speed and versatility.

After several months of deliberation, buying the plans and choosing the right configuration and space made us feel we had begun our project. We chose a fifty foot ketch rigged plan designed by a marine architect named Cecil Norris from British Columbia, Canada. He had brought this concept of Ferro-cement from New Zealand.

Every spare minute was spent visualizing our yacht sailing the Pacific Ocean. We could feel how it would be to sleep, cook and eat aboard. We decided how many bunks we would have and where the storage would be. This was an escape for us from our everyday mundane routine at the business and it was very satisfying.

Wire and woven mesh in place

Once we bought the plans, we had to find the right materials to start our project. Elmer decided on the upright method. Building indoors allowed us to work in any kind of weather. The next step was to construct a building in which to house our yacht. We located the space next door to our manufacturing plant to have it accessible whenever we had any free time to work on it.

After we built the structure, Elmer braced the framework of the hull to the roof trusses of the building, holding it in an upright position.

Then he welded the stations together to make the framework in the shape of the boat. At this point our yacht resembled the skeleton of a giant whale. Now we were ready to begin the tedious job of tying the deformed quarter-inch rebar to this frame. For this we bought a one-ton spool of quarter inch deformed rod for reinforcing steel. To straighten the rod Elmer made a device out of a series of rollers. Then he drilled a hole in the wall of the building.

We would start the wire by pushing it through the hole and then attach it to

Interior wire and stations

the pick up truck outside. I would then drive ahead to straighten the rod. We had a dog at the plant named Ramona. She loved to go for a ride in the pick up so she would eagerly jump in every time I took off. When I only went a short distance her ears and tail would droop as she realized it was the end of the trip.

After straightening about one hundred yards of the rod, Elmer cut it to the exact length of the boat and welded at each end of the framework. The rods were tied to each station two-inches apart horizontally. He continued this system up each side of the hull until he reached the top. The vertical rods were placed four inches apart and hand tied at each intersection. Elmer then attached seven layers of one-inch woven-mesh on the inside that were compressed and hand tied again. Working on the outside he put three layers of half-inch welded mesh, which he compressed, and hand tied together. For all of these jobs Elmer made hundreds of tie wire hairpin shaped pieces. We could occasionally implore some of the family to push the hairpin-like ends through to the inside where Elmer could twist and tighten them against the reinforcing steel. The idea was to stay within a one-inch thickness for the hull of the boat. This makes a very strong, light steel frame, which is then filled with concrete.

Deck with steel enforcing in place

When we finished our day at work, we would eat in the shop lunchroom and then go out to work on the boat. Elmer often said that it was a good thing that the wire tying came at the beginning of the building process, as he would not have had energy to do it at the latter part. His real love and ability is working with wood. While we were tying wire, we visualized the interior. There was a small sawmill in southern Oregon that would custom-saw lumber. We had decided that black walnut was the perfect wood for us to live with. When we visited the mill, we found many recently cut black walnut trees. They were just waiting there for us to perfect our plan for the interior. The mill sawed them into boards and we carefully stacked them inside of our building. They cured slowly for a year and a half with the help of the damp climate of Oregon.

The rod-tying process was finally completed a year and a half after we started. During this time we found the funds to buy each other gifts that would make living aboard a safe and fulfilling experience. We bought a shiny chrome barometer and clock for the pilothouse as Christmas presents for each other. The day we got the compass was the most exciting of all; it showed us all of the directions under a clear magnifying globe. When we set our courses to sail, it would point close to north at all times. Each gift enhanced the vision of our dream.

We took classes in navigation, piloting, and diesel mechanics. We spent hours deciding what charts we would need for the first years of cruising. The book at the chart store filled us with excitement as we decided what ports we would be visiting and what seas we would be crossing. My particular expertise was in nutrition, so it was my job to decide what provisions we would need and where they should be stowed inside the boat. We had heard about boats rolling completely over, so the storage units had to be locked after they were filled to keep everything from spilling out.

Each stage of completion was a celebrated landmark. After the wire tying was complete Elmer spent days and days making certain that the contour was absolutely flawless. The curve on both sides of the hull had to be identical because the sailing hull has to glide along smoothly through the water without any drag. When the wire frame was finished to Elmer's critical satisfaction, it was time to make arrangements for the concrete to be applied.

Hallelujah!! Plastering day arrived, on a Saturday in September, 1973! It had taken a year and a half to get to this point! We hired an experienced contract plasterer and his crew of six men who worked with eight of our crew. Friends and other interested sailors also helped. The entire application of the concrete to the frame of thirteen hundred square feet should be applied in one day without stopping. It was a classic Oregon

Concrete completely cured on hull

day, cool, wet and misty, perfect conditions for applying the material so the concrete would set properly. We set up a plaster's pump under the mixer in our manufacturing plant; the hose from the pump ran over to the inside of the boat. When we pumped the concrete into the boat, the crew that was working in the interior of the hull forced the mortar through the framework with trowels. On the outside, the plasterers smoothed it out with their three foot Darby trowels, moving along like dancers on the scaffolding we had provided for them. They used the impeccably formed wire mesh to shape the hull into a perfectly smooth surface. After eight hours the process was completed and a hungry, tired group of people celebrated the success of the day with food and drink. After the job was completed, we had a keg of beer and a feast.

The next day Elmer rigged soaker hoses that allowed water to run slowly over the entire concrete area, allowing the concrete to cure properly. Over a period of thirty days, the hull dried slowly and perfectly. Not a single hairline crack appeared in any of the thirteen hundred square feet. With the hull completed, the most critical and tedious part of building the boat was finally finished. Elmer then applied a finish of epoxy on the exterior of the hull, giving it a watertight seal. He sanded the entire exterior countless times in order to give it the mirror finish that he required. He was not going to have this yacht look like concrete.

Next, it was time to build the upper cabin frame. Elmer used one-inch square steel tubing framework covered with plywood. After completing the cabin framing we needed to have the entire inside sprayed with polyurethane foam to provide a good noise barrier and insulation. The job of cutting the interior foam back to the bulkheads was very monotonous and time consuming because it all had to be trimmed to shape with a knife and scraper. We covered all of the foam with fiberglass to keep it from out-gassing and to provide us with a smooth interior. To finish the bilge storage areas, we painted them with many coats of epoxy, making them watertight and easy to clean.

Then came the joy of building the interior with the black walnut that we had been curing for a year-and-a-half. We were fortunate at this time to meet someone who had just vacated a wood-finishing plant in Tacoma. We hauled all the black walnut by truck to Tacoma from Clackamas, where our plant was, in order to plane it. As Elmer finished building each area, I applied five coats of varnish and sanded it smoothly between each coat. After this process, I hand rubbed the total surface with steel-wool and hand-waxed it to get a fine furniture finish. We had chosen our walnut extremely well, as many pieces were a beautiful, gnarly, curly grain. When it was finished, my cousin said the interior looked like the finest furniture he had ever seen.

We started the interior woodwork in the stern of the boat. This was our main cabin which was used for cooking, eating and as a social area. At the very back of the boat, Elmer placed three windows so we could look out at the ocean from inside as we sailed. Just inside of these windows was an area that enclosed the hydraulic steering apparatus. Covering this area with wood allowed for a large open surface area with shelving and sliding-door cabinets on each side. Here we spread out a large white cowhide from Argentina. In this space we were to place things like our guitar and baskets full of the local fruit.

Helen in galley

Elmer built bunks on either side of the main cabin above the seating area. In the center of the main cabin, Elmer laminated several pieces of black walnut to make a drop-leaf table where we could comfortably seat eight people. All the surfaces he built had a raised edge to keep anything from sliding onto the floor. We spent hours envisioning what we would need when the water was rough and the boat was tossing around. We used bungee cords on everything we could not lock down.

When we finished the main cabin in the stern, we really felt like we had a home. The galley was just below the stern hatch with a ladder leading up into the pilot area on deck. Elmer used every nook and cranny to build a secure place for everything that we could possibly need. The drawers were very shallow, but we could always get to things when we needed them. He built them that way so when they were closed they dropped down and locked firmly into place, and lifted up to open. We were given a very deep double stainless steel sink with a foot pump that fed water from our tanks below into it. There were bins and cabinets in every available space. He also built special space for plates, cups and other dishes, all of which were held in place with walnut baffles. The stove was stainless steel and gimbled, which allowed it to pivot with the motion of the boat so that the stove top was always horizontal and didn't tilt. There were locking stainless steel rails with clamps to hold the pans down on the burner while it is cooking. The stove also had a big oven for baking. Surrounding the entire interior of the boat at shoulder level, Elmer built grab rails, which we could hold onto when the boat was underway and unstable.

The next area he built was a beautiful head, or bathroom area, with a shower. This head had a chemical toilet that could

View of main cabin

be pumped when we were in port. The storage area had twenty self-locking drawers and several deep bins. Across from the head was the workshop with an oak work-board that had drawers above and below to hold everything that we could possibly need to make repairs. The storage areas behind the drawers on both sides were very large so we fiberglassed and painted them to make storage bins. These bins held things we would need much later in the trip so they were not as accessible.

Up two steps from this bulkhead was the pilothouse that offered a good view to the outside from big windows on the side and front. The idea was that we could steer from down below when the weather made it impossible to be on deck. At the helm we had another compass, wheel and depth sounder. The walnut in this room was exquisite with knurls and strings of all colors running through it. There were two large cabinets that held much of our emergency equipment. On the inside wall were gauges telling us the state of the batteries, oil pressure and a sniffer that went down into the bilge to tell us if there was any propane that had leaked there. Elmer tucked a full bunk and a very comfortable lounge seat on the starboard side. The port side had the desk with my ham radio and a large work area big enough for charts to plot our position. Under this work area Elmer built a huge drawer that held the charts that were needed and the logbook. Next to this he built a chair covered with leather that swung back and forth and locked in place at both ends. I was to spend a good deal of my time in this seat plotting the fixes Elmer would take up on the deck with the sexton and transferring them onto the chart to tell us where we were.

The next area forward of the main cabin held our main bunk. The bed was nearly a double in size. Surrounding the bed Elmer placed rust colored velvet padding to protect us when the boat was rolling. Above the padding the area was finished with walnut paneling, cabinets and a cassette player. On both ends of the bed were drawers containing hundreds of cassettes made for us by our friends. We could lie in bed and enjoy soothing music and listen to inspirational speakers. Below this he built sixteen locking drawers and two big bins. Under the bunk, in the space behind the drawers, was the biggest bin of all. We fiber-glassed the surface of the bin and used it to store all of our scuba gear. We drilled holes in rows under the mattress, because we had read stories of mold accumulating beneath areas where people sleep. I often used an anti-fungal spray to clean the area so that mold would not form. On the wall across from the bunk we covered the whole area with an acrylic mirror. The mirror reflected the incoming light from the two oval port windows, creating a lovely, bright area and making the space seem larger.

Across from the bunk was a beautiful head with many drawers, bins, a shower and a toilet that pumped directly out to sea when we were away from port. Elmer fiber-glassed the area behind the drawers, creating another large storage space. Inside the head, Elmer had curved all of the surfaces so there were no square corners. The curved shower had a black walnut grid that fit over the drain, and we had one oval port above the sink that allowed plenty of light into the room.

The bow cabin consisted of two bunks, two hanging lockers and a seat. Forward of the bunks, in the point of the bow was a large, fiber-glassed sail locker. We encased the entire under-bunk area and the hanging lockers with Tennessee red cedar to prevent infestation and mold. An opening hatch above the bunk area allowed good ventilation, which we knew we would need in the tropical areas.

On the outside of the boat, the toe rail cap was made of black walnut. The cockpit area was enclosed and secured with a beautiful walnut rail encircling it. When a wave washed over the deck, the walnut grid he built kept our feet clear of the water. We had a comfortable rounded seat and a chaise lounge at the upper steering station. Our dear friend Leo, who was an artist at metal work, made all the stainless steel windows and a small stove for us. I took a welding class to make the diesel tanks. Elmer built fifty-two drawers, several bins and surrounds for twenty-five windows, all of which followed the beautiful curve of the hull. The very last thing we installed was our sixty-horse power engine. It was important for us to know that the engine could be removed easily if it was ever necessary. After six years we had practically completed *Elysium*.

While we were building we were searching for a name for our boat. Our daughter, Tori, suggested the name *Elysium*. *Elysium* was the place that the water-people of ancient Greece considered as paradise, a place of pure contentment. As we sat in the main cabin seats, we could visualize the heavenly sights we would soon see through the stern windows.

After six-and-a-half years of hard work, *Elysium* was finally ready to go on a perilous journey to the water. We hired a house mover and obtained a permit to move her on the freeway to Oregon City. A crane would lift her into the water. The policeman who came to check us before the move said, "Just do it and don't tell me about it, and good luck."

The height of *Elysium*, ducking power lines and melding into traffic all made the trip very challenging. There were many stories of crane malfunctions and dropping the boat, the boat taking on water when it was launched or the waterline not being in the right place, but fortunately none of these things happened to our beautiful *Elysium*.

We allowed the crew to be off work that day and we called it a "floating holiday." The Portland newspaper and the Clackamas paper had

Taking Elysium to the water

each printed a story about our trip to the water, so we had a big crowd to watch as we christened and launched *Elysium*. I christened her with a bottle of champagne and she was lifted high into the air by a log crane and placed into the Willamette River. She sat beautifully and perfectly on the water line. We said goodbye to everyone and powered down to our moorage at Parker's marina on Sauvie Island.

The First Sail

*We are changing, we have got to change, and we can no more help it than
leaves can help going yellow and coming loose in autumn.*

– D.H. Lawrence

THROUGHOUT THE TIME that we were building *Elysium*, we were
looking around for the perfect place that would allow "live aboard" in
their moorage. Harold and June Parker's dock in Sauvie Island was the
place. Located on the Multnomah Channel just west of Portland, the
island is at the confluence of the Columbia River, the Willamette River
and the Multnomah Channel. Here, rich loam had been built up over
the centuries by the yearly runoff of the river. Later this was surrounded
with levees built by the Corps of Engineers, making a safe haven for
truck farms that grew all varieties of fruits and vegetables. When we
crossed the bridge to the island we felt we were in another world. We
visited the Parker's and asked to be considered for a slip when we finished *Elysium*. However, before Harold would allow us to be there, he
wanted to be sure that *Elysium* fit into his vision of "beautiful sailboats"
tied up in front of his house. When he saw *Elysium* he told us he would
be very happy to have us in his moorage.

Harold had made his living for many years as a deep-sea diver. One fateful day he experienced a terrible accident. He burned both of his hands on a live electrical cable. He had lost all feeling in his hands, but with the help of several surgeries he learned to hold things in the crevice of his thumb and fingers. He was building the dock slowly, taking his time, but with undaunted perseverance. When we brought *Elysium* into a slip he had no decking on yet so we had to walk on planks to get off of the boat.

Harold, Elmer and I had our visions of the future and we were moving in that direction. When you set your mind to a goal, you can accomplish anything and everything. When we started we had no money to buy a boat, but by building it ourselves we came up with a yacht that would have cost one-hundred fifty-thousand dollars. Even while spending six years building *Elysium*, we were able to run our business and see it grow steadily from three employees to, finally, forty. Although Harold had the funds and the water front property to build his dream, he had to find extraordinary energy and fortitude to build this fifteen-slip moorage. When sailors arrived with their boats and settled down into the tranquility, it gave them a case of what we called, "Parker's Paralysis."

After settling onboard we went back to work. Elmer used his spare time to build wooden masts and booms for *Elysium*. We located clear, vertical grain Sitka spruce out of Canada, the very best wood for masts because of its weight and strength qualities. Elmer built the sixty-foot main mast, the forty-foot mizzenmast and the two booms. They were built by laminating all the pieces of spruce cut to length and glued together into a box shape. The spruce was a beautiful golden color, which was enhanced with three coats of epoxy and three coats Ultra Violet Shield varnish for protection against the sun rays.

All of the electrical wiring, the wiring for the radio antenna and spreader lights, were inside of the mast. On the outside were all the stays that would attach to the chain plates that Elmer had cast into the concrete when we plastered the boat. When we were ready to take the masts to *Elysium* we tied all the wires to the masts and placed them on top of two pick-ups one towing the other. The second pickup had to have a driver steer it because of the length of the masts.

We brought the boat from the marina through to the Columbia River

Our crew moving the masts to Elysium

to a place where there was a crane that was tall enough to set up the masts. Without an over-length permit, we drove the pickup and tow across Portland to a boat yard. The crane lifted each mast and set it in place while the crew we brought attached the stays into the chain plates that stabilized the masts. After it was complete Elmer realized that he had missed putting one of the halyards in the top of the main mast. The crane lifted him up the sixty feet to the top where he swung over to thread the halyard through the sheave on the head of the mast. This was no problem for Elmer as he had been a high climber and rigger in a logging camp when he was younger.

With the masts and stays in place we set off back to the marina. There was a great difference in the feel of the boat with this new weight towering overhead. When we got back to the marina Elmer said, "Helen go to the top of the main mast and take a picture of the deck from up there."

I was torn between being scared of the height and the desire to look down on the boat from the top. This was the first use of our bright yellow boson's chair. Elmer tied an extra halyard to the chair as a safety precaution and then hitched the chair to the main sail halyard and cranked me slowly to the top, like winching up a sail. The view from up there was breathtakingly beautiful but scary. Little did I know I would make this trip up the mast later on under much more harrowing circumstances.

Living aboard was simple because we had been living that way in our minds for a long time. The next project was to build a nine-foot fiberglass tender and line it with walnut trim. We named it *Limbo*. It had a twelve-foot mast and was sloop rigged. *Limbo* would serve as a vehicle to take us to shore when we were anchored out.

Next was the job of installing the emergency gear. We purchased two ten-foot fiberglass poles with lights, whistles, and life rings for our "man–overboard" gear. The purpose of these was for rescue if someone fell overboard. The whole ring and pole would be thrown to them and they could swim to the float, blow the whistle, and use the life ring as a floating device. The length of the pole would be tall enough above the waves to signal where they were and if it was at night, the light could be turned on. Later we learned of a man overboard who did not have this safety gear. The man remained in sight of the skipper who tried for an hour to get him aboard with no luck at all. They finally had to leave the area without him.

For safety there were two five-gallon jugs filled with fresh water fastened to the stern. We filled a styrofoam box with emergency hooks, food, water maker, and fishing gear. Both of these were available to throw overboard in case we had to abandon ship. Last we fastened a self-inflatable Zodiac rubber life raft over the aft cabin under our dingy. Now *Elysium* was nearly ready for our shake down cruise to the San Juan Islands of Northern Washington and the Gulf Islands of Canada inside the protection of Vancouver Island. Every type of circumstance for sailing exists inside the sound: current, tide height, and all varieties of wind.

When the sails were fastened to the masts we were ready to go for our first sail. Bill and Bonnie Broad and their two small girls, Daniela and Tracy, volunteered to go with us. Bill was a seasoned sailor with lots of experience racing small boats on the Columbia River where the winds switch from all directions, reflecting the configuration of the landforms. We set out down the channel with the three big sails up going very smoothly. When we arrived at the Columbia River the wind increased until we were tacking back and forth with more and more speed. We only had fifteen knots of wind, but for us, with our lack of experience, the speed was like sailing in a gale. We were struggling to get the timing of bringing the Genoa across as we tacked letting the main and mizzen boom swing at the same time. At one tack Bill had shouted to release the sheet; however our timing was off and we ended up in irons (unable to sail). We were close to some wooden dolphins set in shallow water and seemed to be drifting perilously onto the rocky shore. I was so filled with terror at the thought of our first sail ending in a disaster that I could not breathe or move. In reality, we had plenty of space and soon gained speed to tack again. This was my first lesson about "don't panic." *Elysium* was immensely different from sailing our *Little Red* sailboat. Sailing now, everything seemed faster, bigger, and more difficult.

Elmer motored *Elysium* back into the slip very smoothly and we were safely home again. Bill and Bonnie said that the boat had sailed very well, which filled us with a great sense of accomplishment. All of our sailing trials after this added to our learning experience, which was never "smooth sailing." After many trials we felt we were ready for some blue water sailing.

When the warm winds of summer came, we set off on our journey to the San Juan and Gulf Islands. Our first voyage was down the Columbia River. When we arrived in Astoria, our friends, Lynn and Deloris Balkan, came aboard to help us with our first trip offshore. We crossed the Columbia bar, which is called "the graveyard of the Pacific" with no problem. We sailed up the Washington coast, finding the first time at sea was a very different experience than sailing in the shelter of the Columbia River. Later in the day I decided that a good hot meal would make everything better, so I cooked some chicken and noodles. I brought the food up on deck and proudly handed the dishes to everyone. Lynn took one look at them and went over to the side of the boat. The noodles were green, spinach noodles and the color was just enough to make him seasick. Not much of the meal was eaten, but it certainly gave me the opportunity to work in the galley as the stove swung heavily back and forth. Thus I began years and years of cooking in difficult conditions.

Westport is the only place that has a good harbor between Astoria and the Strait of Juan de Fuca, and our plan was to stay there overnight.

By the time we got there it was dark and we had to find the navigation lights entering the port. We were exhausted after spending eight hours enduring very strong wind and rough seas. We strained our eyes to see the navigation lights that would guide us in. Finally, Elmer said, "I can see them blinking over there."

I got the binoculars and found that the light he was seeing was a motel light blinking in town. The very bright lights dimmed the pale navigation lights completely, but we finally spotted the red blinking light (meaning stay on the right when returning) and gratefully started toward the channel. This was our very first entry into a port at night. We were very uncertain about this experience, and we slowed down to give it some more thought, we noticed that there was a large boat coming from behind us. "I'll just wait and follow that boat into port," Elmer said. We slowed down and the other boat slowed down. Finally they came along side and hollered over to us. "Do you know how to find the entrance to this moorage"? They were following us! We then all decided to go ahead slowly and watch the depth sounder closely. Finally we entered a berth with the large dive-boat following behind us; the blind following the blind! What a relief to be hooked up to a dock with calm water and a good sleep.

Lynn and Deloris needed to return to Portland, so we were to be on our own from here on. The two of us braved the ocean again and headed for the Strait of Juan de Fuca. We finally found the lighthouse signal on Tatoosh. Suddenly heavy, thick fog swallowed us completely. This was a great challenge for us as we motored along, staying close to the side of the marked channel, hoping we would not meet anyone else along the way. We heard a thump of a motor. The sound came closer and closer; it was a ship, a big ship. The heartbeat-like engine sounded thumpty thump and very close to us but still we couldn't see anything. Finally, when the noise was really deafening we saw the vessel even closer to the channel inside of our route. It was less than one hundred yards to the side of us, a big, black, ghostly shape in the fog.

After this terrifying experience we sailed into the protection of Neah

Bay, feeling great relief. Inside the bay was a small, Makah Indian fishing village, which afforded us a good rest for the night. In the morning we sailed out of the area in clear sunlight to Port Angeles, Washington. Fishing season was on and it was filled with hundreds of fishing boats of all sizes. *Elysium* seemed unwieldy and difficult to steer in the very small margin of waterway between the boats into the dock area. This was another new experience for us, but we managed to enter a slip for the night, glad for the respite.

When we arrived in Victoria there were about fifty other boats moored in front of the Empress Hotel. The procedure to follow was to tie the stern to a buoy and then work the bow up to the dock. Docking *Elysium* was always a time of great stress for me as I could visualize the possibility of us smashing into another boat, inflicting extensive damage. Many harsh words were exchanged between Elmer and I every time we came into a dock. We finally got the boat situated and looked around. It was bright sunshine and we were ecstatic to be in such a beautiful moorage. There we met people who had sailed from many ports around the area. We paid one dollar fifty cents to be in the most beautiful spot right in downtown Victoria. The least expensive room in the Empress Hotel was forty dollars a night. We were living in luxury!

One day the fine looking one hundred fifty-foot schooner *Adventuress* sailed all the way into the moorage and dropped anchor. This took great skill for the skipper and was most impressive, as he did not use motor power at all. The owner was someone I had known from my college days so we hurried over to renew old acquaintances. Ernestine Bennett had owned the *Adventuress* for many years and had often taken young girls for cruises to experience the sea. One year she asked me to sail with them as the water safety instructor and lifeguard.

There were several visitors who had come aboard and were enjoying the spectacle of the *Adventuress* and her crew. Ernestine introduced us to Dick, Claire, and their daughter LeaAnne, who owned a thirty-six foot fiberglass sailboat named the *Wild Finn*. Dick and Claire were school teachers, which allowed them three months annually for a sailing vacation. They had been exploring these waters every summer for the past thirteen years. As we chatted with them Dick said, "Let me mark your charts with all the best places to see and good anchorages in the islands." They were both very knowledgeable, seasoned sailors and obviously treasured the region. They took hours to mark our charts with the great places to fish and anchor in the San Juan and the Gulf Islands. With enthusiasm Dick said, "Heck, we'll just go with you and show you ourselves." So for the next six weeks they did.

We had everything to learn about *Elysium*, including anchoring and putting up the proper sails for the wind conditions. This family turned out to be excellent teachers. We would decide on where we would anchor each night and sail there. When we were securely anchored, Elmer would relax while I made bread. Dick would go out fishing and he always came back with a fish for dinner to share with us. The bread was special for them, as they had no oven on *Wild Finn*, and the fresh fish made a perfect addition for us.

Changing wind and current in the Islands gave us experiences of various kinds. We had to be very cautious when anchoring because of the twenty-foot tides. The current, in some of the passes we went through, was so swift we had to wait for the change of tide to proceed. Even the Orca whales would wait with us, milling around in the water. This was an enormous learning experience for us. When *Wild Finn* came in with the fish, they just rafted, or tied along side of us. This friendship is still one of great value to us.

As we headed up to Prideaux Harbor, following the *Wild Finn*, I noted that the chart showed a very shallow spot at the entrance to the pass. Earlier I had asked another couple about this area and they had warned me not to try to take our boat through there as it was too shallow and the currents were very strong. I told Elmer about this and suggested that he should go around to another entrance. "Would you go below and fix me something to eat," he said because he was very hungry. I went down into the galley and was cooking dinner when I heard his urgent voice. "Better get up here and watch for depth on the bow," he said. Quickly I ran to the bow and looked into the crystal clear water. Right in front of our path was a huge rock that looked very close to the surface. "Reverse," I yelled, just as we hit the rock. Elmer put on the reverse gear and tried and tried to back off with no avail. We were just ten minutes from high tide, the twenty-four foot tide. I felt the panic rise in my stomach and looked around to hear Elmer say, "Now don't get upset." He had chosen to follow *Wild Finn* through the shallow entrance.

Dick had jumped off his boat into his little lime-green plastic sport yak. He rowed over with unbelievable speed back to us and yelled, "Throw me an anchor." Elmer picked up the forty-five pound Northill anchor like it was a toy and tossed it to Dick. Dick grabbed it with the same light hand not noticing that it nearly sunk his small dingy. Adrenalin was flowing in all of us. He tossed the anchor over to our starboard side. Elmer reeled the anchor line in with our sheet winch and *Elysium* began to heel over. Meanwhile someone in another boat had seen our plight and came over in his big powered Avon raft. "If you will just go back and forth as fast as you can maybe we can get enough wake to pull her off," Elmer shouted.

With this effort we moved slowly backward and free of the rock. Elmer pulled up the anchor and stowed it on deck. We went around and into the anchorage. That evening the story was told several times at dinner. When I awoke the next morning, the place where we were on the rock was twenty-four feet high. In my mind's eye I could see what would have happened. I could almost hear the keel scraping down the sharp side of the rock as the tide went down. Elmer remarked lightly "But we didn't, we got off."

We then sailed with *Wild Finn* up to Refuge Cove where there was a dock. We met John and Molly on a small wooden boat called the *Frisky Miss*. Dick and Clare had met them years before and renewed the friendship when they sailed into Desolation Sound. When we got to Powell River, where John and Molly had their home, they offered to watch *Elysium* so we could take a trip back to Clackamas to see how our business was doing. We left *Elysium* alone for the first time, and got on a bus headed south.

When we arrived in the city, we noted that the traffic seemed to be moving extremely fast and everyone seemed to be in a rush. As I started to cross the street, Elmer grabbed my arm and said, "Look out!" He wanted to be sure I looked both ways before we stepped out in the street. After cruising for several months, life in the city seemed hectic to us. When we returned home we were happy to find the business was doing very well. We were not needed at all. We had such a great group of people working for us that they took care of the business like it was their own. After spending a few days visiting with family and friends, we headed back to Powell River ready for more of the life we had chosen for ourselves.

For the second half of our shake-down trip we sailed on without the company of *Wild Finn*. We were now confident on our own. Anchoring was still a challenge for us, but enjoyable. Meeting other couples who had been offshore and listening to their stories about frightening experiences and how they survived was helpful, especially for me. "When trouble hits, stop and think logically before you act," they wisely advised us.

We planned to pick up friends in Nanaimo, Canada, on the way back down to Victoria. When we entered the port, the wind had increased to over thirty knots and the harbor was very crowded. Passengers were disembarking from an Italian cruise ship tender onto the dock where we needed to tie off. At the end of the dock was the ship's crew, dressed formally in black jackets, ready to serve coffee to disembarking passengers. They had set up a big coffee urn placed on a beautiful white tablecloth that was blowing wildly in the wind. We tried to slide in just beyond all of this activity, but the wind was just broadside of us, blowing us away from the dock. We were being blown so far from the landing that I could not jump onto the dock. I was hanging outside the lifelines on the toe rail, with the rope in my hand just a foot or two from the dock, but we were moving away from instead of toward it. On the other side of the boat was a rock wall, which would not have been kind to our toe rail if we were to hit it. Just as I was about to panic, a very old man who was a passenger from the ship, shouted to me, "I will rescue you," and held out his hands. I threw the rope to him as several other members of the crew grabbed him. Together they were able to pull us alongside and I quickly jumped onto the dock to tie us off. As I tied us off, I was surrounded with passengers from the ship wanting to know about our boat and what we were doing. I couldn't help but reflect that when we were in trouble there was always someone there to rescue us.

We sailed back to the San Juan Islands and welcomed aboard several visitors who had come up from Portland. Bill and Bonnie commented that our sailing skills had certainly improved since our first trip together. Our friends Doug and Cheryl Lund joined us, and the six of us enjoyed several days sailing to the park on Deer Harbor and many of the other islands in the chain.

We felt the dry breezes and heard the rustle of the leaves from where we were anchored. The cooler mornings with fog told us that autumn was in the air. Our guests were gone so we decided to head back to Port Angeles. One night we anchored in the bay off Jones Island, noting that most people just dropped anchor and went ashore to spend the evening on the island. We set our anchor carefully to be well clear of these small boats. The other boats used rope to anchor and they swung wildly in the breeze.

As we prepared supper a powerboat came by and asked if we had an airway. This was one of the few medical devices we did not have. The skipper on the powerboat behind us had suffered a severe heart attack and something was needed to keep the airway clear while doing CPR. We had just trained in CPR, so we offered to go help. He said there were several of people there, but if they needed us, they would let us know. As it became dark the situation on the boat worsened and they called for a helicopter to transport the skipper. As the chopper lowered the stretcher, the strong wind from the rotors dislodged many boats. They dragged all around the anchorages colliding with each other. Several times they lowered the stretcher onto the deck where the man rested, but the wind just drove the boat across the water. Unfortunately, in the meantime, the young man died. The eerie light of the red, rotor-beacon and all the sense of urgency around us made us realize how far from medical help we were while sailing. Help would be even further away in the places we planned to sail in the future.

The next day we arrived in Port Angeles where we picked up our daughter, Tori, for the sail back down the coast. I dreaded this trip, remembering how rough the conditions had been on the way up the coast. We had expected to find the same heavy wind and exhausting work going back out into the Pacific. Instead, it was sunny with a steady breeze, and we learned that *Elysium* would sail superbly in the ocean. We did experience the great Pacific swell coming down the coast. Arriving in Westport, this time in the daylight, we felt like we still did not have our sea legs. When we went to the grocery store, we found that the shelves were all moving, like the sea, in waves. When we had sailed in Puget Sound, we had been protected so we had no equilibrium problems. Leaving Westport, Tori sat on the stern and played her flute, making lovely music for our sail home.

We stayed in Astoria for a day or two before starting the trip up to Parker's Moorage. The gill-netting season was on and the moorage was teeming with small, loud fishing boats. Like little hornets buzzing around a hive, they never stopped moving around until well into the night. I asked Elmer if their nets would cause us any problem and he replied, "They have to stay out of the channel, and can only put them out near shore, there's nothing to worry about, Helen."

The next day we sailed out in a vigorous, favorable wind. All our sails were up, including the big Genoa with which I was now comfortable. We reached the Columbia River when I heard a sudden, shocking noise, and we came to a dead stop. *Elysium* started drifting to the side of the channel where there was shallow, rocky water. We were caught in a fisherman's drift net. "Quick, get the sails down," Elmer shouted. That was easier said than done, because we could not come up into the wind but had to pull each sail down, cleat by cleat. Elmer had no choice but to cut the rope that snagged on our rudder. The fisherman was agonized because we ruined his net, but he had fallen asleep and the net had drifted across the shipping channel. If Elmer had not cut the rope we would have smashed against the rocks that lined the channel.

Now, finally in control, we looked down at the bow and saw a small caterpillar-yellow, gill-net boat. The man on deck had no teeth so he was hard to understand, but he let us know he was fuming because we had messed up his net while he was asleep. "You rich people with your fancy yachts don't care about a poor fisherman," he wailed. If he only knew how hard we had worked to build *Elysium*. Unfortunately, we could not explain that to him, so we put up our sails and headed home.

As we sailed on we kept a close eye out for other nets. Sure enough, we had to dodge several more. We looked back and saw a giant tugboat coming up the channel behind us. The tug did not seem concerned about the gill nets as it moved forward, never stopping, but shredding the nets as they moved along. We moved on slowly under short sail for the next few miles until we were clear of the gill-netters. When we got back to Parker's we had a story to tell Harold, who was eager to hear every detail of our trip.

Parker's Paralysis

*If you have love in your life, it can make up for a great many things you
lack. If you don't have it, no matter what else you have,
it never feels enough.*

– anonymous

WHEN WE RETURNED to our mooring space at Parker's Moorage, Tom
and Bobbie from their yacht, *Tomba*, who had leased our space while
we were gone, were still there. They had originally planned to do some
work on their boat and then sail back to their home in California, when
we returned.

"We thought you were leaving," Elmer said.

"We decided to stay around for a while. It's so peaceful here," Tom
replied.

"You have a case of Parker's Paralysis," Elmer informed him.

Tom and Bobbie stayed on another year before they left for their trip
to California and on to Mexico. After they left, they sent information
about their trip down and let us know where we could find good anchorages. As it turned out, we would not catch up with them again for
several years.

Soon we were back to work and our trip was just a memory. We tried
very hard to return to the yoke of work. It was becoming more difficult

to get back into the business, and even harder to stay there. We had always opened the business at six-thirty in the morning and we never left until all of the employees had gone home. Since we returned from our trip, we had difficulty getting to work by eight-thirty and were already thinking about returning to the boat by three in the afternoon. We had sailing on our minds. Even the employees noticed the big change in us. I had been told that Elmer would never be able to let the business go. "He built that business up from nothing. It's his baby. He won't ever be able to leave it," they prophesied. How wrong they were! Initially we had planned to work for two more years before leaving, but that was becoming more and more unrealistic each day.

We began to consider putting the business on the market. Our salesman, Winston, expressed an interest purchasing it even before we could publicly advertise. We checked with several commercial real-estate agents to determine a fair market price before presenting a contract to Winston and his wife, Irene. They wanted to buy the business, but insisted that it must be sold with the property. We decided to sell the business and the lot it was on, and allow him to use the property next door. We decided to keep that land in case we needed it one day. We thought that if we lived carefully, we could manage to live on the interest from the sale and save the principal. That August of 1978, we were free of our responsibilities at the business and able to give our full attention to finishing some details and provisioning *Elysium* to sail the Pacific. How wonderful that felt to us!

All of these years I had never had a medical problem. Now, at a time when we expected to be free and happy, I was faced with quite severe health problem–uterine tumors. We went to our doctor, Luther Johansson, who told me that I should consider having a hysterectomy. He mentioned that if I wanted to treat the problem holistically, I could try by starting an exercise regimen and taking supplemental vitamins. I would need to take extra care choosing my foods and be certain to eat plenty of fruits and vegetables. I had graduated from college with a degree in nutrition and we both knew that our diets could be better. We talked it over and elected to try holistic healing to overcome the problem.

I am certain that if it had been Elmer's problem and not mine, he would not have been so stringent about the protocol that we followed. We began by walking a mile. At first we were so out of shape from lack of good exercise that we were both stiff and sore. But Elmer was on a roll and very intent on walking two miles the next day and three the next. By the end of the week we were walking six miles a day in an hour in a half's time. We chose to follow the US Air Force exercise regimen every morning for half of an hour and took the fitness tests monthly. We did change our diets, stopped eating in restaurants, and began eating lots of fresh vegetables and fruits.

The owner of our moorage, Harold Parker, was always interested in what we were doing. When he heard we needed fresh foods, he plowed a big section of his field for us to plant our own garden. The rich, brown earth was fertile and we grew a good stock of lettuce, tomatoes, beans, peas and everything else we could desire within just a month or two.

Within six months my health problem had disappeared completely. The extra roll around my waist had also vanished. We found that our total outlook on life was much healthier. We never stopped walking, even after we started sailing. It kept us in good shape and ready to face any challenge we might encounter.

Our approaching journey became foremost in our minds. Where would we stay on the way down the coast of the United States? What would we need to know for the trip and how would we learn these things? We decided to look into joining a yacht club. Joining a yacht club would give us reciprocity at other yacht clubs and we would be able to gather information about the cruising life. Unfortunately, there was not a cruising yacht club in our area. The people at the yacht clubs that we visited were only interested in weekly sails, weekend barbecues and cocktails. Fortunately, we knew many people who were planning to build boats and sail the world. We contacted these boat builders and invited them to discuss starting our own cruising yacht club. Of the thirty or so people we talked to, all were ready to join immediately. We called ourselves The Sauvie Island Yacht Club, and began making plans. We met at the school on Sauvie Island and enlisted instructors to teach diesel mechanics, celestial navigation, piloting, and amateur radio.

The first class on diesel mechanics was held on *Elysium* because the engine room allowed everyone a space. We learned that virtually every problem that could go wrong with a diesel engine is caused by dirty fuel or by water getting into the fuel. Elmer installed five fuel filters, two water collectors and three big sediment filters in the engine room on the boat. He was thinking that the engine would always run when it was needed, and he was right. The filters kept the engine almost free of problems for all the years we sailed.

The second class was on celestial navigation and we learned to use a sextant. We had purchased a sextant from a man who had sailed to Spain and back. The sextant was the last keepsake he had of his trip, and when he heard about our boat, he offered to sell it to us. It was a sextant from World War II and had a smell reminiscent of the sea and oil. We took it to a marine store and had it completely refurbished; then we had the difficult task of learning to use it without a real flat sea horizon to work with. The sextant delivers its position by triangulating from a star to the horizon. When we were at sea we found it much easier to determine our position when we had a real horizon to work with.

One of the major items that we needed to add to *Elysium* was a wind vane. A wind vane is an auxiliary steering device that will maintain a selected course. The rudder of the wind vane is independent from the main rudder that steers the boat. The fin of the vane, which is a sheet of metal, is two and a half feet tall by eighteen inches wide and stands on edge. The metal sheet is set so the edge faces the wind to allow the air to flow directly past the edge. If the boat begins to go off the set course, the wind hits the vane and lays it over, which pulls the rudder over to bring the boat back on course.

The material that makes up the vane is stainless steel tubing attached to the stern of the boat. Our friend, Paul Strait, had built one for his boat just like what we required. Paul gladly loaned us his plans, and with a few changes, Elmer adapted them to *Elysium*. Our friends, John and Molly, who we had met while sailing in Canada, came down for a visit the day we had completed our list of materials. John told us that he had a yard full of excess stainless steel left over from his own projects, and that before we bought anything, we should wait until we heard from him. Later that week he called and told us he had everything we needed to make the vane. He declined any money for what he called "scrap," so we chose to name our vane after him. The flag part of the vane was painted white and we put a big J.C. on it. People often took those initials to mean someone other than John Cooper, but that was all right with us. If *Elysium* was paradise, then having J.C. at the helm was reassuring for us.

Harold Parker loaned Elmer his welder and supplied everything he needed to build the vane behind the boat. Elmer assembled the vane standing on a little raft made out of old timbers floating at the stern of *Elysium*. While he was working he had to be especially careful with his tools because anything that dropped would bounce off the raft and be permanently lost in the water. He attached the vane solidly to the boat and fashioned a beautiful tiller out of some spruce left over from building the masts. Now we had an auxiliary steering device if we ever lost the main steering.

In spite of all the work we had to finish every day, we walked our six miles. As fall approached, the scenery on the island began to change. The geese and white swans were migrating south and as they flew over us they sounded their goodbyes. When the geese returned in the spring, we would be starting a similar journey of our own. Each day the honking V-shaped winged legions filled the air. When we walked, we encountered the geese fueling up for their flight by feeding in the fields. These were the peaceful days of autumn and our minds were filled with thoughts of changes to come.

In the early part of our lives, there were many choices about lifestyle, family and career. As that part of our lives ended, the growth in our personal philosophies was beginning. This was the brink of the greatest learning experience of our lives. We would travel and see places we had only read about, like newborn souls with no expectations or goals but to survive this coming experience. Every time I thought of the future, my heart would pound clear up into my head. Leaving our family and friends, the support structure that we had built throughout our lives, would be the most difficult part of our future voyages.

Learning to communicate with the people we would be visiting when we moved south into Latin America was our next priority. The community college taught a class in Spanish, so we signed up. We began studying the Spanish language, and also learned about the culture of the people. On our walks we would practice conversational Spanish. This was limited to the most basic things around us, like the animals, colors and the landscape. It was much more difficult to explore more esoteric thoughts with our limited vocabulary. We learned to respect the people who had knowledge of more than one language and could change from one to another with ease. We would have to use intuition and observation to understand anything more than a superficial conversation.

We invited the Sauvie Island School children to visit the boat. The day of the visit was a sunny warm Indian summer day. There were about forty chattering, excited children lined up on the grass above the dock. We took groups of ten at a time to tour *Elysium*. They had such great flexibility they fit very well into the size and space of the boat. Children were entranced by the thought of being at sea and using the instruments that we demonstrated to them. The compass and the sexton seemed to spark the most interest. We ate cookies and drank punch together and enjoyed the exuberance of youth. Children have the most positive view of life and it was contagious for us to share their sense of adventure.

The plan now was to leave by end of May and hope the weather would be settled enough for our trip down the Oregon Coast. I set up my Sailmaster sewing machine, and made the flags for each country we planned to visit. The flags were made from colored nylon, and I used indelible ink to draw the logos on them. I sewed the flags for Mexico, Guatemala, Nicaragua, El Salvador, Costa Rica, Panama, Ecuador and French Polynesia. As each flag was finished, we researched and learned about each country we would be visiting. We also studied the charts and listed the ports we would likely enter. We bought detailed entrance charts for each port of entry. The extra charts would be our insurance against damage to the boat.

Harold had been doing heavy equipment work for a friend who was tearing down a very large furniture factory. When his friend offered to pay him, Harold said, "Just give me that pile of fir and pine blocks over there."

When he returned to the dock, he had a gigantic pile of the small wooden blocks that were bone dry and would burn beautifully. Harold was pleased we would have plenty of wood to burn in our little stainless steel fireplace that Leo had built us. There were easily two cords of wood in the pile and it lasted us for many years.

As winter arrived, the weather turned colder, finally freezing our drinking water so we had to carry it down in jugs. When we woke up in the morning, the washcloths were often frozen in the bathroom. Exercising and walking would get us warm and the fire in our stove would keep us cozy the rest of the day and through the night while our neighbors, who had a very expensive diesel furnace, could never make it work correctly. After work they would come over to warm up by our cozy fire, before braving their own cold boat.

We needed to qualify for our amateur radio license so we signed up for the class at the community college. We worked hard to learn Morse code because we would have to know it well when we took the test. We easily passed the novice test, but getting the code up to the required fifteen words per minute for the general license test was very difficult. We listened to code from a cassette tape and spent hours sending code back and forth to each other. After listening to the code for so long, we would hear the dot-dash-beeps in our heads for hours afterwards.

Near the first of January 1979, the thermometer stayed well below freezing for several weeks. Elmer had to break the ice around the hull several times a day. One neighbor who had neglected to do this was frozen in place at the angle where the wind had pushed the yacht so he lived on this incline until the ice finally thawed. We would sit in our main cabin and watch the movement of the mammoth chunks of ice, sculpted by the wind. Often they would move so close to the stern of the boat that we could hear them scraping under the rudder.

The local ducks had the very worst experience in this weather. The water that they spent their time on was a protected place in the moorage. This space was completely frozen. When they flew in to land, their flat webfeet would just skate across the ice, and they would squawk loudly and scramble to try to stop. If they were able to find some clear water, they would dip their beaks, and the harsh wind chill would freeze them shut. They would try and try to thaw their beaks by dipping, again and again, until there was such a big lump, their heads would finally be pulled under water. We could only rescue a few of them and we watched helplessly as one after another drowned out of our reach.

Because of this ice coating, the electrical lines were also broken in many places causing the electricity to be out for several days. Many people had to leave their homes and go to places that could be warmed by fires and some had to cook on their camp stoves. The papers told of older people who had been found dead in their homes from the lack of heat. Our families were very worried about us but fortunately we were in a perfect place. We had filled our storage with wood and were cozy as a bug in a rug.

The sailboats were also covered with ice. We came out one morning and bumped into a stay, the wire that stabilizes the mast. The ice came zooming down the wire like a roller coaster and then shot out all over in an explosion at the bottom. This was great fun and we went to each stay to experience the impressive show. The longer the stay was the more spectacular the trip of the ice to the bottom. When we depleted the ice on our stays, we made our way over to the boat next door. Our neighbors came out to see what madness we were up to and happily joined us, going to the next boats on the moorage. Harold had looked down and seeing us playing, also joined us in the fun, laughing heartily as each stay shed its ice.

As the weather became warmer, more and more people came to visit us. Friends told their friends about us, and some of the people that were getting ready to leave came to talk to us about what they needed to accomplish. Seeing us getting ready to depart stirred the wanderlust in them. We enjoyed cozy dinners with big pots of soup and freshly baked bread, which were easy to serve from my galley. The coziness of our back cabin was an excellent place to cement long and lasting friendships.

Before we left we needed to have our physical check ups. Our doctor, Luther Johansson, came to the boat and instructed us about how to deal with various injuries. He said "If anything gets in your eyes get it out immediately, even if you have to dig it out, don't wait." He taught us about how to care for dislocated joints and broken bones. He gave us a list of prescriptions that we could fill all around the world if necessary. With all of this information, we were feeling confident that we could handle any challenge that might present itself.

On the boat next to us in the moorage were two physicians, Ron and Mary Dibble. They came over one day and brought a big red garbage sack of medical supplies. We had splints of every description, bandages, antiseptic patches and lots of tape. They showed us how to use all of these devices and told grim stories, with all of the gory details, of sailing accidents they had read about. Ron had traveled in Asia, and he warned us about cleanliness of food. "We're so clean here in this country that we don't build immunity to the things that infest the poorer countries," he informed us. "The only way to safely eat raw foods is to treat them with a blow torch or to soak them in potassium permanganate," he advised. Now that we were so well schooled, we no longer worried about medical problems. We planned to take good care of our bodies, eat well, and take supplements.

Once in a while my fears would raise their ugly heads and I would imagine fierce storms at sea. One headline in the paper told of the ferocious winds that had roared down the Washington and Oregon coast and had swept the floating bridge across the Hoods Canal completely away. That bridge had been stretched across the bay surviving storms for many years. In my mind, the picture of the winds and water that it took to destroy that bridge was very graphic. I imagined *Elysium* dwarfed by huge seas and strong winds, with nowhere to find safety. The sailor's prayer came to mind, "Help me Lord the sea is so big and my boat is so small." I used mental imagery to cast out the terror. I saw us sailing happily under bright sunny skies. I knew we would have some times ahead that were hard, but decided it would be better to enjoy the good times.

When the end of March approached we moved everything we did not need on the boat to our storage place, and brought everything we needed to take with us onto the boat. More things came onboard than were removed. We found some plastic containers with tight-fitting lids and filled them with wheat and beans. The one gallon buckets were filled with grains, dried vegetables, noodles, honey and various other foods. I didn't want us to go hungry, but Elmer was not sure we needed so many supplies. "We will be in the US for quite a while, Helen, so we will have access to stores," Elmer advised.

The month of May was fast approaching and the feeling of butterflies seldom left my stomach. More and more people came to say goodbye. Knowing that we would not see them for a long time left me feeling forlorn. Harold was the person that I would miss the most because I knew he would never come to visit us.

"I won't go out there with you," he warned me.

I wondered where in the world we would ever find someone who cared so much for the boat and for us.

"I just hate to think of you out in that ocean with all those big waves and strong winds," he often said.

"If it gets to be too much for me, can I come back here?" I replied.

"You just do that. There is always a place for you here," he would reassure me.

This was our little joke, but I found that deep inside it was very comforting to me and gave me a nice warm feeling.

Some weeks before we were to leave a friend invited us over for dinner. As we arrived we noticed several cars parked around the house. This is strange, I thought, because I could see no one around. Everyone was hiding in the other room and yelled, "surprise". What a fun experience this was for us. It made us realize that we were actually leaving in a week! We had such a mellow afternoon reliving old experiences and listening to Harold tell stories about old times at the moorage.

The Sunday before we were to leave Harold and June had a picnic on the great lawn above the moorage. Everyone we knew who had an interest in sailing came. On this occasion we met Howard Radke, who was a friend of our doctor, Luther. Howard was interested in amateur radio and asked if he could see our rig. We had purchased the Atlas 250 and had just set it on the chart table. It was never installed because we didn't know how to do it, even with the instruction books we bought. Howard was a quiet man who did not offer much information about who he was. We could tell by the questions he asked as he fiddled with the rig that he knew a lot about radios. He told us we needed a matching network and a whip antenna, and that when we arrived in Newport he would bring what was needed and set up the radio. We gave him enough money to cover the cost, and felt very lucky to have such a great friend. We were inspired to persevere for our license. "Keep on studying and you can take your exam again when you get to Mexico" he advised.

Our plan was to slip away quietly without fanfare and goodbyes. Wednesday afternoon I went to the big strawberry patch on the island and picked and ate my way across the rows. The warmth on the berries created a smell so intoxicating I'm sure I ate more than I should have. I returned to the boat with a gallon jug full of strawberries. This would be my last harvest on Sauvie Island. That evening our youngest daughter, LeAnn, arrived at the boat to sail with us as far as Astoria. "Down the river is as far as this little chicken will go," she joked.

Finally, Thursday morning arrived. We were finished and ready to leave Parker's Marina. The shed was empty, and we had stored our canoe and red sailboat at LeAnn's house. The dock space was bare of our things. The day was sunny and clear; it was a perfect day for us to sail down the Columbia River. We had not slept much the night before. Each of us awakened to find the other awake, so we just lay there and talked about leaving. As Elmer started up the ladder to the deck, he slipped and hit his mouth on the rail. The cut bled red blood all over his white beard.

"What a way to start a trip," I worried.

"Not a big deal at all," he said as he doused his beard clean and stopped the bleeding.

As we looked up on the bank above the moorage, we saw a crowd of people coming down to the ramp. Our friends had taken the day off from work when they found out we were leaving. When we started to release the lines off from the dock, I began to sob. I looked over at Harold who was untying the boat and he said, "Now don't you say one word." He had tears in his eyes also. More and more people arrived and several of us were crying and telling each other how sad and happy we were and waving goodbye. As we sailed down the channel and under the bridge that crosses over to Sauvie Island, our friends drove onto the bridge to wave to us one last time. What a heart wrenching experience that was! I was totally exhausted and depleted after the emotional good-byes and very sad to leave everyone.

Sailing the Oregon Coast

He, who binds himself to joy, doth the winged life destroy.
He, who kisses joy as it flies, lives in eternity's sunrise.
— *William Blake*

WE LEFT OUR safe home at Parker's moorage on May 31st, 1979, the time of transition from spring to summer. We planned to start our ocean passage when the wind was blowing from the north, and we were hoping for bright sunshine and calm seas. We had a beautiful warm, peaceful day sailing the Columbia River and were tied to a log raft early the first evening. We were still reeling from the emotional turmoil of leaving our comfortable moorage at Parker's Marina. We would miss the daily morning chats with Harold and the inviolability of Parker's Moorage.

The next morning, the breeze was building slowly, coaxing us to jump out of bed and get *Elysium* under sail. We ate a good breakfast and set sail, hearing the sounds of the breeze playing in the rigging like harp strings and then sliding down the silky sails as we pulled them up. This familiar sound erased all feelings of sadness and brought back the excitement of our new adventure as we moved along with a perfect breeze. Near us there was a small sailboat enjoying the river, zipping back and forth.

"Where're you headed?" a voice shouted from the small boat.

"Australia" I shouted back, surprising us all.

"Alright" he replied simply.

To us, Australia was the farthest goal we could foresee.

We arrived in Warrenton, by the mouth of the Columbia River in early afternoon, the sails filled in a broad-beam reach. Elmer took an afternoon nap while LeAnn and I lay on the warm deck in the hot afternoon sun. The air was filled with the smell of salt sea air wafting in from the ocean. We all had a feeling of contentment and gratification, satisfied that *Elysium* sailed as proficiently as we had planned.

Later that afternoon, LeAnn's husband, Steve Tobias, arrived to take her home. She was the last part of our family to say goodbye–now we were alone. We were facing the beginning of the adventure we had dreamed about and planned for such a long time.

The next day we were to cross the Columbia River Bar to begin our voyage down the Oregon Coast. We contacted the Coast Guard on our VHF radio and they told us that there was a twenty-knot wind and no storm warnings. "There is a bit of fog forming but none in the forecast for tomorrow," they said. After we heard the forecast we felt less apprehension about the upcoming trip.

In the morning, looking out from the port, we saw that the weather was foggy. Forecasting weather in Oregon is always questionable. Leaving *Elysium* where we were docked, we went for a walk to look over the conditions. "Surely this breeze will blow this early morning fog away soon," Elmer promised. As we walked, my concern about the fog began to melt away. The last time we crossed the bar it was beautiful, sunny weather. Why should we have anything else? We walked seven miles to the seashore where we were able to look out at the foggy rough sea. "The wind is blowing from the north so we will have the wind with us on good beam reach," Elmer enthused. When we returned to the dock, another sailboat crew was planning to sail out. They told us that the conditions were ideal.

We stocked up the water tanks and decided to leave at noon. We would be out all night and arrive in Newport by the next afternoon. This first trip down the Oregon coast would be over one hundred miles. On the trip we planned to stop and make short visits to the places we had camped and enjoyed so much when we were land bound. Dave and Lee Kincaid on yacht *Leeway* planned to travel at the same time. We thought that it would be reassuring to have someone on the radio to talk with during the trip, so we made arrangements to leave at the same time.

The Columbia Bar is one that is well known to sailors and ship captains because of its many perilous conditions. The well-deserved name "graveyard of the Pacific" spoke of more than a thousand vessels that were lost on this bar. Captain Cook named the entrance Cape Disappointment, because he couldn't cross into the bay for several days.

The Coast Guard trains rescue personal in specially built ships to use outside this bar. This area has waves as high as eighteen feet, which can be spawned by storms out in the Pacific. These waves take weeks to travel and gather speed up to seventy miles an hour before exploding on the Oregon shore. These vessels are built to endure savage, breaking waves that will dump as much as two hundred tons of water on their deck with each wave. A short time before we left, one of these vessels had capsized and sunk under the extreme pressure. Many of the men were able to escape by holding their breaths for a very long time while swimming to the surface. As we were motoring by this spot, a rescue crane barge was raising the vessel to the surface. Four of the men had been unable to escape from the cabin when it went down and their bodies were still inside.

I had these events documented in my mind and recognized my feeling of foreboding. If I really believed in omens, this observation would have sent me home for sure, but I stuffed the uneasy feeling into my stomach as we motored out of the channel. We put up the sails and plowed heavily into the waves with a good strong wind pushing us on to cross the bar. As we met the waves washing into the bay, *Elysium* raised her bow up high into the sky. When the wave passed, the bow crashed deeply down into the trough, and the wave threw heavy spray clear to the stern. The current that was racing out of the river caused the big waves, as the wind was blowing against them. Elmer turned on the motor and pushed the throttle hard ahead to get through this rough situation. While we were pitching about as we reached the bar, we heard the shrill sound of the alarm screaming from inside.

The alarm had been rigged to tell us one of three things: The motor was overheating; we were taking on water in the bilge; or we had very low oil pressure in the engine. Elmer quickly checked the oil pressure and engine heat gauges and found them pointed at normal. Meanwhile I was frantically waving my arm down as far as I could reach into the bilge to check for a seawater leak. With great relief, I saw the bilges were dry. We had still not turned off the alarm, which was now shattering any calm I had conjured up before. As I turned it off, Elmer suggested that we go into Hammond, which was right near the mouth of the river, just to make certain that everything was operating properly.

We were warned previously that Hammond is a very shallow port. As we entered, we had just a few inches to spare beneath the keel. Elmer dropped the anchor and we methodically checked all of the gauges for any malfunction. We didn't find anything that would have made the alarm sound, so we disconnected the nerve-wracking alarm mechanism. We pulled the anchor, which had buried itself deep in the foul smelling black mud in the bay. It then covered the deck with rotted sea life residue, which we had to clean with several buckets of water. We finally continued on to the bar.

This time we made it across the bar with a stiff thirty-knot wind moving us along swiftly as we rounded the last marker buoy in the channel. Bits of fog soon began to form and quickly made a thick soupy wall that we could not see through and we soon lost the dim view of the land completely. We planned to navigate along the thirty-fathom line (one hundred and eighty feet deep) so we kept close track of the depth sounder throughout the night. We heard the navigation buoys, each with a different sound: a bell, a horn, and others with different pulsations. All of these sounds were listed on our navigational chart and indicated exactly where we were in the ocean.

The wind gusted strongly and still did not diminish the fog that clung to us all through the night. Just once, right before nightfall, it did lift enough to give us a good fix on Haystack Rock, which we recognized immediately because it is two hundred and thirty five feet tall and has a very distinctive shape. I had been carefully keeping a dead reckoning position, marking down the compass course, the speed, and the distance traveled on the chart. Although this is never completely accurate, as it does not take into account how the speed and direction of the current could be moving, it did correlate with my place on the chart where we had expected to be. Moving further on we were able to hear a buoy bell ringing, so we were pleased we had another good fix and it confirmed our mark on the chart.

I called *Leeway* on the VHF radio and told them that we had just seen the rock and heard the bell for a good fix. Dave told me that Lee was very seasick so he did not have time to spare for navigation. He was sure that the wind would blow the fog away by morning and he would be able to get a fix on shore. Even when we were sailing along the shoreline with the navigational aids, we always kept a running dead reckoning course and marked our charts, not wanting to leave anything to chance.

We took turns steering through the night in the thirty knot wind and fog. I had on my new bright red foul-weather gear and as the boat swung over thirty degrees each way, I slid from side to side like a pendulum on my curved varnished seat. I noticed that Elmer's face had a yellow cast as he fought seasickness. We alternated staying on the helm while the other marked our position and then slept. The two hours of sleep passed like a blink of an eye; still we woke up just before our watch was due. Each time I came up on deck, I expected to find a bright sky with stars shining. Unfortunately there was only thicker fog. Sailing in a strong wind in thick fog is an unreal experience because the compass light is the only thing visible and it banks steeply two and fro as you try to steer the correct direction. The fog continued with us into the dawn and throughout the morning.

Traveling at about six knots, we estimated that we could arrive at Newport as early as ten o'clock in the morning. Just as the morning light made the fog look even denser it abruptly lifted just a bit and allowed us to see some of the coastline. At that moment we spotted a jetty and the entrance buoy to Newport Bay. We were dismayed that we were so close but still could not to see well enough to navigate the buoys through the channel. We dropped the sails and looked longingly for another buoy, but the fog rushed in and engulfed us again. Suddenly a fishing boat appeared out of the fog with his radar circling around above the cabin. I called to him on our radio and asked him to slow down enough for us to follow him in. Elmer raced to the helm and with the motor purring, we sped up to move into his wake. We followed the boat, but were not able to see either side of the jetty–not even a channel buoy was visible through the thick fog. As we came to the Yaquina Bay Bridge, which spans the entrance to Newport Harbor, an unbelievable sight appeared before us: the sun shone brightly and the wind stopped. It was like passing through a wall of distress into a haven of joy. We quickly shed our foul-weather gear and sweaters to enjoy the very warm weather in Newport Bay and hastened to thank the fishing boat for saving us from an additional night at sea.

We entered the area and turned into the docking site in the Embarcadero where the fishing boats are moored. We tied *Elysium* up on the outside of an old burned out barge that was in turn tied to a dilapidated powerboat. These had obviously been there for years without moving. We left *Elysium* to receive permission from the port captain to stay on the dock and to check into Newport. He told us we could dock there for a dollar fifty a day, but we would have to climb over both boats to get onboard. This was a great bargain for us and we were extremely grateful to be in port. We offered a silent "thank you" for the miracle of arrival.

When we returned to the boat and were preparing for a much needed nap, we heard Dave's voice on the VHF. He was calling for help and sounded very tired and discouraged. When he heard that we were safely in port, while he was in thick fog and completely lost, he sounded even more hopeless. They had come close to shore to try to find Newport, but when they heard breaking surf they headed right out to the safety of the sea again. *Leeway* was a fiberglass fin keelboat, which gave them a much rougher ride than we had. However they did have more speed and because of this they overshot the entrance to Newport. We stayed on the radio with them until five o'clock in the evening to encourage them. Finally, Dave and Lee called the Coast Guard for help and we left their rescue to them because they had instruments to search for a vessel in distress and would find them and bring them in.

We needed to stretch our legs after sitting by the radio for several hours. Getting out on the dock, it seemed to be swaying back and forth and our legs were so stiff that we had to stop several times to steady ourselves to find our sea legs. After walking around for an hour, we were finally able to look at something without seeing it swaying in motion. Returning to the boat we dropped into bed and slept as soundly as if paralyzed, waking up with dry mouths and stiff muscles from lying in one place for so long.

The following morning we found a phone and called some friends who lived in Newport. Our friends were eager to come visit and brought a Swedish exchange student who was living with them. We made arrangements to take them for a sail within the next few days.

When out for a walk again, who should be walking down to meet us but Dave and Lee! They knew we would be worried about them, so they had hitched a ride up from Winchester Bay, the next port south of us. They had spent the rest of the previous night pitching around in the fog because they were afraid to move from their position after they called the Coast Guard. The search took nearly all night before they were spotted and guided in to port. They wanted to stay in port for a while to get rested, which was also our intention.

Before leaving Sauvie Island, many of our friends had asked to go sailing when we reached Newport. I sent letters informing them of our arrival and that we would be there for a while. We did not expect many people to make the trip of more than a hundred miles. However, nearly two hundred people came and signed our new visitor's book, explored the boat, and some sailed. Newport is a great town to visit, with many interesting features; it gave people an excuse for a bit of a holiday.

After we rested for a few days we took our first group out sailing. We had twenty-five knots of wind and big rolling seas and we enjoyed a great sail along the coast. I had fixed snacks for everyone, but people were not hungry. Not being used to the motion of the sea upset their stomachs. When we got back, I got out a big bowl of chili and some bread that I had made. Even though a rough sea dampens the appetite, when the trip is over it comes back with a vengeance. A big one-dish meal with bread and fruit was easy to prepare ahead of time. To hungry people this was a scrumptious meal.

We took friends out every few days for a while. On rough days someone would get seasick and we would have to return early. We certainly were getting familiar with crossing the bar, coming into port and sailing in different conditions. Each evening I would cook a big pot meal of Bouillabaisse or a thick chowder and bread for the next day.

On June 10th, we had a particularly large group of people to take sailing. It was a bright, clear Sunday and the warning flags were out for the brisk twenty-five to thirty knot winds that seemed to come up every afternoon. We had ten people aboard, some family. I got out the life jackets for everyone, but no one wanted to use them. These were all young people eager to go for a sail.

Elysium moved out under the bridge and I was steering with our big stainless steel wheel. I felt something very strange in the way the boat was handling and I remarked to Elmer that the wheel did not feel responsive. "It's probably the current coming in," he said. He and the young boys were out putting up all of the sails so I continued to try to get the sense of what the problem was.

Moving out into the channel, we saw a very large tug pulling a barge coming toward us. The wind made the seas rougher than usual because it was blowing strongly across the channel. The barge was being blown alongside of the tug, taking up most of the passageway. Elmer saw the problem and planned to sail to the first buoy, and then swing around it into the sea to be out of the way of the incoming tug and barge. The wind had increased to thirty knots, which allowed us to sail rapidly. The tug and barge were getting very close to us as we neared the buoy. Elmer was at the wheel now and I was watching with mounting apprehension as we kept moving toward the oncoming pair. I looked back toward Elmer to see why he had not turned. I saw him turning the wheel but the boat was not responding. Suddenly everyone was aware that we were in trouble. Elmer yelled, "Grab the sheet we have to sail around the buoy. We have no steering." I can't say how close we were to the tug and barge, but it was way too close for comfort. Everyone was in a state of shock as we just barely made it out of harms way.

After we were safely out of the channel, several people were leaning over the side losing their breakfast, and the rest were down in the main cabin grabbing life vests. We lay dead in the water rolling from side to side in a big ocean swell. Elmer and I went below and opened the back shelf to see what had happened to the hydraulic steering. There we saw that the steering apparatus had torn away from the bulkhead. He worked on it for a while and was able to jury rig it together with me hanging upside down into the stern section holding a stick in place. This allowed him to resume steering. The boat was undulating sideways in the big swell making my breakfast roll around in my stomach. "If I am ever going to get seasick, now will be the time," I thought to myself. I hung down in this position for the entire trip back to the dock.

Once we were tied up at the dock again, we were very apologetic for the terrible experience we had put everyone through. To our amazement, the crew had actually enjoyed the hair-raising experience. The boat was filled with excited chatter as I prepared the big pot of spaghetti and garlic bread. Everyone ate with a rapacious appetite and we felt a great relief to think we had faced danger and come through the whole thing unscathed.

The next day we walked three miles over the bridge to the other side of the bay and found a marine repair shop equipped with facilities to build a new brace for our steering. Back on the boat, Elmer chipped out an area and installed a steel plate that he bolted into place. This allowed the whole system to be beefed up so the problem would never re-occur. We were so glad this had not happened during our foggy, rough, night sail down the coast from Portland. It was a piece of luck for sure. Synchronicity!

Howard Radke arrived on Friday with the Transmatch for the antenna for our ham radio. He put up a whip antenna and helped us install all the parts, and then we turned it on to try it out. It was thrilling to hear voices on the radio. This gave me the impetus to work harder on the code, so I could legally use it soon. I set aside a time each day to work with my code sender and listen to code being sent on the radio.

On Saturday, we took another ten visitors out for a trip. Tori and her husband Fred were along for his first time at sea. Fred was terribly seasick the whole time we were out, retching over the side. He did not want to ruin the trip for anyone and said, "I'll just sit here on the stern." Every time we looked back we could see that familiar greenish yellow look he had. Finally we could bear it no longer, so we went back in to port. Fred did not recover completely until we had been in port for several hours so we knew he would never be a sailor.

During the next week, we had to return to port three out of the four times that we went out because of someone being seasick. Elmer and I realized how lucky we were that we did not suffer from "mal de mer." We had heard of people spending years building their cruising yacht, only to discover they could never get over seasickness.

While sitting on board in the sun, a reporter from the local paper came by and asked if he could write a story about us. He asked many questions, took notes and pictures. We really enjoyed talking with this enthusiastic young man who had such an interest in sailing. The next day we were quite amazed to see a big picture of us, sitting in the cockpit of *Elysium* on the front page of the paper! The story was very well written with no mistakes or misquotes. His account brought more visitors from town and the surrounding area to see the boat and hear about our experiences.

We strolled down the waterfront, enjoying the sea lions that came up on the dock to sun themselves. They roll around and menace each other with loud barks and snarls, fighting for the best spot on the docks. We looked into the shop windows along the way and decided to go into a ceramic shop. There we admired the beautiful hand turned pots and cups. The potters, Ken and Peggy, recognized us from the story in the local paper and decided to share their dream with us. They had been planning and saving for years to build a kiln and produce pottery. Just recently the dream had materialized and we were in their new shop.

"Could we come visit the boat?" they asked.

"Please come down anytime this afternoon. We'll be onboard," we replied.

That afternoon we welcomed them aboard. They looked with great interest as we showed them around the boat. When they left, they gave us a special "kiln god." "We make this figure when we build a new kiln and fire it for the first time. If it doesn't break we have good luck from then on," they told us. They wanted us to have this good luck charm to keep us safe on our journeys. "But don't break it," Peggy warned, revealing her superstitious streak. We accepted their gift with gratitude.

Two weeks later, on June 19th, we decided that it was time to leave. We topped off our tanks, purchased supplies, and prepared the boat for a long passage. Our son, Steve, and his wife Anjali, joined us for the next part of the trip. Anjali was from the interior of Northern India, so she had never seen a lake, much less the ocean. The first time Anjali had ever been in the water was just months before when she attempted to swim. I really admired her spunk to come aboard for a trip out to sea, spending the night sailing in waters that had the reputation for gales and heavy seas.

The skies were clear and sunny with no fog and a light breeze flitted across the bright blue water. Leaving port is always a happy and sad occasion. We were eager to see the next port, but it's difficult to leave the comfort of friends and a safe dock. Sailing down the coast that first night, the sky was filled with stars and the wind was good for a pleasant sail. Anjali had worried about seasickness, but didn't experience it at all. Steve, on the other hand, didn't think he would be sick, but felt a bit queasy all night. It never got the best of him and he took his turn at the helm, which was very helpful, allowing us each a bit more sleep. We entered Coos Bay near a place the family used to go crabbing at Charleston. We dropped anchor and rowed to shore, walked on the sandy beach and stretched our legs. Back onboard we ate a good dinner and we all slept well through the night to prepare for our next sail to Brookings, a one-day trip down the coast.

An ideal wind was blowing and we were sailing at a good speed passing Bandon, near the lake cabin where we had spent our summers. My mother used to live on the coast here and we could even see her house on the bluff. This was where I had spent my summers when I was young and I knew all of the rocks and crannies of the beach for miles and miles each way. Bandon Beach on down to Cape Blanco was where we had walked so often to watch the far horizon and imagine our sailing plans. What a joy it was for us to be out here with our own *Elysium*.

Sailing on, the weather began to change rapidly and the sea conditions were showing signs of a stronger wind. With the wind at thirty knots and in a very rough sea, we were now sailing too fast, so we made the sails smaller by reefing them. The wind reached a full gale, as we rounded the fabled Cape Blanco, which Oregon claims is the westernmost point in all of North America. The extreme protrusions of rock jutting out from land created a harsh, unforgiving environment. As we sailed around the Cape, the waves were over ten feet high, the roughest sea we had been in so far. We decided to seek refuge in a protected place near Port Orford for a night's rest. As we rounded Port Orford Heads, we felt a change in the weather as the wind seemed to compress and mix with warmer air south of the Cape. Arriving safely at anchor, we felt that the crew and the boat had performed extremely well, and we were very pleased.

Once around the rocks and in good protection, we anchored and lit the oven as we prepared and cooked a salmon we had caught on the way in. Soon the whole boat was filled with the smell of fish baking. We relaxed as we ate dinner gratefully and were happy to climb into our bunks for a good night's sleep.

The next morning the sun was streaming into our ports early. We started out eagerly with a fifteen knot breeze and we sailed well as the wind steadily increased. We experimented with our wind vane, J.C., but it would not work efficiently long enough to make it worthwhile. It would sail off course suddenly and have to constantly be reset. The steering vane was not as dependable as we had hoped it would be. We were now in heavy seas again, with over thirty knots of wind. It was so cold that we had to put on all of our warmest sweaters and foul-weather gear. The weather report from Brookings, which was our next destination, reported that it was warm and sunny, but for us it was so cold that we had to take turns going below to thaw out our hands and feet. As we rounded the corner and saw Brookings through the binoculars, sure enough there were people on the beach enjoying the very warm day in their swimsuits.

As we sailed into the protection of the bay, we could not get our heavy clothes off quickly enough. It was very warm and calm, as the report had indicated. This area is called the banana belt of Oregon, and rightly so. Steve and Anjali had to be back in Portland the next day, so after tying up at the dock we went for a walk to see a bit of this quaint little town. We finished the salmon for dinner and fell asleep quickly as evening approached.

The next morning we saw our guests to their bus and said another goodbye. We would not see them again for over a year. The life we had chosen was going to be one of meeting people, seeing family for a short time, and then leaving–so many goodbyes.

To stay tied to the dock was very expensive, so we decided to move into the Chetco River along with Dave and Lee, who had arrived shortly after we had. We had noted that as the tide came in there was plenty of depth to motor into the deep part of the river. We carefully anchored stern and bow and tied *Elysium* to trees on shore. It took us a good two hours to get this all done, but we felt very happy to be in such a verdant, beautiful place. Dave and Lee came in also, and tied *Leeway* onto our port side. The river was crystal clear, with beautiful trees lining the shore.

Around midnight I woke up suddenly, hearing the scratching of branches going by the boat. The tide had come in so swiftly it had lifted the anchor we had onshore. I grabbed Elmer and yelled, "We're dragging anchor." Elmer was up and running to the helm before he was completely awake. We started the engine immediately so we would not drag into the shallow inlet and go aground. Then in the pitch-dark night we anchored the boat again. Lying right along side of us, Dave and Lee had slept through this whole nightmare and did not hear a thing.

The next morning we rowed our dingy, *Limbo*, over to the dock area to see who was moored there. A big powerboat had just come in and a white haired lady and her husband stepped onto the dock. Their names were Dick and Karin Latham. We talked with them for a while and found that they were not used to being on powerboats; they were cruising sailors. A friend had asked them to help him take the big, unwieldy boat from California to Alaska. Dick and Karin had sailed to the Marquises from Hawaii and now had their sailboat in Oahu harbor. We had lots to talk about and invited them to visit us. They loved the interior of our boat and the way we had designed it. We traded notes about the Marquises, as we intended to visit there in the future. After taking them back to the dock, I made a loaf of bread and took it over for them. Karin said to me "When you get to the Marquises, I want you to get a tiki for me," and gave me twenty dollars. I told her we would not be there for several years, as we planned to sail clear to Panama before heading over to French Polynesia. The twenty dollars stayed in my wallet for several years. I think that she gave it to us so we would stay in contact, which we did, and they became very close friends.

Now that all of our commitments to family and friends were over, we were free to be lazy for a while. We stayed in Brookings for a week, swimming in the river and walking on the beach. We were reluctant to leave this small town where it was so easy to get provisions of fresh fruits and vegetables. We actually had no schedule except to leave San Diego near Thanksgiving, because that was when the cyclone season would be over in Mexico. From here we were going to sail down the coast of California, counting on warmer weather and calmer seas.

California Here We Come

Where great whales come sailing by, sail and sail with unshut eye.

– Mathew Arnold

WHEN WE SET out this time we were rested and felt none of the anxiety that had plagued us on the Oregon coast. We left early in the morning and enjoyed a beautiful sail to Crescent City on the northern Coast of California. Crescent City is famous for the Tsunami in 1968 that damaged much of the coast and town. Elmer and I explored the harbor area and the remains of the giant jackstraw, a heavy concrete formation made to keep the jetties stable, standing as a monument to the great surge of water. The terrific force of water had washed the jackstraw right off of its foundation.

Our friends, Dick, Claire, and their daughter, LeaAnne, joined us in Crescent City and were planning to sail on to San Francisco with us. We set sail the next morning for a pleasant trip to Eureka on Humboldt Bay. It was a warm hazy day and, just as we crossed the bar, thick fog quickly formed and followed us into the harbor. We had originally planned to only anchor overnight but the forbidding fog rolled back in the next morning. We decided to wait out the fog, although Dick and Claire were feeling restless and eager to move on to San Francisco. On the second day they urged us to sail, but we resisted and chose to wait for the weather to clear. They finally decided they couldn't wait anymore and hopped on a bus to San Francisco. "We'll see you when you get there," they hollered to us as they departed.

We stayed in Eureka for an entire week and enjoyed exploring the historic city of the Redwood Empire while waiting for the weather to clear. We would walk for miles admiring the Victorian style architecture of the houses. The city had given homeowners a tax break to refurbish their homes and more than fifteen hundred of the houses had been restored to their original pristine condition. The homes were brightly painted and finely detailed and as we strolled through the city for hours, we enjoyed the individuality and uniqueness of each residence.

When the sun finally shone brightly again, we were eager to continue down the coast. We stopped in several small towns and sheltered bays that we had visited before, by car, on earlier trips along the coast. *Leeway* was still sailing with us at this point and we decided that we would pass Shelter cove together. Unfortunately Dave called when we drew near and informed us that Lee was sick again. We had heard that Shelter Cove was a safe anchorage, so we ducked in and anchored. What an awful anchorage! The Pacific swell rolled all the way into the cove. We swayed back and forth feeling the cadence of the swell, rolling constantly all night long. Loose items rattled around in their drawers. Shortly after we were anchored, a fisherman approached and asked if we would like a salmon. He called it a shaker because it was too small for a commercial fisherman to keep, but because it was already dead he did not want to throw it back into the sea and waste it. We accepted and enjoyed a tasty baked salmon while rolling around in our less than comfortable anchorage that evening. I noted with astonishment that Lee was not at all ill while in the anchorage, despite the heaving sea.

Our next destination was Fort Bragg, a fishing village not often visited by pleasure boats. We raced a thick fog to the entrance of the channel and were thankfully motoring through the narrow waterway when we passed a fishing boat.

"Is there some place where we can tie up at a dock?" we asked an unhappy looking skipper.

"Not for sailboats," he angrily replied.

His response was a bit daunting, but we looked back at the fog rolling inexorably toward us and carried on to the docking area. We tied up to the outer dock and looked for a port captain. The office was closed, so we asked someone in the area about the dock that we were already tied. We were assured that it would be fine to stay there. That evening after we had taken our walk, we heard a very loud motor just outside *Elysium*. A giant fishing boat had pulled up along side us and we saw a man with a heavy black beard at the helm.

"You're in my space," he said briskly.

"We're sorry" Elmer said, "We were told that it was OK to tie up here. Would you mind rafting on the outside of us?"

"That would be fine, we'll be going out at dawn tomorrow," he replied, sounding friendlier.

We put our big red buoys over the side and he tied off to us.

Later that evening we had a chance to talk with the skipper. We learned that when fishing boats encounter rough weather, they are often not welcome to dock at yacht clubs. "That makes for some bad feelings between us," he concluded. The crew was pleasant and interested in exploring the inside of *Elysium*. Fishing boats are strictly work-oriented providing none of the luxuries we enjoyed. The crew apologized for having to cross our deck before dawn, but we expressed our gratitude to be in their slip and were happy to have them cross over at any time. It worked perfectly for everyone and we welcomed the opportunity to meet such wonderful people. It was our policy to get along with the people we met since survival at sea makes everyone an essential neighbor.

We stayed in Fort Bragg until the fog lifted. In the meantime, we learned about life in a small fishing village. We finally sailed from the village to a small bay near the Little River at Van Damme State Park where we found protection in the great kelp forest. The kelp beds are nourished by the California sun and can grow a foot or more a day. They function as nurseries for spawning fish and enable the fingerlings to take cover and to survive. Our next stop, Bodega Bay, is a well-protected, calm and peaceful place near the Sonoma Coast State Beach Park, where we enjoyed meeting several campers who expressed interest in *Elysium* and our voyage. This would be the last opportunity to provision for a while so we walked the four miles to town everyday to buy fresh fruit and vegetables. We would fill our backpacks with the beautiful produce and eat fresh peaches as we walked back to the boat. We had no refrigeration aboard, but Elmer had built a very large icebox. We would buy a chunk of ice that would keep our food cold and fresh for quite a long time.

We approached San Francisco Bay with some trepidation because we had heard many tales about the difficulty entering this busy port, "So many ships coming and going there's hardly even space for a small sailboat to enter," they warned us.

As we sailed over the legendary Potato Patch, a small shallow stretch of very rough water, the wind blew more than thirty knots, creating a mass of tossing swirling currents. Then as we entered the channel, there were, indeed, many large ships. We had been out to sea with no one nearby, and the ships in the channel seemed perilously close to us. In actuality, the proximity of the ships was more of an illusion than a reality; we had plenty of room. Envisioning the worst scenario, I began to feel very apprehensive; heavy fog was forming behind us. With the fog chasing us inexorably into port, Elmer said, "I know this is uncomfortable, but when we are in the shelter side of the bay, we won't even feel the wind."

We sailed in and found a buoy at the Sausalito Yacht Club, where instead of protection, the wind shot down the hills screaming like a dragon through the rigging. Because the water was so rough, it was three days before we could take the dingy to shore. In spite of a thirty-knot wind, long arms of fog reached down over the mountainside, taunting us with its interminable presence.

"We just won't go out until it clears up," Elmer assured me.

When we finally reached the shore three days later, we received reciprocity at the Sausalito Yacht Club with our Sauvie Island Yacht Club membership. We were welcome to use the showers and the dock for our dingy for as long as we wished to. We had realized on the voyage thus far that we desperately needed an autopilot. The hours and hours of steering a compass course had been almost unbearable and we were happy to meet one of the members of the club who sold and installed autopilots. He agreed to install one for us right away so we could stay moored while they worked on the boat. During the installation, we happily took a ferry over to the city of San Francisco. We were tourists in this beautiful city again. We took long walks and hiked in the Golden Gate National Recreation Area. One day the fog was pouring into the bay and we decided to cross the Golden Gate Bridge on foot. We walked half way across the bridge to a thick wall of fog and watched as the cars did not even slow down, but plowed into the dense invisibility of the fog-wall before them, literally disappearing before our eyes. We could stand on one side of the fog bank, then take a few steps forward and be entirely enveloped by the eerie white haze, suddenly invisible even to each other.

I let the family and friends know we had arrived in San Francisco. Howard Radke visited us on the boat and worked on our radio while some of the family came down to enjoy sailing with us in the protection of the bay. When Tori arrived, she was so eager to see us that she jumped into the freezing waters and swam out to the boat! LeAnn arrived and happily informed us she was expecting her first baby in December. Elmer and I were both enthusiastic and wistful: keenly aware of the fact we would miss the birth of our first grandson while we were at sea.

Conditions in the bay were ideal for sailing. We enjoyed a strong wind and no swell, perfect for exploring the many protected anchorages and historical sites in the bay. We sailed around Alcatraz Island, an uncomfortably eerie and haunting place. We spent some time at Angel Island, the point of entry for the United States for one hundred and seventy-five thousand Chinese immigrants in the 1930's. It was also known as the "Ellis Island" for Asian immigrants, where they often had to wait for over two years before entering the country. We tested our new autopilot, and, to our relief, we found it to be unbelievably accurate. We could set our course and leave it, so we didn't have to be at the helm all of the time. It was going to set us free.

Since the conditions were still not great for going out to sea, we decided to sail up the Sacramento River. On the way up the river, we decided to stop at a dock in Antioch for the night. But as I looked at the chart, I noticed that it was too shallow for *Elysium* to safely enter. "I know we can get in," Elmer said confidently. "Look at that big boat over there." We started into the docking area where the depth sounder indicated that we were already hitting ground. Despite the depth sounder, Elmer successfully steered *Elysium* to the dock. On shore was a group of people watching us enter.

"How much water does your boat draw?" one person asked.

"Six and a half feet," Elmer responded.

"This moorage really doesn't have enough depth for you" said someone else.

"What about that big boat over there," he asked?

"Why that boat has been stuck in the mud for years," they replied.

Meanwhile *Elysium* settled into the thick mud as the tide went out. Fortunately the next morning we were able to leave because the tide was higher than usual. We had lucked out. "Next time listen to me when I tell you that we shouldn't go into a place because it's too shallow," I advised.

We motored off the river into Steamboat Slew, occasionally skimming along the muddy bottom. We noticed a large boat motoring ahead of us, made from the same design as *Elysium*. Mud was stirring up from beneath the boat, but the tide was low and we knew that there would be more depth soon. We followed them in, and as they anchored we came alongside and introduced ourselves to Guy and Irene La France. Guy had built his boat *Alon'zy* from the same plans that we had used to build *Elysium* a few years before. When he was ready to cruise, Guy, who had hailed from Vancouver, Canada, placed an ad for a crew member interested in travel and adventure. Irene from Southampton, England, responded, thinking anything would be better than her boring job. She had never been on a sailboat before, but Irene was plucky and adventurous, and she and Guy made a tremendous couple. We learned that they were headed south, to Mexico, and then on through the Panama Canal to sail the Caribbean Sea.

The four of us shared information. They had sailed *Alon'zy*, out of sight of land from Vancouver to San Francisco Bay. Elmer and I had plenty of experience of crossing bars and anchoring, but we had no experience navigating or offshore sailing. We shared experiences and practiced using the sextant, which we hadn't even touched since taking classes in Portland. Now that we were on the water and had a real horizon to work with, some of the troubling things in class finally made sense to us. We enjoyed their company very much and planned to meet at the anchorages ahead. We would never sail together as we had with *Leeway*, but if they were at an anchorage when we arrived it would be great! If not we would see them later on.

When we re-entered San Francisco Bay, we anchored outside of the Sea Scout base in order to provision while in the city. A key to the base was given to us so we could leave the dingy at their facility. We had heard that it was not safe to leave a dingy onshore because of potential theft. We were able to walk to town from the boat near Ghirardelli Square to visit the San Francisco Maritime National Historical Park, Fisherman's Wharf, and many other points of interest along the busy waterfront.

San Francisco Bay is a gathering spot for cruising yachts that are heading both north to Canada and Alaska, and south to Mexico and through the Panama Canal. We met people who had been to Mexico and asked them to mark our charts with the safe anchorages they had found on their voyages. We listened to each person's experiences with interest even though we found people who enjoyed telling scary stories about Mexican villains and dreadful seas. Now, as I look back, we were very inexperienced and made excellent targets for scare tactics.

At the end of September we set out with *Alon'zy* for the next leg of our trip down the coast. We expected to have a north wind, but as we went along toward the Golden Gate Bridge, we felt it turning to the south. We had a fast current that sluiced us under the bridge and out of the bay. When we turned south, the wind became stronger and stronger until it was blowing right on the nose. We beat into a miserable sea that was slopping up over the bow with a big spray for eight hours before finally giving it up and turning around. We were back at the anchorage within an hour, sailing with the wind and sea behind us. This would be the last time we would beat into weather.

We spent one more night in San Francisco Bay to see if the wind would turn around as forecast, and sure enough we had a good north wind. As we left and were approaching the heavy current near the bridge, we heard a mayday call on the radio. The man sounded terrified. "H E L P" he cried in a very shaky voice. Thinking he needed help, we motored over to where he was calling. We saw him just outside the entrance of a large yacht club and all that happened was that he had lost the power of his motor. He was terrified that he would be swept to sea, but he was in no trouble as the people from the yacht club came out and towed him in.

After San Francisco we had good sailing in beautiful sunshine and we found a good anchorage each night just as dusk arrived. We would go into a harbor, intending to stay the night, and sometimes stay for several days. We anchored off the coast of Santa Cruz where there is an amusement park right on the beach. This is the oldest amusement park on the west coast of the United States and it still has some of the original carvings on the carousel. The Boardwalk is now a State Historical Landmark and the old-fashioned carnival games and snack booths still preserve the integrity of the original arrangement. The town is very attractive; we took the opportunity to browse through the many interesting shops in the mall. We rode a few rides in the park and met local residents on boats who had been anchored there for many years. One man lived on a very poorly suited sailboat without even the most basic safety features. His lifelines were made from plastic pipe, which was decorative, but would not stop a strong wave. He enjoyed a frugal lifestyle with a snug little home in a safe anchorage.

We looked forward to visiting Monterey by sea where we found a safe anchorage just off of the Embarcadero that provided a good place to leave the dingy. As we walked ashore, we observed that since John Steinbeck's day, the city had turned into a rather wealthy retirement area. Condominiums and malls dominated the historical sites. The canneries he wrote of were idle and in a state of ruin because over fishing had closed them down years ago. Monterey was a city in transition; people without jobs had to move away, and good climate and access to the sea had drawn affluent people to take their places.

Two hundred and seventy-six miles of this coastal area is a federally protected National Marine Sanctuary. The California sea otter, which is now a protected species, had been hunted nearly to extinction in the past. The desirable fur that has one hundred thousand hairs per square centimeter makes a very luxurious fur coat. We watched the otter's playful antics as they clustered around the boat every day. We observed them preening their fur to get oxygen into their heavy coat; they have no fat to keep them warm in the water, like a seal does, so they rely on the oxygen in the fur to keep them warm. They would dive down and retrieve shellfish, storing them in a pouch under each flipper. Then, when back at the surface, they would lie on their backs in the water and use a stone to crack them open while holding the shellfish on their chest. Otters are very beneficial as they are grazing on the crustaceans that do great damage to the kelp forests. We never tired of watching them clown around.

Another protected species found in Monterey is the brown pelican. We loved to watch them sail out to sea and dive down for fish and when they fly, they have a look of complete confidence and peace. We counted on having good luck if we had a pelican nearby. We hated to leave this peaceful anchorage with all of the sea life around, but a strong south wind was rising, creating an untenable anchorage.

We arrived at San Simeon after an overnight sail to see a beach full of nude sunbathers. Irene was shocked, and threatened not to go ashore at all. "There are only two kinds," Elmer kidded her. We decided to go to shore because we wanted to see Hearst's Castle. While most people see this as an opulent beautiful place, we saw it an obscene marble tribute to wealth and materialism built by Chinese slave labor. We stayed several days at San Simeon beach to swim and hike. One day we were surrounded by a massive migration of thousands of monarch butterflies. Some didn't survive the trip and had fallen along the roadway. I gathered as many perfect butterflies as I could find and displayed them on a piece of driftwood in the aft cabin of *Elysium*. They looked as though they had landed there and stayed flawlessly preserved for many months.

Our next stop, Moro Bay, an artificial harbor built by the U.S. Army Corps of Engineers, had a narrow passage that is often impossible to enter. When we arrived at the entrance there were waves breaking all the way across the channel. We waited for a while and could see that after several waves there would be a relative calm. "Lets go over and see if we can make it," Elmer said. We cautiously approached, waiting for the calm; when it came we allowed a wave to carry us in.

When we entered the port captain's office, we saw the famous picture of John Wayne's one hundred foot yacht with its bow in the air engulfed by a breaking wave near Moro rock. As we walked over to the jetty, I wondered how we would ever be able to sail out, as the waves were swirling and breaking everywhere on the bar. We read the warnings signs on the jetty that told of the unpredictable waves that swept sightseers and fishermen off the slippery rocks to their deaths into the sea. When the time came to leave, we anxiously watched the wave action. Guy and Irene went out on a breaking wave and we followed closely behind to take advantage of the subsiding tide. We were glad to be safely on our way.

A gale was brewing as we sailed out once more, which made life onboard very difficult. Even something as simple as fixing a meal in these conditions was a gymnastic feat. I had to hold onto the grab rail at all times. Everything that was set down had to be placed in the security of the sink to keep it from sliding onto the floor. But Elmer was so appreciative to have a hot meal when it was cold and windy that it made all my work worthwhile.

Coming into Santa Barbara we had a fierce northwest wind of thirty-eight knots. The currents become strong in this area as they are influenced by the Channel Islands close offshore. The sea was whipped up into furious foam, swirling around the mouth of the channel where we intended to enter. We were most eager to get out of this rough, untenable sea, so we decided to go into the moorage area for a rest. As we approached, we saw that the whole area was rimmed with logs and that a dredge was working on the channel. The strong wind had caused the logs to form a barrier to the entrance so it looked like we were going to have to sail on down the coast. We were watching closely and saw a small powerboat navigate around the logs and move safely into the docking area, despite the big waves breaking clear across the channel. We decided to venture nearer to see what kind of chance we would have to enter, because we needed fuel and water. As we drew closer, a small tender came out and signaled us to follow him into the docking area. The logs were dipping and diving close by, but we stayed very close to him for safety. He led us to a slip where we gratefully tied up to a dock lined by buildings for the first time since leaving Newport, Oregon. The moorage was so well protected that the wind just whistled over the top of the buildings, leaving us in a peaceful, quiet space. Even though we had to pay to stay there, we were not going to go out until the wind and seas abated. We were able to supply our storage with food, water and fuel, and to hike around the waterfront exploring the city before we left.

We were approaching Los Angeles, which is a very heavily populated area. We entered Marina Del Rey, referring to a special chart to give us directions. The channel is like the Los Angeles Freeways with throngs of boats both entering and leaving. The charge to stay at the public dock was more than twenty dollars a night, so we went to the California Yacht Club to see if we could receive reciprocity. Because a member was going to be gone for a month, they kindly gave us permission to occupy that slip. The slip had electricity and water and they gave us the key to their opulent clubhouse with access to a large swimming pool. The members came to visit us and admired Elmer's work on the interior of the boat. There was also an ice maker, so we could safely preserve the fresh produce we bought. Besides all of this, there was no particular time we had to leave and did not have to pay to be there.

The weather was getting cooler; it was now the first of November. We had been at sea for about ten hours after leaving the yacht club. We sailed around Point Loma's Cabrillo National Monument, an old lighthouse at the entrance of San Diego Harbor. Next to San Francisco bay this is the best-protected and busiest port on the west cost of the United States. All sorts of military and pleasure boats were moving in and out as we rounded the U. S. Naval Air Station on the north island. Shelter Island is inside the bay and provides a visitor dock for yachts for three days to provision and take fuel.

We intended to stay in San Diego until Thanksgiving, so we could get supplies and wait for the cyclone season to be over in Mexico. The constant mandatory movement in the San Diego Bay anchorages is known to sailboats as the "San Diego Shuffle". Each boat has a few days to anchor before the water police come by and ask them to move. The Bay area is always crowded with cruising sailboats preparing to go south. The sailing lifestyle does not conform to the mind set of the conservative military-based town.

We anchored at the Coronado Yacht Club where we could stay in front of the club for a limited time. From there we went to Southwestern Yacht Club's guest dock, which allowed yachts three days to dock. Each day we hurried to shop for what we needed before the time was up. On our third day we were starting out early in the morning when we met a vivacious, very friendly lady. We told her that we were provisioning for Mexico and we were in a hurry because it was the last day we were allowed to dock there. Her name was Joanne Mitchum and she told us that their sailboat was on the outside of the dock and that we were welcome to raft to it until it was time for us to leave for Mexico. We gratefully accepted her kind offer. We would not have to move again and we could relax and enjoy the rest of our time here.

Now there was time to visit the Star of India, a maritime museum on the bay. The sailing vessel is two hundred and five feet long and has an iron hull that was built in 1863. This is the oldest active sailing ship in the world. The ship is known for its many stories of lost sailors and ghosts that haunt the decks and cabins. The beautiful cabin for the officers is graced with rich hardwood furniture and a beautiful brass and glass skylight arching over the dining salon. This luxury is a stark contrast to the sterile bunks below for the crew. The smell of these old boats always filled my imagination with images of stormy times at sea with only the oil lamps and a warm oil stove offering sanctuary inside.

We called on our friends in San Diego to drive us to Price Club where we could buy the rest of the supplies we needed for our trip south. We had learned that toilet paper, some canned goods, and mayonnaise were scarce in Mexico. As I stocked up with these goods and much more, Elmer said the water line on *Elysium* went down a full inch. We also found a marine supply store called Pacific Marine, a place where sailors met. Tommie and Steve, who owned the store, sailed a beautiful Alden sailboat each year to Cabo San Lucas, Mexico. Pacific Marine not only collected mail and forwarded it to the cruising sailors as they requested it, but also carried everything a sailor could want or need. While we were there we met Steve and Elaine on *Flicker*, who were leaving the same time as we were. Because it was a new experience for us to leave the United States, we decided to stay in radio contact with them. We had heard so many tales from other people about the awful things that would confront us: there are no aids to navigation; when there is no propane there are no navigation lights; fishing boats are out at night with no lights; theft and bribes are widespread; conditions are anything but clean and there are cockroaches and rats that come aboard. "What pleasant things to look forward to," we thought. We were feeling a bit apprehensive about the voyage ahead.

Goodbye United States of America

*Accepting others as they are brings a wonderful
freedom to your own mind.*
— The Peace Formula

WE SAILED OUT of San Diego at 3:30 p.m., Thanksgiving Day, and arrived in Ensenada, Mexico, the next day, mid morning, with our good luck pelicans guiding us into port. Our philosophy was to never be in a hurry when checking into or out of a country. We found that dealing with authorities in foreign countries is a more relaxed and friendly experience than we were accustomed to in the United States. We checked in with no problems and were given permission to stay for six months and sail the waters of the Pacific and the Sea of Cortez. Back on *Elysium* we looked forward to exploring the Pacific waters of Mexico.

Our charts were marked with the safe anchorages along the Baja California coast. We sailed out with several other boats in a very light wind and decided to stop earlier than planned for an unexpected visit to Santo Tomas a short distance away. As we were anchoring, the Pacific swell began to approach the bay, suggesting an uncomfortable anchorage and the return of wind the next day. As we had anticipated, the wind was blowing the next morning and we departed at daybreak for a full day's sail. There are many beautiful bays and jutting land formations on the Pacific side of Baja that would offer excellent protection for anchoring, and we looked forward to stopping nearly every night if that was our choice. When traveling at a good pace we would often attract a pod of dolphin that raced over and would swim beside us. Each time the dolphins joined us, Elmer and I would take turns lying on the bowsprit to watch them swim and play beneath the bow. They frolicked in the water, seeming to smile up at us, making eye contact, suggesting to us that they were enjoying themselves.

We sailed around the perfect hook of land that juts out of Puerto San Bartolomes and protects Turtle Bay from the north wind. There are kelp forests all around the outside, further calming the swell. Several of the boats we were traveling with arrived at the same time to enjoy the protected anchorage. The crew on one boat needed diesel and went ashore to buy it from a local entrepreneur named Gordo. We had been warned that buying diesel in these small places was risky because water tended to get into their drums, and since we were not running the motor often we wanted to wait until we got to a large supply station to fill our tank.

There was a good size fish on our line so we invited Guy, Irene, and Steve and Elaine over to join us for dinner. Everyone brought something to add to the meal; while we ate we enjoyed sharing stories about our experiences. That evening we heard a tapping on *Elysium's* hull. A young man selling abalone stood in a small wooden boat. Elmer and Steve bargained with him for some time, thinking that we could divide the meat and we could also have beautiful shells. When they agreed on the price and the man left, they lifted the box up onto the deck to see what they had purchased: there were twenty-five pounds of abalone meat that had been removed from the shells. This was an enormous amount for six people to eat! We were able to buy ice to keep the meat cold for six or seven days. As the days passed, we discussed ways to prepare and eat it for breakfast, lunch and dinner. We were also able to catch small tuna using the abalone scraps for bait.

Leaving very early in the morning on December 9th, we sailed overnight to our next stop in Santa Maria Bay. Pods of dolphin jumped high out of the water before us as the afternoon sun shone on their sleek bodies. The happy swimmers stayed with us all evening; just as they left us we caught another yellow fin tuna. These delightful animals always seemed to bring us good luck with our fishing.

Elmer and I decided to keep two-hour watches because the longer watches were exhausting. We started our first watch at eight o'clock, with one of us at the helm and the other sleeping, changing every two hours all through the night. I was on watch when Irene called on the radio. "Wow wasn't that something! To have a big ship cut right in between us?" she exclaimed. I was chagrined, as I had not even seen the ship. I must have been asleep. I promised myself that it would never happen again while I was on watch.

As we enjoyed a peaceful anchorage and a warm comfortable day in Santa Maria Bay, we all decided that it was time to take a swim in the ocean. We walked to the white sandy beach and put our flippers on at the waters edge. I was having a hard time fastening mine, so Elmer and Steve waded out into the water first. Just as I was finally able to get my strap fixed and started out to follow them, they quickly turned and immediately headed to shore as hastily as they could, running clumsily in their flippers. They were in hip-deep water when an enormous hammerhead shark swam in between them. We hadn't considered sharks a danger because we hadn't seen any for the entire trip. Later on that year we heard of someone being killed by a shark on that beach.

A gentle breeze was blowing the next morning so we decided to leave for the short hop into Magdalena Bay. We were slipping through the water at a very good clip when a Mahi Mahi, or dolphin fish, hit our line. The dolphin fish is not to be confused with a porpoise, which is a species of the whale family. The Mahi Mahi is a beautiful fish with colors flashing bright gold and shimmering with brilliant blues and greens when caught. The prominent forehead on this fish indicated that it was a male and he weighed about eighteen pounds. Just right for an evening feast. I went below to heat the oven and bake bread while Elmer threw our three hundred test-line with baited hook back into the water. We had room for more fish in the icebox if he happened to catch another one. Just as we were sitting down to enjoy the fragrant white fish, we heard the fish line snap on deck. Elmer rushed on to deck and began to pull on the line. He was having so much trouble that I helped him tug. As we hauled the line in, we could finally see the fish that was giving us such a fight. A beautiful silver king mackerel was struggling and jumping as we brought in the line. When we finally pulled it up alongside the boat it was flopping violently and Elmer could barely hang onto it. I grabbed a hammer from below and gave it a few blows on the head so we wouldn't lose it. I can still see Elmer cleaning the colossal sixty-pound fish, slipping around on the decks, drenched with blood, as the boat sailed along at five knots. We had never before pulled in such a magnificent catch. We were very fortunate that we had enough ice left in the icebox to keep the flesh cold.

We radioed ahead to Magdalena Bay to see if there was anyone there. "We just caught a sixty pound King Mackerel" we bragged. "Anyone up for a fish dinner?" We would be in the bay in thirty minutes. Several hungry sailors replied, and offered to bring a potluck dish. Elmer cut a

sixteen-pound roast from the middle of our prize catch, so large it would barely fit into the oven. It was baking as we anchored in the beautiful, protected Magdalena Bay.

Sixteen people enjoyed the feast, but because of the crowded conditions, they were seated in every available place on the boat. We filled each plate with a big chunk of delicious fish, a very moist white meat that had a taste similar to halibut. Before the crowd left, the table was emptied of every scrap of food. Everyone enjoyed a delight-

Sixty pound Wahoo

ful meal and good companionship, and we enjoyed the opportunity to meet new friends.

That evening I cut another ten pounds of the fish into small cubes and pickled them with the tasty Mexican limes that we found growing on the shore. Some distance away from the other yachts was an eighty-five foot Chinese Junk rigged sailboat at anchor, called *Intrepid Dragon*. We had never been inside a Chinese Junk before so we thought that if we took over some steaks from our fish perhaps they would invite us aboard. We rowed over the next morning, and when the crew saw what we had for them, they asked if would like to come aboard and see the yacht "We would love to," we replied enthusiastically.

A notable Hollywood star had purchased it and hired a delivery crew to deliver it to San Diego from the east coast. The room that held the three hundred horsepower engine was as big as our aft cabin. In the next space stood a gigantic generator. This lovely old yacht was not modern, and the hand-carved teak that adorned every part of the interior, even the curtain rods, spoke of an era long gone by.

That afternoon our friends gathered to walk the wind-swept dunes that lined the remote beach. In one area there was a large section devoted to drying salty fishy smelling shark fins. The fishermen who caught these huge sharks were extraordinarily brave. The massive body of a single shark would occupy the entire inside of their little fishing prams. Once they caught a big hammerhead, they needed to immediately place a blow in the right spot to kill it! There were many tales of severe shark bites occurring during this risky process. The fins for Shark Fin soup were in great demand at that time, making it possible for this remote fishing village to survive.

Later we all set up a picnic on the beach and enjoyed our pickled fish with some salad. The entire ten pounds of fish were eaten very quickly. We resumed our hike and spotted several species of birds living along the mangrove-lined lagoon. The mangroves protect the sandy shore from washing away and also give many species of small fish and crustacean protection to grow and feed. The mangrove forest is a complete ecosystem with one species depending on another for survival. Egrets and herring gulls also enjoy the mangroves as they can pick up a tasty dinner without having to fight for it.

The six of us went snorkeling together. We saw for the first time the bright orange garibaldi shining like a spotlight in the verdant sea grass. Lobsters hid under the rocks, their antennae waving around, suggesting a fight if we were to try to dislodge one of them. Steve and Elaine dug up fallen angel clams and prepared a clam chowder dinner for all of us. It was a perfect ending to a beautiful day.

It was near the end of December and we felt the desire to situate ourselves in Cabo San Lucas before New Year's Day. The anchorage tended to fill up with yachts near the end of the year. We sailed for three days to the tip of the Baja Peninsula, enjoying a five-knot breeze that suddenly turned very warm. We had finally reached the tropical zone! As we approached the anchorage, the sight of dozens of boats bobbing around at anchor greeted us. After anchoring, we turned on the radio to hear someone droning "another day in paradise." The voice went on to report the weather, the activities at the beach and the conditions at sea. This was the afternoon news from Mike, on the yacht *Starbuck*, who returned to Cabo every year in December. He told us about the New Years Day pig roast for all the yachties. The cost would be ten dollars per person with a potluck dish required to compliment the feast.

The Panaderea, or taco bakery, had agreed to cook the pig for our New Year's Day celebration. We were told that the pig would be ready for lunch between one and two o'clock in the afternoon. The New Year's Eve celebrants from the anchorage were drinking cheap Mexican alcohol called *canya*, pure one hundred-proof alcohol mixed with limejuice. New Years Day, because of all the festivity, everyone was ravenously hungry. The potluck dishes were in the tent and the fire was lit, and we were more than ready for the pig at two o'clock. We saw people sampling the potluck dishes, but did not realize that they were hungry campers raiding our food. The potluck had disappeared and still there was no roasted pig. At four o'clock someone went to see what had happened to the costly meal. We learned that in Mexico, two o'clock means anytime after noon, so it was dusk before the pig arrived. We divided it up and everyone else began to eat. I watched as very hungry people gnawed on the tasty bones, but I saw red blood. "We're not eating any of this raw meat," Elmer and I decided. Raw pork can cause Trichinosis, which is a cyst that is formed by a larva that infests an animal's muscles and transfers to humans. Increasing the danger, the Mexican pigs we had seen foraged for anything, including worms and human feces. So much for the long awaited feast; we returned to the boat and baked fresh bread to eat with canned meat and vegetables.

We needed to fill our diesel tanks so Elmer made us backpacks out of five-gallon containers in order to carry diesel from the service station. Every day we labored along, carrying the forty-pound load a mile and a half from the Pemex station back to the boat, doing our best to avoid the Mexican dogs that found great joy in barking at us as they drew so near that we could feel their hot breath on our legs. Guy and Irene also joined us carrying backpacks of diesel for *Alon'zy*. It was a rewarding labor because diesel only cost eighteen cents a gallon and was exceptionally clean and would guarantee no problems with our injectors while tossing around at sea.

The lazy days drifted into a week, which happens easily when the weather is balmy and there is warm water lined with relaxing white sandy beaches. One morning we left the boat and went sightseeing with Steve and Elaine. As we were walking, a very strong wind suddenly began to blow. We rushed back to the anchorage where fortunately Steve had a big motor on his dingy. We would never have been able to row little *Limbo* through the breaking waves back to *Elysium*. The rest of the day and into the night *Elysium* plowed and tugged as the wind and sea tried to dislodge her from our anchor.

After this, we gathered with our friends and agreed to leave for the difficult trip into the inner Sea of Cortez. The voyage is particularly challenging because of a strong predominant head wind that blows from the northeast. The combination of the wind and the tide produces what are referred to as square waves. We each decided how we would make the two-day trip up to Cabo San Jose. Some would tack out and back going to windward, others would motor close to shore. It turned out to be a dreadful trip indeed, as we chose to motor into a constant twenty-five-knot wind. When the tide changed, we encountered a sea of green water broaching over the bow. We arrived at the anchorage first, and then the others, who had been drenched inside their boats on the journey, came in and anchored. They had to remove everything from their boats and hang it out to dry. As we listened to their stories, we realized what a dreadful trip it had been and that we had made the right choice, especially with the inexpensive diesel. The motoring time had been worth the comparative comfort.

After a few days rest we pulled anchor for the sail up to Los Frailes; we collected a delicate little tan seahorse that had been attached to the chain. This was the first one we had ever seen and its unusual head and fins were perfectly shaped to propel him forward into the water.

The next few days were comfortable as we had good winds and no tide to hold us back. We stopped each night at good anchorages and snorkeled, delighting in the brilliantly colored angelfish and striped blue and gold grunt. It was like standing in a tropical fish aquarium.

When we reached the city of La Paz, we found another bay full of yachts and large fishing boats. It was now the end of January, and we had not been able to get fresh fruits and vegetables for quite some time, so we enjoyed shopping at the well-stocked stores of La Paz. The people of the city were very friendly and they spoke English so we did not have to use our very inadequate Spanish. Now we had all the food we desired and were ready to explore the many islands in the upper reaches of the Sea of Cortez.

As we motored out of La Paz, two gigantic grey whales rose out of the water right beside the boat. It was a breathtaking sight to see an awesome creature of this length and girth leap completely out of the water with such ease. This is an area where pods of whales come in order to bear their calves in the warm waters. We had the opportunity to see many more of these gentle giants as we sailed around the islands in the Sea of Cortez.

We left our friends and went on alone to explore the stunning bay at Los Gatos, which is surrounded by dark red rocks patterned against dark green cactus blooming brilliant orange flowers. This was the first time we had been alone since leaving San Diego. We had been warned several times about theft and other dangers in Mexico, so we were glad to have the bay to ourselves. We rowed ashore and were walking along the beach when a brightly painted open motorboat entered and sped over to *Elysium*. We watched from our vantage point helplessly as they tried to get someone to answer their knocking. Then one of the men saw us onshore and sped over to where we were standing. "Hola" they greeted us. They offered us a ride back to *Elysium*, so we accepted and returned to our home with them. We invited them aboard and began practicing the few Spanish words we knew, asking them how the fishing was and how many children they had. These questions elicited a warm response as they pulled out pictures of their fine looking dark-eyed children. We had a picture board of our children and they looked at each one with interest, exclaiming "muy bonito!" We all enjoyed a small snack together, and then Elmer pulled out some of his treasured Mounds Bars for them to give to their children. We had such a warm friendly exchange that our whole attitude about meeting local people improved considerably. We cast away any apprehension that we had previously felt. They took us back to our dingy onshore and as they left, they gave us two big fish from their catch. We thanked them from the bottom of our hearts.

The inland sea of Cortez is highly populated with many species of birds and fish. We caught several different varieties of fish each day. A big yellow- fin tuna would strike the hook, and then we would pull it in, dress it out and enjoy fresh fish each night for dinner. We sailed to small islands with white sandy beaches where we could walk on shore and collect a variety of shells. I wanted to make a puka shell necklace, so I spent time lying on my stomach in the hot white sand, sifting though it to find them. I finally found enough of the varying colored shells to complete a long string.

Sailing into the small island of San Francisqito, we found that our friends were already anchored there. We shared a big barbecue on shore and explored the island together. We were each headed to Puerto Escondido, which is close to Loreto and is a good size town. It was good to be reunited with our friends again, sharing stories and experiences. During this time, passing the ham radio code test was constantly on my mind. I wanted to be legal; the people that use the radio without a license are called pirates, which certainly did not appeal to me. During the last few months I had been studying the Morse code and I was determined to get my license. Now that we were close to Loreto, where we could catch a bus to San Diego, we decided to take our amateur license exams.

The proper procedure for leaving a boat in Mexico is to transfer the title for the boat over to the Mexican Government. This seemed like a lot of fuss when we were just leaving for a few days. It was not as if we were going to be gone for the entire season. Guy and Irene said they would stay in Puerto Escondido with the boat and care for it while we were away. With this decided, we went to town, purchased a bus ticket for San Diego, and left the next day.

We were only able to get seats on the bus because we had made reservations the previous day. The bus was packed with people because the road had only recently opened having been washed out for at least a month. There were so many passengers that the aisles were filled with people standing through the twelve-hour trip. It seemed to us that everyone had a cigarette in his mouth and was puffing furiously, creating a miserable blue haze. I opened my window so I could breathe, but when I dozed off someone would sneak up and close it. Still, when the smoke became too overwhelming I would have to open the window again.

While in San Diego we stayed with Elmer's brother, and from there we made arrangements to take the test for an amateur radio license the next day. I spent that evening and all night listening to a recording of the code. I was exhausted the next morning and my head was ringing because I was so focused on passing that exam. When the test began and I heard the code, I panicked. I could not even think clearly because I was so nervous, but I finally pulled myself together and just barely passed the test. Elmer decided that since I passed it, he would not even bother with it.

As we returned to Mexico, the bus was stopped at a checkpoint one hundred and fifty miles south of the border. An officer boarded the bus and questioned each person.

"Did you leave Mexico on this trip and go into the United States?" he said, looking me straight in the eye.

"Yes" I answered sleepily. A person can cross the boarder within one hundred fifty miles without a visa or passport, but you must get one if you go further. We had gone further, which I admitted.

"Come with me" he said, leading us off the bus and into the station.

Now my stomach was rolling and I was alarmed. What would they do to us, I wondered?

"The next time someone asks you if you went over the border you say NO!" the officer said as he looked at me sternly.

Then he laughed and gave us permission to leave. I was amazed! I had often heard about corrupt officials asking for bribes, and I have blessed this man in my thoughts ever since that day.

We were extremely relieved and absolutely exhausted when we returned to the boat. Getting into our bunk was like slipping a tired foot into a comfortable slipper. We had brought back some wine for Guy and Irene to thank them for taking care of *Elysium* while we were away. We were glad that we had been successful in obtaining a radio license and were safely home again.

A few days later a customs boat entered the anchorage. It sped directly over to us in a little tender and the men in it requested to come aboard. As they climbed on board, we felt extremely relieved that we had returned when we did. The young officer and his crew sat down in our lounge. One crew member had a machine gun pointed carelessly at me as he sat tapping on it on his lap, which made me quite nervous. The officer spoke excellent English and asked to see our papers. After he inspected the boat, he asked if we had any alcohol on board. I told him we did not drink alcohol because it was bad for our health.

"No," he said. "Do you have a dictionary?"

I brought him our dictionary and he found the word alcohol in it.

"See," he said, "alcohol is a preservative". We all laughed and enjoyed a savory snack together.

Meanwhile our friends had seen them come aboard and were worried about what was taking so long. They thought that we must be in trouble and that they were searching the boat, or something even worse. The officials had just jumped into their tender to leave when we heard Irene on the radio.

"We were worried about you. What did they want?" she asked.

"We were just showing them through the boat and having some refreshments" we said.

She sighed with relief. How wonderful to have friends close by that care and help.

Escondido Bay was a secluded, comfortable bay and we enjoyed our time there. When we were walking on shore we met Fred and Dot Burdon who came from Iowa to spend the winters in their little trailer that they parked on the beach. Fred was an avid fisherman and they both enjoyed bird watching. They came out to the boat and were amazed at the homelike comforts that had been built in. Fred was concerned that we would not be able to store enough food onboard during the time when we were away from stores. I showed him the storage areas under the floor and in the lazeretts that contained buckets of food.

Several days later they invited us over to have dinner with them. After dinner, Fred brought out his pride and joy—fish jerky. It was superb, and we asked him for the recipe. We often pickled fish and it kept for a while on ice, but this dried fish would keep for months without refrigeration. After he gave us the recipe, we said our goodbyes, planning to begin our trip south the next morning. Just as dawn was breaking, we heard a tapping on the boat and there was Fred, with fifty pounds of filleted fish. He had stayed out nearly all night fishing and had filleted what he had caught so that we could make jerky. We were very moved by the extraordinary effort he had gone to for us. We followed the recipe, soaked the fish and hung it from every possible spot on the boat to dry. We motored out of the bay looking rather strange with the fish dangling from all parts of the boat as we waved goodbye to our wonderful new friends.

We had not gone far when the wind increased to a good strong blow. We quickly gathered all the fish and stowed it below so we could unfurl the sails and not knock the fish off into the water. Later, we checked the moisture content by putting the fish in plastic bags in the sun. If moisture formed at the top of the bag we would turn the bags windward to dry some more. It took a long time to completely dry all of the fish, but eventually the job was complete. We had some of this jerky with us for nearly a year and enjoyed it in countless meals. Because of this wonderful couple's kindness we kept in contact for several years.

When our scuba tanks were empty, we always found someone to take them to be filled, but we found that some of the stations were not as careful about air quality as they should have been. In La Paz, we found a marine store selling an air compressor that would be perfect for us to have onboard. We wired home for money and bought it. We stowed it below in the bilge until we could build a box on deck to make it more accessible. Now we had safe air for our tanks and we could fill them at any time necessary without having to pack the heavy tanks to town. Having the compressor aboard improved our ability to fish and clean the bottom of the boat because we could stay under without constantly coming up to the surface for air.

Hurricane season would be starting soon and we needed to be heading south. We had spent February and March in the Sea of Cortez, relaxing in protected anchorages, walking the beaches and just being lazy. We swam in the crystal clear water, watching for the bright blue sequined spots that warned of tiny stinging jellyfish. Our plan was to return to our first anchorage in Baja, Los Frailes, and sail out to Isla Isabella to visit the bird sanctuary, home to the magnificent frigate bird and the blue-footed booby. These are two of the most distinctive bird species in the world, and we were eager to observe them and their habitat.

We left early in the morning for a three-day sail to the island's anchorage. While taking my first midnight watch, I summoned up my nerve and turned on my radio to try a CQ, calling for anyone who was willing to answer. It was the middle of the night, so I thought I could practice without disturbing anyone. I called CQ, CQ, CQ, and gave my call sign KA7 EKO in a pretty shaky voice. I received an immediate answer! The man answering me was in a police patrol car in California. He was genuinely interested in the fact that we were sailing and that this was my first call. I was happy to have made my first contact someone who could help me with procedure and give me good feedback on my use of the radio.

On the way down we had several days to gather more information about the birds we would be seeing on the island. The Blue-Footed Boo-by has distinctively colored feet, which one might believe were covered with blue plastic. We often saw them in the inland sea, but we never had a chance to get close to them. The boobies are about the size of geese, with close set, piercing eyes that stare curiously forward. Usually only predators look forward while prey animals have eyes on the sides of their head. The Aleutian Tern also has nesting areas on the island along with the frigate bird, which nests there because it must take flight from a tree or a bluff. This strange bird can't walk on land or take off from the water. Their distinctive flight is like a black kite flying through the air as they glide in the updrafts. They can stay aloft for more than a week, stealing food from other birds' beaks while in flight. They glide within inches of the water to pick up a fish or crab in their lethal curved beak. The Frigate bird has the largest wingspan to body weight ratio of any bird in the world. To lure a female, the male finds a spot to nest and brings a few sticks to that area. He inflates his big red throat pouch to attract a female partner who finishes the nest building and mates.

When we arrived at the island we found a beautiful protective bay in which to anchor. Going ashore was like entering an extraordinarily crowded city of birds. The black frigate birds contrast starkly with their environment, roosting and nesting in the white-barked trees. We arrived at the beginning of mating season and were privileged to witness the big red balloon-like appendage extending from the throat of the male, advertising for a mate. We were able to approach the booby and gaze into their amazing eyes. Elmer came within ten inches of one curious male and some females sitting on their nests. The Spanish conquista-dors named them *bube*, meaning stupid bird, but we found this sociable bird's friendliness extremely engaging. This was an unforgettable ex-perience for us and we were unhappy to leave, but we felt the need to continue sailing south.

The Mexican mainland has numerous protected bays giving us an opportunity to stop for a good night's sleep and some exercise on land. There were cool, rushing streams from the mountains that allowed us to take a refreshing bath, removing the salt spray we had acquired on our sail. On shore we were able to observe the exotic pink roseate spoonbills and striking egrets fishing along the outlets. The largest port we had entered so far was Puerto Vallarta, a thriving tourist city, in contrast to the lazy, friendly atmosphere of Baja. The water in the bay was dark brown and filled with garbage so we looked at the local handwork, and provisioned with food, then planned to leave the next day. Just outside of the bay in Puerto Vallarta we found the sparkling clean little village of San Juan de Juanacasta. There was fresh, clean drinking water and beautiful clear blue-green water to anchor in. We decided this was a perfect place to stay for a while to rest.

The next morning we saw three boys swimming near a boat next to us. The skipper yelled at them to stay away, so they swam over to *Elysium*. Many people on foreign yachts fear the local people because they don't understand their curiosity. We invited the boys aboard, instructing them how to climb up using the wind vane for a ladder. Their names were Benjamin, Carlos and Juan. We invited them to share a snack and together we carried on a halting conversation. When it was time for them to leave, they said to us, "We will come back tomorrow."

We were grinding wheat in the morning to make bread and looked up to see someone swimming toward us, but not making much headway. As the swimmer came closer we saw that it was Benjamin and that he had a line in his teeth with ten small fish attached. He was very proud to bring us fish, and we were delighted to think that he would do this for us. Benjamin came out to visit every day while we were there. He told us that his father had died and his mother worked hard at one of the resorts in Puerto Vallarta. We would greet him in the morning, receiving his gift of a fish or a mango. He would stay with us most of the day, proudly walking around on the deck, showing his friends that he was welcome on a yacht. Benjamin had patiently instructed us in pronunciations of Spanish and had taught us many new words. When it was time to leave we were sad to say goodbye.

We were in radio contact with Guy and Irene who were anchored in Puerto Vallarta, and we decided to leave with them for an overnight sail to Zihuatanijo. We had been on our way for five hours when they called on the radio telling us they were both violently ill. They were vomiting and experiencing what Americans refer to as "Montezuma's Revenge," and they were barely able to control their boat. We entered Tentacita Bay, and suggested that they follow us in. For the next four days we provided food and helped them with boat chores as their health improved. While they were in Puerto Vallarta, they had given in to the temptation to drink a milkshake. The local dairy products caused their illness, as they were unaccustomed to this genre of microbes. To be safe when eating in foreign countries, you need to cook or peel all food before ingesting it.

While we were there we hiked up into the hills above the bay. We found luscious mangos growing thickly in the trees, and picked up several from where they had fallen to the ground. Their color was lovely, blushing from bright red orange to purple on the outside and a deep golden-yellow inside. The fragrance of the ripe fruit filled the air as the sun shone down on them. We peeled and ate the fruit with the sweet juice dripping off of our chins.

Our next port, Zihuatanijo, was a small town with a quiet lazy atmosphere. There were several small stalls selling handcrafts and various foods, all manned by friendly people. We filled our backpacks with a bounty of fresh fruits and vegetables. Returning to the boat with our heavy backpacks and struggling to carry a fifty-pound block of ice between us we heard the entire town come to life behind us: people were hurrying around; lively music started playing; the entire peaceful, lethargic atmosphere changed as quickly as switching on a light. Looking ahead to the dock we saw a big cruise ship arriving and letting people off into motorboats to come ashore. As we struggled down the dock with our heavy load, the people being discharged were coming toward us. The clean-scrubbed, perfumed people looked at us with disgust as they passed by on their way to the now lively town. Not one person answered our smiles or hellos or made way for us to get back to our dingy. As soon as the ship departed a few hours later, the town settled down and was as quiet as when we had arrived.

Moving on to the big city of Acapulco, which provides one of the best harbors on the Pacific coast of Mexico, we learned that we had to anchor out in the bay. The city is situated near the ancient historic ruins of Mexico City, so it draws local visitors. Years ago, engineers from the city of Acapulco cut through the Abra de San Nicolas Mountains in order to allow the cooling sea breezes from the other side into the stifling city, bringing the temperature down to the high eighties from over one hundred degrees. The city is built on a narrow strip of land a half mile wide, with a waterway leading to a circle of pristine beaches where people enjoyed many water sports. Some were kite flying behind a motorboat, presenting an incredible image of colors, their brilliantly multicolored sails flying over the dazzling blue sea and sky.

The main tourist attraction in this part of southern Mexico is the La Quebrada Cliff Divers, who are known for making the famous leap into the shallow stream of water during the high tide. We had seen pictures of these divers, but nothing can compare to the thrill we experienced while watching them perform.

One day a small boat near us began moving around erratically. We discovered that a whale had entered the bay and decided that the boat bottom was an interesting shape to rub against. The skipper had frantically tried to scare it away, fearing for the integrity of his boat hull. In desperation he pulled anchor and motored around the bay. The gentle giant followed for a while, but was finally discouraged and left. The whale was a breathtaking sight for us, but a most frightening experience for the skipper because it weighed eight to ten times as much as the yacht.

The dreaded Gulf of Tehuantepec, which lay ahead, would be our next challenge. This is where the well-known Tehuantepeckers, or fifty-knot crosswinds come up and blow without warning. The fierce winds come across the narrow strip of land from the Atlantic onto the Pacific Ocean. Numerous small and large boats have been capsized, and some lost to the sea without a trace. The recommended route to follow for safety is to leave the Port of Hutulco exactly at daybreak and motor sail close to the back of the waves breaking on the shore. Timing is strategic because there are two rivers that flow out into the gulf. The course must be set to travel around both of these shallow, uncharted rivers' mouths before nightfall. We were uneasy about this journey because we had heard of so many problems this great hazard presented to every boat traveling this route.

We left at daybreak on May 17th, 1980, and we reached the first river mouth at six o'clock in the morning. We could easily see the large lagoon and the flow of the river moving into the bay. We watched the depth sounder closely as we cautiously moved around the shallow area. We were doing very well, even able to sail a bit. Then we motored a good ten hours on to the next river with an increased wind adding a few knots to our speed. As we cautiously proceeded, we were astonished to find that a big fishing boat was motoring even closer to the breaking waves than we were.

The anxiety was broken when we caught two Bonito and a Dorado. We pickled some and ate the rest. We easily reached the next river off of Tonala Bay at five o'clock in the evening, with enough light to see the shallow spit coming out from the mouth of the river. Beyond this last river the width of land between the two oceans widens and the danger from the destructive offshore wind is no longer a menace. With enormous relief we continued on for three days to Puerto Madero. The very risky trip was behind us and we had no more problems.

Puerto Madero is an oil port and not a very attractive place. We stopped long enough to prepare for the next part of the trip to visit Nicaragua and El Salvador. We met a skipper from a yacht who had just returned from that area and he gave us some frightful information. When he stopped off the coast of Nicaragua for a rest, someone on land shot at them. There were several bullet holes in the upper cabin of the boat to substantiate their story. The frightening experience motivated them to leave immediately and sail out as far from land as they could for the rest of the way into Mexico. There was a military conflict going on in both Nicaragua and El Salvado, so we determined we would sail south also avoiding the sight of land until we got to Costa Rica.

We looked forward to the rest of our voyage with apprehension. What would be encountered on our trip? How far away from the coast would be safe for us?

Looking for Costa Rica

Some day after we have mastered the winds, the waves, the tides and
gravity we shall harness the energies of love.

—Teilhard de Cardin

IT WAS VERY nice to have Guy and Irene for company when we left
Puerto Madero; two boats sailing together were safer than one traveling
alone in these dangerous waters. As we entered into Guatemalan waters,
we had a nice variable wind until nightfall when suddenly a horrific
tropical storm descended upon us. The lightning flashed constantly at
the same time as the deafening thunderclap sounded. The flashing light
illuminated the whole area and was so brilliant we could clearly see the
nearby fishing boats. The continuous electricity in the air caused our
depth sounder to stop working so we had no idea of our depth, which
the charts indicated was shallow in this area off of the coast. We dropped
the sails and decided to lay to until the storm passed by us. "It can't last
very long with this ferocity," Elmer assured me, as I lay huddled on the
floor with a pillow over my head to block out the colossal vibrating
pound of thunder. The unremitting brilliant ferocity of the lightning
was like my idea of what the primordial birthing of the earth must have
been. The storm lasted for ten hours, rendering us limp with exhaustion

and throbbing headaches. At last, when morning dawned, the storm gradually faded away. During the night we had lost radio contact with Guy and Irene. The last we had heard was Guy telling us that the boat was well grounded, but they didn't intend to touch their metal steering wheel. We later learned that they had reached the shore further down the coast, so we would not see our sailing buddies again.

We were to face the dangers of Nicaragua and El Salvador alone, so we headed out to sea to avoid any possible problems along the coast. We sailed well with good wind and calculated that it would take seven or eight days to make our next landfall on the Rock Islands of Costa Rica. The first three days we enjoyed very comfortable sailing and the sexton shots indicated that we were off El Salvador on the 27th of May. Another tropical storm with dark clouds and myriads of rainfall caught up with us, obscuring the sun, so there was no chance for us to take a celestial shot for the next two days. Our dead reckoning suggested that we were sixty miles off shore, somewhere near Nicaragua.

When at last the clouds parted just long enough for Elmer to get a noon shot, we had a discrepancy of sixty miles off of our dead reckoning location. With our lack of celestial navigation experience, we decided to sail in close to shore in order to locate an unusual cinder cone formation that was indicated on the chart and that would give us a true location. As we approached the coastline we saw the unique shape of the Ceres Nicaragua volcano. This position confirmed that the sextant shot was correct and that the current had held us back for the last several days.

As we sailed close enough to see the shore, a small craft flying a large Nicaraguan flag sped toward us. We were concerned that this was an official coming out to check our boat in these unfriendly waters. As the boat drew closer we saw a man who had a very large hammerhead shark's body taking up most of the space in his boat.

"Cigarettes?" he yelled.

"No tengo, don't have," we answered with a sigh of relief.

We waved goodbye to him as we headed further out to sea, happy that cigarettes were all that he had wanted.

Later that afternoon the wind died completely and the air grew extremely warm and humid. As we lay on deck to cool ourselves, the boobies joined us in the quiet water, demonstrating their elegant, acrobatic flight. The coloring of these birds was stark white with black trimming around the white wings. They contrasted marvelously with the azure blue of the sky and were so tame that one bird roosted on top of the main mast while the others rested in the water near the boat. We were also greeted by a red-billed tropic bird with its two long feathers flowing a foot behind his body. The presence of this bird traditionally indicated to sailors that they were nearing a tropical coastline. To further welcome us, gray and black-spotted porpoise frolicked in the calm waters, chasing the frisky, flying fish that zip in and out of the sea. Some flying fish go on and on as if they are striving to see more of the world, while others seem content to sink back into the sea to become a meal for those hungry mouths waiting for them. A few complacent looking turtles floated by the boat, lifting their heads from the water seeming to scrutinize us.

We planned to make our landfall on Mala Point; a rocky outcropping that juts into the sea and lies between two bays. When we were able to spot that point, we could sail south of those rocky islands and be south of the border of Nicaragua. We looked at the position on the chart, which indicated we were twenty miles off Mala Point. It was 3:00 p.m. in the afternoon and when we figured the time and the speed we were going, we discerned we wouldn't reach shore until after dark, so we pulled down the sails to wait for morning.

At night the full moon lights the water like an immense spotlight, then suddenly disappears behind a cloud and the night becomes totally dark. As the moon slowly returns, the rim of the clouds shine with a silver glow and the returning light reflects like tiny diamonds on the small gentle waves. At the first rosy, pink glow of dawn we anticipated that we would be able to see the rugged, rocky coastline of Costa Rica.

We had a slight wind in the morning so we maintained a course that would bring us to a landfall in Culebra Bay. Very suddenly a storm hit us with thirty knot winds and laid us over thirty-five degrees, blowing us completely off course. We charged through the water at an unbelievable speed with the hydraulic gear screaming from the pressure. The seas were incredibly rough and disturbed from the sudden shift in the wind. We put on our harnesses to go aft and take down the mizzen sail, and were soaked to the skin from the heavy downpour and the huge waves slamming into the hull. When we got our second breath, we worked our way forward to take down the big headsail. The rain was coming down so heavily that it was difficult to breathe. We could only gulp at the downpour, hoping to breathe at the same time. As suddenly as it came, the storm cleared away and the seas subsided. In the distance we could see Santa Elena. What a welcome sight! We set our course for the Gulf of Papagayo and then sailed into Culebra bay. At anchor the weather was peaceful and calm, and what a pleasure it was to relax after the grueling hours in the storm.

Due to the storm all of our other traveling companions were blown further on down the coast. When we sailed into the bay, *Bungerai* was the only yacht anchored there. The crew called out "hello" as we anchored. Our friends Mike and Steve brought over some cooked shrimp, which we gratefully accepted. We chatted about our trip and they told us that Papagayo means a bird that dashes back and forth, just like the conditions we experienced at sea, which were very prevalent in this part of the ocean. Shortly after they left we collapsed into a very deep, restful sleep. We had traveled by log six hundred and ninety-nine miles, but according to the chart we only covered four hundred and seventy four miles over the ocean bottom. We had experienced a two hundred and twenty-five mile reverse current, which would have been tremendously helpful if we had been going the other way.

All we accomplished the next day was to haul out our washing when the heavy rain came and to rinse everything. The rain dissolved the thick salty crystalline shapes that the sea spray had formed on the mast and deck. I turned on the ham radio Mariners Net and found George WB7 OYD, a friend of Howard's who had been looking for us on this net. George and Donna were neighbors of LeAnn and Steve in Portland, so they were able to complete a phone patch through for us. It was good to hear voices from home, to tell them about our voyage, and that we had arrived safely in Costa Rica. George suggested that we meet at a regular time each week in order to receive news from home and speak with the family. This arrangement with George was rejuvenating and the tired feeling faded away completely.

We went on shore to stretch our legs and to feel the earth beneath our feet again. Looking into the thick jungle growth we could see a stream with a little clearing beside it. As we started up along the stream we heard a piercing roar just above us. We both expected to see a fierce animal spring out at us so we jumped into the middle of the stream. Looking high up into a tree we saw a black howler monkey looking down on us. We had read about them, but never expected to hear such a startling roar come from such a monkey. As we walked further, we disturbed a large flock of bright red and green parrots who joined in the chatter, admonishing us for invading their territory. After our heartbeats returned back to normal, we came upon a small group of semi-wild pigs running through the water. "I guess I won't have a drink here," I thought to myself.

We soon came to a space where the creek widened into a pool and there was a local woman scrubbing her clothes. We used our limited Spanish to express our greetings. She had a gourd in her hand and was scooping the sandy bottom aside to get a drink of water. She scooped again and held the water out to us. We were thirsty, but remembering the pigs, we declined. She insisted that we drink. Not wanting to hurt her feelings I took a big drink of the sweet, fresh water. Elmer was not drinking any of this and looked astonished that I would consider it, much less actually drink it. The sand must have filtered out any contaminates because I didn't get sick. We went back to the boat refreshed by vivid impressions of the unique flora and fauna here in this beautiful tropical land.

Just as soon as we returned onboard, a man selling ice in a small *pongo* (a dugout canoe made from a local tree that has been scooped out) came by. He came out to see if we would be regular ice customers. This enterprising young man would come out every few days to deliver ice to the fishing boats and was willing to deliver ice to us as well. It was twice the price we would have to pay at the nearest icehouse but the convenience of having it delivered was a blessing to us, and we admired the ingenuity of the young man. We enjoyed his visits because he spoke very good English and told us about the local happenings.

Culebra Bay felt like paradise. Everything we needed, and then some, was available. Only a short walk away was Playa Los Bananos, a small enterprise that served lunches, kept mail for travelers and sold cold drinks. There was heavy rain everyday about four o'clock so we could take fresh water showers, collect abundant water for our storage tanks, and wash and rinse clothes. Fernando, who owned the shrimp boat, *Donya Julito*, was more than willing to supply us with shrimp and camaraderie. Another wonderful thing about Culebra bay was that it was just a short walk through a heavy forest where we could catch a bus that took us to the little town of Liberia. In Liberia there was a great variety of fresh tropical fruit and vegetables available and they also sold superb fresh beef raised on the nutritious and abundant grass that grows in Costa Rica. The anchorage in Culebra Bay was very well protected and seemed like a safe place to leave the boat, making it possible to fly to the states and visit our family. To top all this off we had clear ham radio contact. We were set up with everything we needed in the restful bay.

The lively porpoise swam into the bay chasing the myriads of fish we could see so clearly in the water over the side of the boat. When we cleaned the bottom of the boat, brilliantly colored fish would fight for pieces of the barnacles as we scraped them off. The sea life in the bay was very plentiful, but in order to catch a fish dinner we had to put on our scuba tanks and get out our spear gun to chase them.

The second evening in Culebra Bay we heard that a yacht had been hit by the same storm we were in off of Santa Elena. The skipper had been trying to get a sextant shot and had fallen overboard. His wife had tried to get him aboard, but she had lost him in the very disturbed seas. She never saw him again. He had fallen overboard with his sextant and she had no way to figure out where she was. She made a mayday call. A big ship responded and came to her rescue. When she arrived in the port of Puntarenas, there was a problem with customs because the ship's papers did not show her as part owner of the boat. Her son had to fly down from Seattle to help her prove ownership. These was an explicit lesson for all of us on yachts–put on the harness whenever you go out of the safety of the cockpit and always have your boat papers in impeccable order.

We were invited to a gathering of the yachties at Gwen and Crystal Dougherty's Los Bananos. There were four of us in Culebra but ten in the Cocoas Bay further south. We arrived to find quite a crowd of people, many of whom we knew but several people we had not met yet. When groups of yachties get together the conversation inevitably turns to sailing, the voyage, the boat and each person's sailing experiences. We were enjoying meeting new friends when we spied a couple sitting at a table on the fringe of the crowd, looking alone and left out. We introduced ourselves and sat down for a chat. They were Kathy and Ross Smith, medical students from the United States going to school in the capital, San Jose. When they heard about the party, and that there would be American and Canadian people there, they came down to join in. They didn't want to intrude so they just sat silently watching everyone. We particularly clicked with these two young people and we introduced them around so they could join in the fun. They told us if we were to come to San Jose, we were to stay with them. They gave us their phone number and a place we could leave a message for them. Returning to the boat, we were enthusiastic about all of the new friends we had met.

At 5:30 a.m. the next morning we caught the bus to Liberia. When we arrived in Liberia, we ate a very tasty and satisfying breakfast at a tiny restaurant that served the local specialty–pinto and dos huevos a mixture of black beans and rice and two eggs. Each time that we went to town we ate at that the same little place so we could become friends with the owner and the patrons. While there we exchanged our money for Colones and bought as many fresh fruits and vegetables as we could carry in our backpacks and bags before heading back to the boat in Culebra Bay.

The plan to visit the family was materializing very rapidly. Dale and Kathy, on a yacht named *Crystal Dolphin*, were now anchored in the bay and they told us that they were willing to take care of our boat if we would bring supplies back for them. Fernando, from *Donya Julito*, also said he would look out for *Elysium*. We went to the Port Captain and checked the boat into the country to be legal and found out about the bus system to San Jose. We contacted the family on the radio to tell them where and when we would arrive in Portland. At this point we were ready to go San Jose to buy plane tickets. While we were there, we contacted Kathy and Ross to tell them about our plans. They invited us to stay the night at their place before the flight and they offered to drive us to the airport. All of the necessary preparations were now complete for our trip home.

On July 8, 1980, we moved the boat down the bay closer to a small store and house called Playa Panama where we were advised that the anchorage was a safer place to leave the boat. Before we left, several people came over with lists of items to bring back from the states and also things take with us to mail there when we arrived. We caught the bus to Liberia then waited four hours for the bus to San Jose. We called Ross and Cathy and they picked us up. The next morning we got on the plane and were off to visit Portland. The plane stopped for four hours in Guatemala where we had a chance to buy some beautiful hand woven items for our family and friends. We arrived in the States that evening.

The next three weeks we were on a whirlwind of visits and catching up with family and friends. We spent time with both of our mothers and saw to it that they were taken care of. It was important for us to visit Elmer's mother who was in a nursing home and not well. We had medical appointments to make sure we were in perfect health. Our friends threw several parties for us to visit with people we had not seen for over a year. We were able to see our first grandson, Joshua, who was now eight months old. Our time just whizzed away, not at all like our lazy days on *Elysium*. It seemed like days instead of weeks when were on the plane going back to the boat in Costa Rica.

We arrived in San Jose, Costa Rica on Pan American airlines and found fog over the city. We could only see two big mountain peaks sticking out where the airport was and the lady sitting near us was crossing herself in prayer for safety. As we broke through the fog we saw another passenger plane had crashed on the other side of the runway. We felt very relieved to be on the ground and to see that Ross and Cathy there waiting for us. We went to pick up our excessive amount of luggage, and found that it had not made it off of the plane. They told us it would be here in a week and gave us fifty dollars in U.S. money to stay in a hotel while we waited. Ross and Cathy insisted that we stay with them and we were more than happy and grateful to do that. We spent a quiet time meandering around San Jose during the day and getting to know Ross and Cathy better each evening.

After the luggage arrived, Ross and Kathy took us to the bus station. We loaded the luggage aboard the bus and were off to Liberia. The bus in Liberia was smaller but not full, so we were able to occupy the entire back seat of the bus with our two boxes, two suitcases, two backpacks and two handbags. We were relieved to be on the bus and relaxed for the drive to Panama Beach. When we got there, we walked from one shady spot to another lugging our one hundred sixty pounds of goods. Finally, when we reached the bay, we were able to signal Dale to come help us. Everyone who had requested something for us to bring back to them crowded over to get his or her treasures from us. Dale had speared a big Dorado fish, so we had a great dinner and were happy to be home at last and tucked snugly into the familiarity of our world.

The next day we could not seem to wake up. The muggy, drenching heat was like stepping into a steam bath. The trip and the happenings of the last few weeks had left us with very little energy. At nine thirty the next morning we finally roused ourselves and began to clean our dirty boat and put all of our newly purchased items away. We went swimming several times to relax and cool off trying to motivate ourselves again. The big fishing boat, *Donya Julito*, came in and Fernando brought us shrimp and some small fish he had caught. I cooked them all into a bouillabaisse. The delicious seafood meal and cool air after the rain brought us out of our stupor. We busied ourselves by scraping off the green scum and purple bunches that looked like a tropical garden coating the bottom of the boat. We shook off the anchor chain that was spectacularly populated with barnacles and sea slime enjoying a space to catch their daily meal of plankton. Satisfied with our day's work, we were ready for a good sleep that night.

Later that week we went into Liberia to replenish our vegetable bin. As we were coming back, we noticed that there were several people on the bus who looked like they could be American. I went over to sit with a lady clutching a big stuffed animal in her arms. "Hi I'm Helen and we're here in this area on a sail boat in Culebra Bay," I said, to begin a conversation. Her name was Barbara and she was an archeology student from Los Angeles. She and five others were traveling to Culebra Bay to meet their instructor who was already stationed there. I could not imagine where he could be. We had not seen anyone in the very dense jungle around the bay. In fact I could not visualize how these people were going to get around with their unsuitable shoes and heavy luggage. "If you have a problem when you get there, we're anchored near Panama Beach down the shore about a half a mile from where you'll reach the bay from the bus," I told her. We said good-bye and hauled our groceries back to the boat without giving it another thought.

After we fixed our meal and were resting on the deck, we saw the whole crew on shore waving to us. We went over to the shore in our dinghy, *Limbo*, to find out what the problem was. They told us no one had met them, so we offered to take them across the bay to the site. They were quite befuddled being in a very hot, foreign land and not knowing where they were going to stay. They had dragged all of their gear down the sandy beach, the huge suitcases and the many stuffed animals, which seemed so out of place for this area. We loaded them and all their gear aboard *Elysium* and ferried them five miles across the calm bay to Nagascola.

Nagascola had supported a small church colony at one time, but the government moved them all away when the area was made into a preserve. The only current inhabitants were two semi-wild pigs that lived on the beach flotsam and bathed themselves in the gentle waves. The archeologists who had come to dig up artifacts had planned to use the very dilapidated camp to stay in while working on the digs. The professor in charge had been there for some time with a few Costa Rican men helping him. He had really become a little wild in the jungle, forgetting completely that he had a crew coming. We got them ashore and they looked hesitantly at their new quarters. We wondered what they would have done if we had not been there. The last bus had left and they would have had to sleep on the mosquito-infested beach without any protection. Finally Dr. Dillon emerged from the jungle and greeted his students. He showed them the screened building that was to be their home while they were in Costa Rica. We left them and went back to the boat, promising to come back in the morning for a visit and to help if we could.

Barbara fitting shards to make a pot

We were exceedingly interested in what they were recovering from the digs, which had been previously raided several times. We stayed a week off shore, inviting them out to the boat several times a day for a cool drink and relief from the mosquitoes. We learned about archeology and were privileged to visit the site and view the shards that they were working with. Six of the students took us to visit a new site. The two pigs went along, crashing through the brush ahead of us, hopefully frightening away any poisonous snakes lurking there. We wore long boots to keep our legs safe in case the pigs missed one.

The site was cautiously scraped away with brushes and small knives to unearth the delicate pottery shards and figures. Each layer was measured and recorded as the archeologists completed the dig to ascertain the dates they were buried by the heavy soil. Each layer is a different time and date. This area was thought to be pre-Columbian Mayan and Aztec. The painted designs still were clearly visible on the pottery. When we returned to camp, Barbara, who was a student, took the shards and pieced them carefully together to restore the whole pot. The patience and perseverance of the archeologist was awesome to us.

We were reluctant to leave this interesting endeavor, but it was time to get to Puntarenas to check in with the port captain again. Our new friends came for a final visit and we wished them good luck on their diggings. They thanked us profusely for the afternoons they had spent on the boat away from the mosquitoes and scorpions that inhabited Nagascola.

It was a sad day for us to leave Culebra Bay where we had spent several months and met so many friends. This bay had been a wonderful refuge for us and we would miss the visits from the iceman and Fernando on the shrimp boat. We sailed off early in the morning in mid-August for the trip to the Gulf of Nicoya and the big city of Puntarenas, Costa Rica. After several stops at well-protected bays when the wind died, we would be out again when a wrinkle in the smooth water foretold a sailing breeze.

With fifteen knots of wind there was fine sailing circling Tobago Island. Passing the island, we anchored in front of Hacienda Nicoyana where there was complete protection from the weather. This island was the stopping place for the yachties traveling south. There were no yachts in the bay when we arrived, so we went ashore to see the signs that were made by the people who had visited previously. Guy and Irene had their names on a carved piece of wood near the path. We met Norman and Sue who had bought some property and were now residents. Further up the hill Dean and Ginny Kennedy had built a magnificent ceramic tile house after retiring from the Panama Canal, where he had served as an engineer. They owned the ferryboat that took people from this spot into Puntarenas, on Monday, Wednesday, and Friday. They brought back the ice and supplies that were needed by the folk who lived there and also received and held the mail for the yachties who were anchored in the bay.

We thoroughly enjoyed the abundant seafood that we obtained on our travels. In addition, the inexpensive, lean and tender Costa Rican beef that we bought would be good protein for us. I would be able to can the meat in tins with the pressure canner we had on board. One day I told Dean that I was going to buy beef and pressure can it in my galley. He said that it would be miserable and hot in our small space, so he and Ginny invited us to come up and use their open kitchen cooled by the sea breeze. This worked out extremely well for me. We went with Dean to buy twenty pounds of beef, and loaded it into the cockroach–laden bilge of the ferry. Back at the boat we put it on ice until the next day when we pressure canned it. The cool breeze that drifted though Ginny's kitchen made the task easy. I continued canning meat until I had filled one section of our storage space. This wonderful beef lasted for several years and added plenty of diversity to our meals. When the bins were full of canned beef, I decided to make one more trip to make beef jerky using an easy recipe someone had given me before we left. The jerky turned out to be the snack of choice on long, dark passages.

Soon the anchorage crowded with yachts headed down to the Panama Canal to cruise the Caribbean Sea as well as other points west. We would have a large flotilla to sail with and to help us explore the versatile coast of Panama. Our charts were marked with well-protected anchorages indicating that we would have a place to stop each night. The weather was calm with light breezes so it looked like a perfect time to make the trip. We took the ferry for one last time to check out with the authorities and say goodbye to the many Tico's, local people who were now friends.

Our last stop in Costa Rica was Gulfito. Gulfo Dulce is famous for its lush green hills that rise steeply from the bay and provide a naturally protected anchorage. The fruit company in the town of Gulfito provided lots of jobs loading bananas and also supplied the workers with housing. When there were problems with a strike, the American government came in and took over the United Fruit Company, making unions illegal. While we were there, all was quiet again. As we entered the bay, the water was crammed with damaged bananas floating out to sea. We scooped them up and found them to be ripe and delicious.

We anchored next to Captain Tom's grounded PT boat that he had brought to Costa Rica after World War II. Tom was well known to all of the yachties because he provided everything that they required. There was a large waterfall behind his little grass hut called a *palapa*. He fenced in the area and built up a small dam for laundry and a comfortable bath. There was a store that had every item that we needed, from drinks to canned goods. Tom only asked for a donation to use all this marvelous retreat and the appreciative sailors were generous with their contributions.

We were enjoying our anchorage the next day when we heard a very slight bump on the boat. We looked out and there was a small dugout with five young children aboard. We invited them in and served them a limeade and coconut macaroon. They sat down very politely, and after they had eaten I brought out a game of colored monkeys for them to play. The object of the game was to pick up each monkey by the tail using one hand until they were all gone. The children played the game, taking turns with each other, for over an hour. When I told them we needed to go ashore, they quickly scampered into their small dugout and went home, which was only a short distance away.

The next day we had a visit from the oldest girl, Sara, who was thirteen and Henardo, who was twelve, along with three smaller children: Raphiel, five; Nelson, four; and Siomada, three. They brought us a gift of fish and we brought out the monkey game again. They played until we decided to go ashore for a hike. The children were very polite, sensing when they needed to go home and showing genuine joy at being able to come aboard. We were amazed by their ability to quietly play with the monkeys and never cause a stir of trouble or argument. They visited

Gulfito children with monkey tail game

each day, never bringing out more than five of the family, which now we knew by name. Besides the group above, there was Juan, eleven; Idelina, ten; Magdeleno, nine; and Oldamar, seven. There were ten children in all, and they became our daily visitors but never imposed on us.

It was always hard to pull anchor and leave our friends but we had been there for several months. We went to shore for the last time and hiked up into the mountains to look down at the peaceful bay and see our boat at anchor. Then we washed all of our clothes and took a luxurious bath. We had a last visit from our Costa Rican family who brought everyone out in two dugouts to say goodbye. They each drew pictures and signed their names on the bottom for us to take as a remembrance of them. We found small tee-shirts that fit each one and said our sad goodbyes. We slipped out early the next morning setting our course for Panama, leaving the beautiful Rich Coast, Costa Rica.

The Lush Panama Coast

...until you have become really, in actual fact, as a brother to everyone,
brotherhood will not come to pass.

–Dostoyevsky

THE WATERS OFF the Panama coast are crystal clear with magnificent coral towers swarming with a kaleidoscope of brilliantly colored fish. We sailed around the impressive Burica Point that is lined with huge breakers rushing up onto the rocky shore and anchored in front of a small village built on stilts. The shore was surrounded with crashing surf so we stayed onboard and watched the sunset project beautiful silhouettes of palm trees lining the luminous sky. As evening approached the waters calmed and small *pongas* with candles lighted came out to fish. It was a beautiful scene of peace and contentment.

The next morning the seas were very calm and we sailed along peacefully. The light wind tapered off at noon, so we decided to stop at Parida Island. We went to shore and snorkeled around the rocks, admiring the abundant sea life. Then, returning to the boat, we spent an hour working on the failing autopilot and found electricity everywhere except where we needed it. When we met George that evening on the radio, we asked him to contact Benmar, the manufacturer, to see what they suggested about repairing it so we would know if we needed to send it back to the U.S.

Later that afternoon, a young couple came over to the boat bringing some vegetables and a squash as a gift. Siomada and Antonio lived on Parida Island in a grass and palm leaf hut. Siomada told us her father had built a large dugout fishing boat all by hand on the island. They were interested in how *Elysium* was built so we showed them our boat building pictures. They went through each part of the boat exclaiming "que lindo, how beautiful." They told us that although there had been many yachts anchored there, they had never been invited aboard any of them. They stayed until the sun set and treasured the few bars of soap we had given them in return for the vegetables. Just as they were leaving a heavy rain began to fall which gave us an opportunity to take a bath and collect water in our large, yellow plastic water catcher.

Early the next morning Antonio arrived with two very large lobsters. What a gift! In return, we found some packets of shampoo and other small items that would have been difficult for them to obtain. He invited us to come ashore to see their dugout and to meet his father. After we ate our lobster and squash for lunch, we rowed over to their little palm leaf hut. Siomada had a two year old baby, Lucilla, so we gave her one of the toys that we carried onboard. We met Filomar and Eralda, the grandparents. Filomar took great pride in showing us his twenty-foot long dugout with added sideboards that he found necessary because he paddled so far out into the sea. In the following days we became regular visitors to their home. Nearly every day they brought us lobster or shrimp and we found something from our provisions that we could give them in return. This was a delightful exchange for us and we learned about their simple way of life on their remote island home.

Several of the other yachties anchored nearby told us that they would like to buy lobster also, but Filomar chose not to sell to them. They had visited the other yachts that first day, but had been told to "go away." Because of this they wanted nothing more to do with the yachties, not even to sell them lobster or shrimp. Often people traveling on yachts were afraid of the native people and would not allow them to come aboard. Each encounter we had erased more of our fear and in turn we learned all about the local customs and their efforts for their continued existence. In this way fear did not divide us from the understanding we gained. Each encounter enriched our lives and made it easier to open up to the next person that was to come and visit.

Going over to tell them that we would be leaving soon and say good-bye, they showed us how they planted dry-land rice and hand picked the grains. They hung the bundles of rice under the eaves of their hut to dry and then pounded the dried grain in a hollow stump with a big pestle to winnow out the chaff. After showing us all of this, they brought out a large bag of the fragrant rice to give us as a parting gift. "No," I said. I couldn't accept a gift that had entailed so much labor for them. They asked why and I attempted to tell them that the gift was too precious for us to accept. Their faces brightened and they insisted that we take it for our journey ahead. We brought gifts to give them, but they had given us a part of their survival food so much more than we could ever possibly reciprocate. It was indeed a bountiful gift to receive.

Reaching the Secas Islands we skimmed over massive coral heads into a secure anchorage. The water was the clearest we had seen so far on our voyage. When the water is so clean, it magnifies the bottom and makes it difficult to determine the depth. There was no swell because we were completely protected from the ocean by the reef. We snorkeled and gazed with amazement at the complex ecosystem of iridescent fish and vividly colored sea worms inhabiting the safety of the delicately colored coral heads. The coral heads rose from the sea floor to a height of as much as ten feet and formed great voids which afforded sanctuary for a vast diversity of sea animals. When we finally tired and went back onboard *Elysium*, we gratefully ate the last of the shrimp and some of the rice we had been given.

Just as we had finished eating, a lady came out to our boat in a long dugout. She explained that the babies on the floor of her boat were all very sick. I went with her to look at the six babies who all had a croupy cough and were so weak they were not able to cry. She begged us to give her medicine to make them well. I didn't want to give them penicillin because it can cause an allergic reaction, especially in children so young. Without any other safe drug available, I gave her a bottle of orange flavored vitamin C powder and some mentholated oil. I instructed her to diffuse the vitamin C in water and to give it to them in their bottle several times a day. I also instructed her to rub their chests with the oil. I felt very helpless because I was not sure whether this meager remedy would be enough to ease of their illness. This was a heart wrenching experience for both Elmer and me. We would never know if our efforts helped those little children.

The next anchorage was another protected bay with similar coral formations. This time we found yellow, green and purple angelfish, and many others with royal blue bodies, white stripes and an orange tail. We also saw brilliant blue damselfish with iridescent spots on their heads, striped parrotfish that shone like a blue blaze, and dazzling yellow puffer fish. We were in the largest aquarium we could imagine and we wondered how there could possibly be more variety in the sea than we had seen in the last two anchorages. We drifted around the area and found some rock oysters for dinner and also gathered a large conch to use for fishing bait.

We explored the area onshore and found a refreshing natural waterfall to wash off the salt that had dried uncomfortably on our skin. We washed our clothes and all of our salty diving gear. After we boarded *Elysium*, we pulled anchor and sailed out into hot sunshine, enjoying a very light breeze, fishing with the bait we had found. When the wind died completely we chose to anchor in a large empty nearby bay. Just as we were settled, a massive rusty shrimp boat motored by and anchored near us. They hollered 'hello" to us as they went by and we waved back. They quickly boarded their little tender to paddle over for a visit, eager for some company and conversation. As they came aboard they brought the smell of stale fish and sweat on their clothes. We offered them some refreshments and found that we communicated with them quite well, as our Spanish was improving. Most of them were from Columbia, where the boat was based. They showed us pictures of their families and we took them below to see the pictures of our children and showed them the interior of the boat.

The man we supposed was in charge said something to one of his crew, and he jumped into the tender and paddled away. While he was away, we found some tee shirts that fit the men and some magazines that they particularly liked. When the crewmember returned, he presented us with eleven pounds of bright pink shrimp encased in ice. We were amazed by the generosity of these men as this gift represented so many hours of hard work on their part. We thanked them profusely as they left to return to their home on the water.

Elmer enjoying shrimp

Pat and Gordon, on the yacht *Alphora*, who we had met in Costa Rica, had just entered the bay as the shrimp boat crew was leaving. They had also given up trying to sail and were ready to get out of the hot sun. They were worried about us, seeing the men leave our boat, so they quickly came over to see if we were all right. We shared our shrimp with them, enjoying the feast until we could eat no more.

The next day was calm and hot without a breeze. We rowed over to shore and found another waterfall to cool off. I don't think I ever had such a sensual bath with the cool fresh water pouring over my body as the sun broke through in small patches, highlighting the lush greenery. Thoroughly refreshed, we climbed high on top of a rock to view the blue green Pacific Ocean.

In the morning the wind was blowing again, so we set sail heading for Honda Bay. As we motored through a colossal downpour of rain, it rendered our surroundings invisible. We moved ahead slowly, closely watching the depth sounder to avoid the hitting the shallow reef. The depth sounder indicated depths swiftly changing from ten feet to eighty feet. To be sure there were no dangerous tall coral heads, we had to wait for the rain to let up before we could safely anchor. We had just set the anchor when an old man came over with oranges, plantain and bananas to sell. He wanted to trade for fishing gear, so we set him up with hooks and hootchies, plus a small hat to keep the rain out of his eyes.

In the evening the old man returned and invited us to come ashore to see his home and to meet his daughter. He had been born just a few miles from his present home. Thirty years before, he had acquired the isthmus to plant his orchard where he had orange, lemon, mandarin, mango and papaya trees. He planted maize and rice on the hillside to supplement his diet. He also had chickens and some pigs. His home was made from palm fronds with a very steep roof to keep out the torrential rains that were common in the area. The inside of the hut smelled like smoke and there was fish drying near the roof. The floor was very muddy from the recent rain. His wife had just washed their meager supply of worn and patched clothes. Before leaving the next day, we got into our huge cache of Goodwill clothes and were able to supply them with dresses, shirts and shorts that fit them. They, in turn, brought an abundance of fruit and some vegetables for us. This was a very agreeable trade for all of us. These self sufficient people only needed what we had onboard and we always wanted fresh fruit and vegetables.

The next four days we experienced good sailing and anchorages, catching a fish for dinner each day. We would swim with large schools of fish swirling all around us, just out of our reach. The sun shining down into the water produced a brilliant rainbow of color reflecting from their bodies. On the last day, just as we were anchoring, the rough murky water warned us that a storm was approaching.

We were awakened in the morning by big waves rushing into the bay creating a surge that jerked at the anchor so harshly that the heavy stainless steel bow rollers that fed the anchor chain were bent down. Elmer had to lift the chain by hand as I worked on the windless to pull up the anchor. As we left the anchorage, our journey was dreadful and becoming worse by the hour. The seas were violent because of the swells running in one direction and the squalls blowing the other way across the shallow water. We were sailing with our Genoa only, when suddenly the boat pitched forward and the wind hit the sail so hard it was torn clear across the full width of the sail. We had a time getting it down without further damage. We desperately needed to find shelter from this storm!

We were near Isla Naranjo where someone had marked our chart with the location of a dangerous reef. Just then another squall hit us with full force. For nearly an hour the heavy rain came down so hard we could not even see one hundred feet ahead. As the squall rained itself out, we saw an area on the island where an anchorage was available. We corrected our course to beat into the very large sea and a headwind. It took us three hours to go three miles, but we decided the anchorage was fit enough for us, even if waves washed in a heavy sea. We dropped anchor, very relieved to rest and find warmth below in the sanctuary of the cabin.

Just as we were getting ready to prepare our evening meal, we heard a distress call on the radio. I replied to find out what the emergency was. The man shouted, "I am the captain of the Greek Ship, *Nastoporos*, and I need you to come and help me," When he told me that he was calling from a five hundred and ninety-six foot cargo vessel that had gone aground in the storm just north of us, Elmer and I knew that we could be of no help to him. We asked why he had not called for help on his ship's radio. He said none of his electronics were working except the VHF radio. The ship was pounding on the rocky coast and they were beginning to take on water. I told him I would call for help on my ham radio.

I turned on the radio and got on the emergency calling channel. "Mayday, Mayday, Mayday!" I called. Immediately there were answers from San Jose, Costa Rica, Howard Air Force Base in Panama, Caracas, Venezuela, and Long Beach, California. I arranged with them to send rescue helicopters from Balboa and got a telephone call to the ship's agent in Colone, Panama. For two hours I relayed information from the captain to the people providing the rescue. Finally at dawn, they were finished rescuing the crew. We had been on the radio all night, but the squall brought in such big waves we would have never been able to sleep anyway.

In the morning a McAllister tug arrived and the people who were waiting for the captain to abandon the ship swarmed in to pillage everything. The radio now was filled with the cynical talk of the tug operators who had no mercy for the Greek crew. We said goodbye to the captain with whom we had been in contact all night. He sounded very sad and we both knew he would lose his post when he arrived back home.

The day was still stormy but not quite as threatening, so we decided to sleep and wait for better weather. In the afternoon the weather calmed down a bit, so Elmer was able to fix the bow roller. He had to remove it and take it to shore, heat it with a torch, and beat it back into shape with a sledgehammer. It was not completely straight, but he was able to attach a small piece of steel to brace it from the bottom so it worked again. Next we got out the Sailmaker sewing machine and mended the seven-foot tear and the other hole in our headsail. We finished just as another squall hit with a downpour of rain. It rained so hard that it completely smoothed out the swell that had been rolling in.

In the early morning we finally saw a small break in the weather. Even though there were still some squalls around, the enticement to leave this place was unconquerable. We sailed around the dangerous reverse current of Punta Mala, but the wind kept us from moving forward, so we just watched cows grazing on the green grassy hills dotted with small grass hut *palapas* nestled among the short coconut trees. The beach was lined with stark white sand and jagged black rock. We enjoyed the view for an hour or so as the wind and current continued to oppose each other, keeping us stationary.

On November 17th, we sailed into the Balboa Yacht Club where a club motorboat came out and led us to a mooring. After we were tied up, the man who drove the boat showed us to the office where we received information, our mail and paid sixty dollars for four days moorage. We were able to get a good radio signal, so we could talk with LeAnn, share news and ask her to send our mail. She told us that Winston and Irene, who now owned our business, were coming down for a visit as his sister lived in the Canal Zone. He would bring us the cash we needed and take Christmas presents home to our family.

We explored Panama City and bought hand made *molas*, a major form of art, from the Cuna Indians. They hand stitch reverse embroidery in brilliant colors with a noteworthy message displayed on each quilt. When we went over to look at them, quaint little women with wide rings in their noses mobbed us. "This one, this one" they shouted at me, pushing their exquisite handwork forward. We had a difficult time choosing, but finally determined which eight pieces we wanted to purchase. We chose not to bargain with them because the price they asked was so reasonable, especially considering the time and effort that had gone into creating them. When we got back to the yacht club, the secretary commented that we had paid twice what we should have.

We woke up early the next day to catch a bus to Sears. As we waited, a yellow Toyota Jeep stopped and the driver, Dr. Carlos Andrade asked if we wanted a ride. Yesterday on the dock we had seen Carlos deep in thought coming down the dock. We had spoken to him and immediately his whole face broke into a big smile and he answered warmly, inquiring about where we were from. He was most interested in our trip and *Elysium*. He wanted to know how long we were staying and where we were going from Panama. He cordially accepted our invitation to visit the boat. He had done some carpentry work himself and was tremendously appreciative of how Elmer had finished the black walnut.

When we got into the Jeep, Carlos asked where we were headed. "We're going to Sears but let us off anywhere," we said. "I will take you there and if you want, I'll come down to the moorage every morning at eight o'clock and show you the city until nine thirty. At that time I must be at my hospital to begin work," he said. We thanked him and accepted his generous offer. Riding in an air-conditioned car instead of catching the crowded bus was a real treat for us. Carlos showed us places in the city we would never have otherwise found or known about. True to his word, he was there every morning, enjoying the fact that he could show us his country.

Another good contact for us was with Dean and Ginny's son, Mel, and his wife, Roz. Dean and Ginny were the kind folks who had provided us with a place to can our meat in Costa Rica and ferried us over to Puntarenas. We brought them some pictures that his father wanted to send to them from Costa Rica. When Mel came to pick them up at the yacht club, he asked if there was anything he could do for us. We told him about the autopilot that needed to be mailed to Portland for repair. He was an engineer for the Canal and offered to use his American mail privileges to send it. This gave us an inexpensive American freight, saving us hundreds of dollars. Also, the people working on the canal were able to mark urgent business on the package for even faster service. We were relieved to get this underway because we did not want to face a month's sail without the aid of the autopilot.

Our social life got even busier when Winston and Irene came for a visit from Oregon. Winston's sister, Bonnie, was married to David, a clergyman who had a parish in Balboa. Their three children, Melodie, Shanna, and Evie, all came with their parents to visit us on the boat and go out for a sail. No one in the group had ever been aboard a boat before, so we sailed out in a pleasant, gentle wind. We don't know which of us enjoyed skimming across the bay more, because this time we had no destination; we were just out to enjoy a day sail. While we were out in the water, Bonnie told us that they had a membership to a wholesale grocery outlet and would be glad to take us there to provision for our upcoming trip.

Nearly all the yachts that arrived at the club planned to transit the canal into the Caribbean Sea to cruise. We enjoyed big dinners together at the yacht club and I ran phone patches for people who wanted to tell their families where they were. A man in Florida offered to put a phone patch through for me, so I decided to say hello to my mother in Portland, Oregon. He explained to her that he was in Florida and was patching, or bringing through his set, the call for us in Panama. After our conversation, she called LeAnn and told her that we had just arrived in Florida. This was a big shock to the family and there were lots of questions the next time we met George, our contact, on the net.

Gordon and Pat on *Alphora* had made arrangements to go through the canal and needed line handlers to come aboard to help. Four rope handlers plus the skipper were required, so they asked us if we would be part of the crew. We agreed to go. It was interesting to watch the operation of the canal. Despite the big ship in front of us barely fitting inside the parameters of the locks, they made it through with no problems. There are three lifts totaling one hundred and seventy feet in height. The entire twenty mile journey took us ten hours to complete. Each vessel has to pay the owners of the canal in cash, which attracts pirates, as hundreds of thousands of dollars constantly change hands. We arrived at the other side that evening and returned by train back to Panama City.

I told George that the autopilot was on the way and that we had only a few months on our Panama visa before we had to leave. He said he would personally press the company to get it repaired and ready to send back quickly. He would keep a schematic, so he would know what was going on with the machine if we had further problems with it.

There were also many repairs to do on the boat before we left for the longest passage we would ever make. I took the ham radio apart and cleaned everything. Elmer took the bow roller off, brought it ashore and really beefed it up. We wanted to fill our gift box again, so we bought tee shirts and inexpensive hand embroidered dresses and blouses in the Chinese stores. Balboa is a city with stores reflecting all of the countries in the world and we perused many of them. We slowly prepared the boat and ourselves for the long voyage ahead.

We needed to obtain a visa for French Polynesia. We were warned that the embassy was in a very dangerous part of town and we would be taking a great risk to be on the street. We hired a taxi to take us to the embassy, but as we would be there for several hours we couldn't have him wait. When our visas were finally stamped, we decided to walk back to town. We were met with smiles and encouragement from each person we met along the way. We wore old clothes and were not carrying a camera, as we did not want to look like tourists. We walked along single file so we could tell if someone was stalking us. We never were threatened and we walked all over the city from then on.

While we waited for the autopilot to arrive, we took time to take our dear friends out for a sail. Carlos, our doctor friend, his wife Rena, and their son, Juan Carlitos, really enjoyed being on the bay outside of Panama and looking back to see the big city. Carlos told us about his history: he was born in the Darian Jungle, the most primitive and obsolete part of southern Panama. His mother was a Choco Indian and his father was a black Columbian. His mother wanted a better education for her two boys, so she separated from his father and came to live in Panama City. She taught school to educate her sons and sent Carlos to Spain where he could train as a doctor. He told us about arriving in Spain and waiting in a room filled with men applying for the scholarship for medical school. By the time they were through with the interview, there were only two people left, Carlos and one other young man from Spain. He had to work very hard to maintain the grades expected of him and finally graduated with honors from the school to become a well respected

Elmer, Rena, Juan Calitos, and Carlos

M.D. in Panama City. When he returned to Panama, he built the clinic Santeria Santa Teresa.

They took us to their home above the clouds, high up on a mountain where it was cool and green. Carlos wanted Elmer to plant a coffee tree to remember us by. The house was filled with glossy black, hand carved, inlaid teak furniture. It was completely different from any place we had been in Panama. Small farms and lush grass for the cattle made the cool spot an important getaway for him and his family. Carlos and Rena became such close friends that it was like leaving family when it was time to say goodbye.

We had to get an extension on our visa because the autopilot did not arrive on time. We learned that it was sent from the United States on the sixth of February and it was now the twenty-sixth. With so little time left, we thought Elmer would have to fly to Los Angeles and buy another autopilot. The very day we planned to buy tickets for the flight, Mel came out and brought the autopilot with him! Finally we were ready to sail out to the Perles Islands and start our trip to the Galapagos.

We had several parties with our friends to say goodbye. It was very hard to leave these wonderful people who had driven us around, taken us shopping and treated us like we were part of their families. Each farewell dinner was harder for us than the last. Finally we had to make the break with everyone and sail away from the city, twenty miles to the Perles Islands.

While at anchor at the Perles Islands, I bit down on something that had a bone in it and broke my molar. This would give us a lot of trouble because we were going to be at least thirty days at sea with no one nearby to help. Reluctantly, I called David's wife, Bonnie, from the airport and she said to get on a plane and that she would meet me at the Panama City airport. The Shah of Iran was on this island at the time, so planes were going back and forth regularly. When I got to the airport, Bonnie took me directly to a dentist in town with whom she had made arrangements to perform a root canal on my tooth. The dentist told me to come back the next morning to finish placing the tooth together. She told me that if I had not repaired the tooth, it would have become abscessed, making me very ill and causing a great deal of pain. When she was finished, Bonnie drove me to the airport to catch the plane back to the Perles. Elmer met me and we returned to *Elysium*, ready to start our journey away from the coast of Central America the next morning.

Crossing the Pacific Ocean

*Lowly faithful banish fear, right onward drive unharmed. The port, well
worth the cruise is near, and every wave is charmed.*

— Emerson

THE TIME HAD come for our greatest adventure yet—crossing the broad
Pacific Ocean. This passage of over five thousand miles would take us to
the Marquesas Islands, the land that is the farthest from any continent in
the world, sixteen hundred miles northeast of the Tahiti ridge. The trade
winds would carry us over the waves with no opportunity for us to duck
into the safety that we had found along the coast of the North American
continent. We felt a great accomplishment in coming this far, down the
coast of the Americas, and though there was a thread of apprehension,
we were eager for this new experience.

We began the sail with light winds that increased in velocity by the
hour until we were sailing at six knots. We took several sextant shots,
and found that the current was pushing us along to the southeast, not
directly south as our course had indicated. A dangerous mountain, Malpalo Rock, was situated alone out in the ocean, positioned right on our
course line. If we followed that course and maintained the speed we
were going we could possibly slam into the rock at night, so we altered

our course to sail west of its location. As morning dawned on the second day, the gigantic rock was clearly visible rising out of the water only about a half of a mile from us. We were near the Equator and the changing declination made the sextant shot very difficult to take. Even though Malpalo surprised us by being so close, it did give us a very precise indication of where we were. As we passed close to it we knew exactly how much the current pushed us so we could chart our course more accurately.

Near the Equator we noticed a sailboat following us all day, staying just on the horizon. We tried to contact them on the VHF radio several times during the day but received no answer. At dusk they dropped their sails and motored quickly over to our boat. Not knowing who they were, I grabbed our flare gun in case it was an unfriendly group. Their sudden approach concerned us. As they motored closer, to our relief we saw a young crew waving and calling g'day. This was yacht *Acushla* that was being delivered from Florida to Australia. The crew were glad to see someone else sailing on this lonely journey. Rowley, Bobbie, Jeannie, Peter, and Mizzie made up the crew and wanted to say g'day before dark. We had no communication on the radio because Australia uses different frequencies on the VHF radio than we do in the States. We traded experiences and plans and then we both went on our way toward the Galapagos, where we planned to meet again in Academy Bay.

Elysium was sailing at a good clip of eight knots with a strong wind and a relatively calm sea when I heard a crashing blow on the side of the hull. I ran up on deck pleading with Elmer to cut the sail because I thought we had hit a sea turtle. Elmer protested that we were sailing perfectly, but he reluctantly cut some sail. At the moment he did, the wind stopped completely, just like turning off a fan. This was about three o'clock in the afternoon. Elmer believed that our cutting sail had sent the wrong message to the wind. Because we had not been appreciative, it stopped blowing and never reappeared throughout the entire evening and into the night. I was looking back at our wake to see if there was an injured animal floating in it. There was no body in evidence, so whatever it was must have sunk into the sea.

The next day there was still no wind and we drifted slowly on a flat sea. Far ahead of us we saw the rocky, rust-colored islands that marked the perimeter of the Galapagos Islands. With such a long trip ahead of us we decided not to start the engine, but spent the day moving in the gentle breeze amount the outer islands Dolphins swarmed around us, joined by sea turtles, and seals. Pelicans, blue-footed boobies, and an unusual gull with red streaks were flying along, welcoming us. We had never encountered animals that were so accessible and tame. We understood that this was their home and we were only guests. They came out to observe us, as if deciding whether we were worthy to be allowed into their space. What a delightful experience this was for us after spending seven days at sea.

As night descended, the water became completely flat. We couldn't see the horizon, only the stars reflecting themselves on the water's surface. As I lay on the deck enjoying the warmth of the evening, I thought of the nursery rhyme, "Winken, Blinken and Nod one night sailed off in a wooden shoe." The picture in my childhood book was exactly like the sea; I felt like we were sailing in the heavens among the stars. Alongside of us several dolphins lay near the boat and we could hear their gentle breath all around us. With the light of dawn, we could see the entrance to Academy Bay on Santa Cruz Island of the Galapagos. We were accompanied by a pod of dolphin joyfully leading us into the entrance of the bay. Seals jumped out of the water, curving their sleek bodies and diving gracefully all around us. The pelicans, albatross and a sandpiper flying near us filled the blue sky with their white wings.

Since we didn't have a visa for the Galapagos Islands, we were only allowed to stop in the islands because of the provision of the International Harbor of Refuge Law. That law gave us permission to stay in port for seventy-two hours to take care of getting fuel and water and any emergency that we may have encountered. The red rock and rust colored earth glowed above the dazzling blue-green water that washed up over the pristine white sand lining the beach. The entire island chain was breathtakingly beautiful. Coming into the port, jet-black iguanas over two and a half feet long swam out to the boat. Their bodies were a stark contrast to the pale colors of the clear water.

As we neared the bay, the port captain came out to meet us in a small boat to show us where to anchor. We were tired from being awake all night so we both napped a bit before going overboard to scrape off the gooseneck barnacles that had grown thickly all along the side of the boat. When we awoke, the authorities came out and asked us what our emergency was. We told them that we needed fuel and water, and we were allowed to stay as a result of the Harbor Of Refuge law.

We rowed ashore and found the crew from *Acushla* just arriving. We were pleased to see our new friends again so soon. We all walked up to the Charles Darwin Educational Center and met Fritz Angermeir's son, Frederic. The Angermeirs were the original settlers of the Galapagos and Frederick and Fritz were their descendents. We invited them and several more of the local people to come out and visit us on *Elysium*.

On shore there was a set of six concrete laundry tubs that provided fresh water and a tin roof for protection from the hot sun. I loaded up sheets and clothes to take advantage of this great facility. When I got to the tubs, there were several Ecuadorian women washing their clothes by beating each item with a large wooden club. Just as I completed my washing, the lady who was using the tub next to me took my clothes and, with a disgusted look, beat each one of them also. Evidently my method was not satisfactory, so she felt I needed a lesson. I thanked her profusely and gave her a toffee candy as I gathered everything up to take back to the boat to dry.

Mrs. Angermeir came to the boat and brought us a basket-full of avocados that she wanted to trade for a bottle of sunscreen. I seldom used sunscreen because the sweat always washed it off, so I gladly gave her two bottles for the trade. She was very pleased and when she got home she sent her lovely daughter, Monica, out with pineapple, papaya, lemons and some coconut. I got out my cache of gifts and Monica chose some fishhooks, a bar of soap, and some baking powder. We always had a good supply of the things that we had learned were in demand in our gift box. No matter what we gave others, we always seemed to get back even more from them. We found the generosity of these people to be incredible.

We invited the crew from *Acushla* over for dinner that evening. While they were there, we pulled out our charts of Australia so they could

Galapagos laundromat

mark the best places to stay. We planned to arrive in Australia in about two or three years. "You come to Mooloolaba and we will have a place for you to stay at the yacht club," Bobbie told us. This crew was such a diverse group: Bobbie had masses of curly black hair and a big, bushy beard; he was very outgoing and friendly; Peter was a soft-spoken intellectual from New Zealand; Mizzie was Jewish and had immigrated to Australia from New Jersey; while Rowley was comfortable and charismatic; and Jeannie was very much her own person, bright and outspoken. They were enjoying the trip together and learning a lot about living and working in close quarters. We told them we would see them in Australia in 1982 or after! We looked forward to spending more time with this jovial group of young people.

We had one more day to spend in the Galapagos, so we went up into the hills to see the giant land turtles. It is very difficult to describe these gentle creatures that are as large as a small pony. While sitting on their backs, our feet barely touched the ground. These beautiful animals were nearly extinct before they were protected. The sailors of yore would stop at the islands and take them for food. They would lie helplessly upside down in the bilge of the ships until they were slaughtered for fresh meat for the crew.

We hiked further along the trail and saw many of the birds we had read about in Darwin's book. We also found the large trees that looked like a pine trees with prickly pear cactus-like limbs. The whole island showed evidence of adaptation for survival. We observed the cormorants that did not have adequate wings and could not fly, but they had no predators. We were not ready to leave this unique place yet. There was so many more extraordinary things that we wanted to explore and observe and we knew we would probably never be able to come back.

It was March 7, 1981, when we checked out with the port captain. As we sailed out, the boat was loaded with delicious fruit, full diesel and water tanks. We spent all of the Ecuadorian money we had exchanged for when we entered. Just before we pulled anchor, Monica Angermeir came out again with a whole stock of bananas and a melon that we traded for a roll of nylon fish line. She gave us some tips about the strong current taking us east around Blanco Point where there is a navigational light.

We were headed out for a very long journey that had taken some sailors as long as sixty days. In the days ahead we would have to conserve food, diesel and water to make them last the entire trip. When we left, we put up our biggest sail, the drifter, and sailed comfortably with a very light wind for the entire evening. We took turns sleeping and watching the light on Blanco Point, caught in the current, making little progress. As I lay on deck relaxing in the warm evening, I suddenly heard a loud whooshing noise. A whale that was the size of the full length of the boat came up right next us, inhaling a big breath of air, then drifted slowly down into the depths again, leaving a brilliant lime green phosphorescent glow the magnificent animal descended.

Elmer and I set up a routine of two hours on the helm and two hours off with extra time for me to cook meals. Our plan was to head south of the Equator until we picked up the westerly trade winds that were indicated on the Pilot Charts. We drifted along for several days with light winds. Finally a bit of wind came up and the islands disappeared from sight. Elmer tried to get a shot with the sextant at noon and found it was ninety degrees in all directions, indicating that the sun was directly overhead. We were only one hundred thirty miles from Santa Cruz. We were able to get a good signal on the ham radio so that we could to talk to George. He was eager to hear from us and to maintain contact with us as we made this long journey. This contact made us feel much less alone as we were so far away from land.

When we finally picked up a bit of wind, we put out our big fishhook to catch a fish for dinner. When Elmer looked back he saw that we had caught a pair of big sea turtles instead of a fish. We lowered our sail and Elmer stepped down on the wind vane to gently draw them in toward the boat. As they came closer we saw we had hooked two turtles mating. The large female was just able to keep her nose out of the water while Elmer took the hook out of the flipper of the male. It was obvious that we were being a nuisance to them as they blinked their big watery eyes at us, but they still they did not stop mating. Elmer said he didn't want to "disturb the piece"!

In the evening as the wind died down, there was only a playful foam swirl to break the monotony of the vast expanse of sea that goes on as far as the eye can see. The sentinel of the mast moved forward into the sunset and began the night watch. The 4:00 a.m. watch was my favorite time because I was able to see the first brightening of the sky in the east. At 6:00 a.m. I could go below to lie on the bunk and look out the back windows and watch the waves try to overcome us, but *Elysium* always rose up to them and floated free.

We sailed over beautiful patterns of foam as the sea monotonously moved up and over itself. Then, as the wind picked up, the sea became alive, moving, flowing and resisting the waves slapping alongside the hull. They pushed and swelled, whipping the sea foam like a thick white frosting. We began to see whiskery clouds that promised a strong wind aloft and was a forewarning of powerful winds to come.

Each day we obtained a sun shot and I would go below and mark the chart to see how far we had come in the last twenty-four hours. The chart covers the whole Pacific Ocean, so even the one hundred mile mark is less than an inch. Then I would predict how many miles or days we had left to go. When we had been out only six days it already seemed like a dreadfully long time with the wind increasing and extremely difficult steering. When I figured the distance ahead, I realized our journey required twenty-five to thirty more days. That seemed like a time without end in this area, void of anything but water.

One night, just at midnight, we saw a bright glow behind us that stayed with us until a squall came and moved it away. Later in the day we heard someone speaking Spanish on the VHF, then a big four-seated helicopter flew over and circled us as I lay nude, sun-tanning on the back of the boat. The light must have been from a fishing boat and the people in the helicopter were looking for fish, but shocked me instead. That evening we saw the light from the boat again and we watched until it faded out of sight, hoping that they had good radar so they would not run into us at night.

Just as evening arrived, a pod of three small black whales covered with barnacles swam by. The wind died completely so we lay down on the lounges on deck to sleep. When we woke up, we saw the light from the fishing boat again. The whales had signaled to them that there were fish nearby. We must have been in a group of fishing boats. We watched closely in case they drew near so we could shine a light at them to avoid a collision. Then we got a call on the radio from Carlos on the yacht *Brazilerrino*. They saw our sails and contacted us to tell us they were on their way to the Marquesas. We were happy to have the contact and we planned to see them when we all arrived in Hiva Oa.

Finally, on the tenth day, we started to make some good mileage. There were periodic rain squalls in which we bathed and washed our clothes. At last we reached the trade winds that were blowing eighteen knots from the southeast, where we picked up more speed. Elmer obtained a good sun shot and we discovered that we were less than two hundred miles from the Galapagos. We had been held back for several days because we were in the Horse Latitudes. The huge stalk of bananas that were on the stern of the boat had been green the day before; all turned bright yellow at the same time. The autopilot had been doing a lot of the steering, but as the wind increased, the electrical breakers were blowing so it stopped working. The heavy sea and rapid speed had been too much for it. We would have to be at the helm every moment to steer, night and day, for the remainder of this very long voyage.

When I went below to prepare breakfast I found the lower tier of eggs in the bilge were broken and rotten. The bananas were now all very ripe and we hadn't even eaten half of them. In order to save some we dried them in the sun. The ice was gone and the food left in the icebox was a sickly color of green with orange spots. I wistfully threw the cheese and pepperoni overboard. The flour was filled with small worms that had to be sifted out before I could make bread or pancakes. When I made pancakes, the lumps that were left in the batter wiggled, but quickly died as the heat overtook them. "Just protein," I decided, and didn't tell Elmer. We were now sailing with thirty knots of wind, which kicked up a much rougher sea. I knew we needed that wind to complete the long journey, but the rough sea makes everything extremely difficult. I needed to have one hand holding tightly to the grab rail for every move. I fixed Elmer a cup of hot chocolate and started up the stairs when a sudden heavy jerk of the boat threw me backward, spattering the dark brown sticky mess all over. But taking a noon sextant shot, we found the discomfort was worthwhile because we had covered one hundred and fifty-eight miles in one day. "Hurrah"!

Now we moved along swiftly in the heavy sea. On our tenth day out, several black and white false killer whales joined us. They were about fifteen feet long and stayed with us, surfing around the wake of the boat for nearly an hour. At the time, I was reading about a boat that had been wrecked by these big black and white whales in the same area we were sailing. I took comfort in the fact that the boat they had sunk was made of wood instead of concrete and steel. The crew had written a book about many days' survival at sea in a life raft. I put the book away and found something to read that was not so similar to our situation. A few sea birds kept us company and occasionally we saw a large flat sunfish on the surface of the water. The steering had become much too difficult for either the wind vane or the autopilot to handle, so we had to take turns steering for as long as we could. With the constant twenty-five knot wind and heavy sea, Elmer was much more capable of handling the helm than I was. When I could no longer handle the steering, I went

Elmer with cinnamon rolls

to the galley and made him a big pan of cinnamon rolls to assuage my guilt.

We were able to get a good signal from George and talk with LeAnn in Portland, which was fantastic. I felt some sadness stemming from my childhood when my father died, and I often felt alone and abandoned. Being so far off in the desolate sea heightened those feelings. The radio contact erased those uncomfortable thoughts and I was able to acquire a more positive outlook again. Elmer and George discussed the autopilot, but there was no solution to make it run again. We figured we still had nearly twenty days until we arrived at the Marquesas. The thought of fighting the steering every day for twenty or thirty days and nights was overwhelming to me and I wondered if I could maintain my strength.

One thing that broke the monotony of the days was the sea-life. We had a black tipped albatross stay with us for several days. The wingspan of these birds is nearly six feet and they can soar along using the wind off of the waves to support their flight. They very seldom moved their wings, but seemed to be able to glide with the wind like the sails of the boat. In the middle of the night, when we were changing watches, the sky suddenly lit up like daylight for several minutes. We could see everything on the boat and the whole ocean around us for miles and miles. Then just as suddenly the light blacked out. We thought that a meteor must have hit somewhere, and that it was probably notable around the whole world, so we were eager to ask George about it when we had our next chat.

On March 19, we had to advance our clocks an hour because we changed time zones. We were still not half way to the Marquesas yet and had at least eighteen to twenty days left to go. We were taking half an hour watches during the day because the steering was so difficult and tiring. At night we took down the main sails to make it easier to steer and get some rest. When a heavy rain squall occurred, bringing with it extremely difficult winds, we dropped all of the sails and lay to for a night of much needed sleep. To sink into the pillows that lined the walkway and know that we did not have to wake up was ecstasy beyond belief. We both sunk into unconscious sleep for eight hours with no worries about hitting a boat or any other danger. Sleep was all we cared about.

The next morning the skies were blue and there were white fluffy trade wind clouds. The autopilot was able to function for a short while and the trailing generator produced some current to keep the autopilot going. We were able to get well organized before a big wave stopped the autopilot from working and a gusty twenty knot wind brought the heavy seas back. When we tried to take the main sail down, the halyard got twisted in the sheave so we couldn't drop it. The wind vane rudder was making the steering nearly impossible, so we just wrapped up and tied the sails and went to bed thinking we would have work to do in the morning.

In spite of the very tumultuous sea and twenty knot wind, Elmer climbed down on the wind vane rudder to detach it and bring it on deck. He planned to work on it later when the weather conditions made it possible. Next, the main sail halyard at the top of the main mast would have to be repaired. The autopilot was able to handle the steering for a while, indicating that the problem had been the wind vane rudder over-riding the main rudder. We could only use the headsail so we couldn't maintain a good speed. The log showed us that we were moving ahead at four knots, but when Elmer finally obtained a good noon shot it showed we had achieved six and a half knots and had traveled one hundred and forty miles in one twenty-four hour period. The improved steering was manageable, so we could endure one and a half hour watches at night. Whenever there was a calm moment, Elmer worked on the autopilot so we could hold the boat steady to repair the mainsail.

Our supply of potatoes was gone but we still had a few onions to eat with our canned food. I used the last of our eggs in the pancakes we had for breakfast. When I broke them there was green mold inside, but it stayed with the shell so I cooked the pancakes well enough to kill anything that might have been harmful. Carlos Andrade had taken us up to an egg farm in Panama where we had purchased eight-dozen unwashed eggs that had never been refrigerated. In this state, eggs will keep a long time as a film protects them when they are laid. Now they were responding to the warm damp bilge and rough movement and were becoming very stale. When I was in college I had studied microorganisms that caused food poisoning. We learned that if the temperature were high enough, this type of mold would not be dangerous. We made it through the day without being sick and I was relieved that I had been right.

The wind decreased enough so Elmer could get the wind vane back into the water and working properly again. It took him two and a half hours standing on the two wind vane braces on the back of the boat, pitching up and down like riding a wild bronco, to get it back in place. After he finished and put it back in the water, the boat stayed on course until 10:00 p.m., allowing us the ultimate freedom from the drudgery of steering. After this short rest, a squall piped up and we had to hold onto the wheel for dear life all the rest of the night. We were able to take the sail up with the anchor winch so at least we were moving ahead. Advancing was a great priority. Each time we lay to without sailing we had to add all of those hours to our time at sea.

The next morning several animated bottlenose dolphins swam up and surrounded the boat along with storm petrels and another albatross, allowing us some diversion. Our noon shot indicated that we had traveled one hundred and sixty-two miles since the last shot yesterday, which was very good news. The bad news was that we were going too far south and would be at the same latitude as Hiva Oa in twenty miles. We were sixteen days out of the Galapagos and had one thousand, two hundred and sixty-one miles to go according to my figures. Elmer rigged up the headsails with a broom handle and with some diving weights holding the sails out so we could have our big sails catching the wind from behind us. This is called sailing wing-and-wing and would help us to hold a course sailing directly west instead of tacking back and forth. The wind vane held and took the major effort off of the steering so Elmer could finally get a good sleep.

We were able to get a clear contact with George that evening and eagerly asked him about seeing a meteor, but he said that there was nothing in the news about any sighting. I was extremely disappointed because the light had been so bright that we expected that it must have shown around the world. This told us how far away we were from everything and everyone, but talking with George helped take away the sting of the isolation.

In order to sleep, we stuffed pillows in every empty space around the sleeping bag to keep us from rolling around with the motion of the boat. It was truly ambrosia to slip into that bag when the time came to go off watch and be able to fall asleep almost instantly. One morning, just as Elmer was waking up for his watch, a very energetic flying fish zoomed right over the rail and into his sleeping bag. The fish are able to fly such a distance because they exude fish slime all over their bodies and flying fins. The fish ended up sliding down right under his chin and well into the bag. "Ugg!" he cried, as he jumped up, bringing with him the wriggling fish. He was covered with the slime, so he threw a bucket overboard to bring up water to wash it off.

The sea was so rough and turbulent that it caused the boat to slam back and forth, eventually snapping the sheet to the headsail until it finally broke, pulling out all of the main grommets in the sail. The wind was maintaining twenty-five knots so at least we were moving ahead at a good pace, but it was putting a tremendous pressure on the sails and the steering. Our routine consisted of pancakes for breakfast made with powdered eggs, canned bacon, snacks of dried apricots and some jerky. A main meal would include dried fish or canned meat casserole. Then the dreaded endless night and the lonely watch would begin. When each of us could maintain two hours on the helm, the night went much faster. During the day, cassettes of music were helpful to boost our spirits a little. The next shot we took still put us eight days from the islands at the speed we were traveling. Eight days felt like an eternity because our yearning for land became almost unbearable. We did not know for sure if it would only be eight days. What if it took ten or more? How would we be able to hang on to our sanity? The contact with George is what took us out of the routine and brought us back into the world of home and people.

Just when we thought the sea couldn't get any worse, the action of the ocean became almost untenable. The wheel jerked from side to side as the waves smashed into the side of the hull, each one throwing us completely off course. The sextant shots were virtually impossible for Elmer to take because the boat careened from side to side. At this point, we were on constant look-out for any sign of land in the far distance, although our best guess was that we were as far as two hundred miles away. Just as we were feeling depressed, a beautiful white albatross flew over and sat down in the water next to the boat. Several other sea birds were also gathering. A storm petrel flew over the waves like a butterfly, winging from side to side to avoid the wave peaks. This could be our sign that land was closer. The wind abated for the first time in many days and we noticed some strange clouds ahead. We thought we saw something solid at the base of those clouds. When darkness came we could hardly sleep because of our anticipation and excitement. What we saw might be a mirage, but what it would look like in the morning? We decided to lay to and get some rest before morning to discover if we really had seen something. We were thirty-nine days from Panama and it was April 3, 1981.

The next morning I came up on deck to hunt for some sight of land and as I searched the sky to the aft of the boat, I saw a small rocky is-land. Elmer said "No, look over there behind you." I turned and saw the breathtaking green island of Hiva Oa rising up three thousand feet into the air, with its deep sculpted rocky ridges sweeping down into the sea. The very closeness and reality of its being was overwhelming to me. With great excitement we continued into the harbor and were in Taa Haku Bay by 9:30 a.m. Our friends from *Acushla* were there to greet us for a very happy reunion. We had completed the trip! We all could hardly believe it was over. No more sleepless nights, and no more pas-sages that took as long as this one!

We went ashore to the gendarme to check in. It was ecstasy to be able to walk on the land again. The fragrance of the frangipani and of the other earth smells was awesome to us after a month at sea. The crew on *Acushla* suggested that we accompany them to a farm where they were able to get fresh fruit and vegetables. It was a four mile hike up a very steep and muddy road, but one bite of a fresh watermelon made it all worthwhile. Due to the isometric exercise while we were sailing, we still maintained excellent physical condition even though we lacked sleep. After eating as much as we could hold, we loaded our backpacks and bags to overflowing and started down the road again. Each vantage point gave us a magnificent view of the bays around the island. When we returned to *Elysium* we collapsed into an extraordinarily restful and long sleep, filled with joy that we were at last at anchor.

Every day there were new arrivals in the bay while many yachts also left. It was very sad for us to say bid farewell to our good friends on *Acushla*. They all came over to say goodbye and brought us gifts to remember them by. Bobbie wove a bracelet onto my arm and said that it should be left there until we arrived in Australia. The new arrivals to the bay were from France, Italy, Holland, Denmark, and other countries from around the world. We greeted them as they arrived and enjoyed the international conversations on-board *Elysium*. It was a very social time for us and we enjoyed the camaraderie very much after so many days of seeing no one but each other.

Now that we were safely in port there were chores that needed to be done on *Elysium*. Elmer went to the top of both masts to unsnarl the tangled pulleys, we tediously mended the torn headsail, and I did prodigious loads of laundry each day. Everything on the boat was stiff with salt from the sea spray, so the fresh water faucet on the shore was a blessing to use and I could wash and rinse everything without waiting for rain. We filled our scuba air tanks and began cleaning the bottom of the boat. Elmer put a new circuit-board in the autopilot that we hoped would perform properly. We knew that from then on, we would have shorter trips where we could give it a good work out; we hoped the seas would be kinder.

We made several more trips up to the fertile vegetable garden to fill our packs and show others the way. The French yacht, *La Belle*, had two young girls aboard whom we had met in Panama. They agreed to help us build a French vocabulary, so they came over often and we progressed, learning some of the very basic greetings and questions. We invited all the people we had met to come over for a potluck so they could meet each other. We had twenty-eight people in all on the boat. That was a record for the number of people onboard at one time.

We moved to another bay on Nuku Hiva, about eight miles away. We planned to move from bay to bay for a while, as the Marquesas has several islands that are close together. There was a well-known wood carver here so we went up to meet him. We ordered two small masks, two little swords and two tikis, which are the carved, large-eyed likeness of a spirit. The tiki was for Karin in Hawaii. Manu, the carver, did not have good sandpaper and had difficulty finishing the hard wood that he used for his carvings. His fingers were just small stubs because he had lost them to leprosy. Still, he was able create very intricate carvings. We

Manu and Elmer with tiki heads

had a whole ream of sandpaper on the boat so we took some to him for a gift. He was delighted and in return he made the masks twelve inches and the swords thirty-six inches, much larger than we had ordered. He was pleased to do this extra work for us. We accepted them and thanked him profusely and then had to find places on the boat for them.

We stopped for a chat with several people on the boats that were now anchored in the bay representing so many countries in the world. We all got together to talk and discovered that we were very comfortable in this international community. Terry and Phillip, on *Vataroy*, had sailed from England and had stayed in the bay for several months. Their idea of cruising was to make the trip and stay put in a place that suited them. They became fast friends with all of the local people, including one couple from the United States who had established a local restaurant. These new friends, coupled with the friends we had met ashore, expanded our perception of the world every day. One day we looked up and saw a boat that was from Sauvie Island Yacht Club. Some young friends from Parkers moorage! Tom and Becky Coffield sailed in on *Cabaret*. What a surprise to see them and to catch up on all of their experiences.

We sailed over to Daniel's Bay with several other boats. The bay has towering green cliffs and is better protected than Hiva Oa. Françoise and Helena lived along the shore and had eighty-one fat and sleek French Charlais cattle. Helena had names for each of the cows browsing on the bushes that grow rapidly all through the valley, fed by the daily rain on the inland. They directed us to the path that led to a spectacular waterfall, pummeling down four hundred feet from the rocky cliffs above. Lining the path was a wall with carved boulders expertly placed, some standing eight feet high. On the side were square foundation rocks with doorways that suggested a civilization as large as two thousand people long ago. There was an abandoned church that was slowly slipping into the mud. The local dogs accompanied us and enjoyed swimming in the stream as we walked along.

Helena and Françoise lived under an open shed with a large king-size mattress covered with bright printed sheets and many pillows. They had boxes set up near the bed with a place for us to sit as they served us hot tea with a staggering amount of sugar. They spoke very good English and told us about their intriguing life on the bay. As we visited, the animals came around to be watered. First was a large dog with seven new fat, furry puppies. The pigs arrived scratching their backs on the shed supports, coming right inside to look around under the bed. These were very different pigs than we had ever seen before; they were all black with the longest snouts imaginable, much like wild boars we had seen. One pig was quite aggressive and pushed the other pigs around, biting them soundly on the rump. Finally, about twenty pigs congregated around us as we drank our tea.

When Françoise and Helena came out to our boat for dinner, they told us about their lives. Françoise was in the French Army three years before finding this beautiful spot on Daniel's Bay. They had taken their savings and purchased this beautiful spot where they could be away from the traffic and noise of the city. They both especially liked the crystals we had hanging in the windows to catch the sunlight, so I gave them one we had in a port. Françoise asked if it was a diamond and I told him no and showed him the one on my ring. He asked what a diamond cost us and we said anywhere from two hundred to a thousand dollars. "No good, too small, better buy cows with that money," he said. As they were leaving they asked us to give water to the cows the next day, as they needed to go to town for supplies. We went to shore with them to get the directions for all of the animal care we needed to perform. When they returned to the bay in their motorboat that evening, they brought us mangos, oranges, tangerines and a big lobster Françoise had caught.

We said a sad goodbye to our friends and sailed with a perfect breeze over to the small island Ua Pou, which was only twenty miles away. We planned to anchor there for a few days to prepare to leave the Marquesas for the Tuomotos Islands. As we anchored in the small bay, a woman and little boy came by in a dugout with six cleaned fish to give us. We invited them aboard and found a tee shirt that fit the boy and a hat that was made in Panama for her. She had a hat on that she had woven out of palm fronds. The tightly woven hat was new to her and with delight she snatched her hat off and gave it to us, and admired herself in the mirror with the new one. We told her we were leaving the island for a long trip to the Tuomotos the next morning. She wrinkled her brow and shook her head saying, "Very long way and dangerous"! She asked us to come to shore and see her little house in the village when we were finished cleaning the boat. When we got to her house, to our complete amazement she had piled up pineapple, green beans, lettuce, two stocks of bananas, a basket full of limes, a large squash, two pots full of the starchy tuber that is the mainstay food, manioc, which she had cooked, and bundles of flowers that smelled so lovely that the whole boat was permeated with them when we put them in vases.

We tried to tell them that this was more food than we could eat, but they insisted that we all carry it back, so they came to *Elysium*, laden down with all the supplies. We found a tee shirt for each of them, needles, sandpaper, socks and a good pair of shiny scissors, which brought lots of sighs and "ahhhh's." They stayed on the boat and taught us some Marquesan words and played the ukulele for us. When they left, they told us that our journey would be blessed and we would have a safe trip.

Very early the next morning we pulled anchor and sailed out of the bay, waving goodbye to our friends on shore. This little island did not have the visitors that the other bays did because there were no stores or shops. It was a charmed stop for us, loaded with too much food and filled with the love that these beautiful Polynesian people gave out so fully.

Atolls and Coral Reefs
Marquesas, Tuamotu Atolls, Tahiti, Huahine, Tahaa, Riatea, and Bora Bora

Do not follow where the path may lead. Go instead where there is no path and leave a trail.

– Emerson

WE LEFT THE anchorage on my birthday, May 16, 1981. We blessed the lady and her friends as we sailed along eating green beans and manioc. Manioc takes such a long time to cook; she must have boiled all day over a fire giving it a wonderful smoky taste.

We were very fortunate to have good wind and to be able to take such an accurate navigational noon shot. We were now headed for the low-lying Tuamotu atolls. An atoll is a perimeter of coral that is built on an old volcano caldera, and is only the height of a palm tree. The entire area contains hundreds of atolls surrounded by extremely unpredictable currents, making the approach by sailboat very hazardous. At the edge of these atolls, the water plunges without warning to a great depth. In this circumstance the depth sounder gives the approaching boat no indication that shallow coral is directly ahead. We made good headway and covered over four hundred miles in four days of easy sailing, but could not spot Takaroa, a very large atoll that we should have reached on the fourth night. We must have skirted it because we could hear our friends on other yachts talking on the VHF radio where they were anchored inside the atoll.

We missed taking the next strategic navigational shot because clouds formed just when we needed a fix. We decided to take all the sails down in order to move more slowly and avoid running onto the coral reefs at night. When the sun was just barely up again, we sighted the atoll, Manihi. We sailed over to the pass and as we started into the area where the water drains from the interior of the atoll, we found it was flowing out extremely swiftly. To our relief, three native men who saw us approach came out in a powerboat to help guide us in. The current aggressively swung the boat back and forth as we motored against it. The water was so clear that it had magnified the clarity of the sea floor making it appear that we might scrape the bottom of the boat.

That evening a big squall came in with forty-five knot winds, but the anchorage had complete protection and no waves formed inside. When we entered, we saw sailboat skeletons strewn on the outer reefs, wrecked because they were unable to avoid the wind and current. We were very relieved to be inside and safe from the heavy wind and sea.

In the morning we went on shore to walk along the reefs where we found beautiful shells. Wading ankle deep in the surf we saw the most amazing marine animals: sea slugs and anemone type animals laid out with fingers extended. The wavy mouths of the giant clams glowed all colors of the rainbow, an iridescence created by tiny animals that live along the lips of the clams in a symbiotic relationship. We hurried back to the boat to get our scuba gear in order to take advantage of the low tide. The animals living on the reef tend to live forty to fifty feet from the surface of the water. We were entranced, examining the different types of animal life at each level of the reef, and I didn't notice a shark come by, but it caught Elmer's eye right away. When the shark swung around for a closer look at us, Elmer grabbed me and pulled me right up on shore. The shark was a black tipped one and was not supposed to be dangerous, but Elmer said he didn't know if the shark knew that. The shark put an end to our diving, but the colors gleaming on the sun-drenched reef would be a memory we would have forever.

When we returned to the boat, we received a call on the radio from some friends in another atoll nearby, called Ahe. Our friends told us that it was gorgeous there and more of our friends were arriving every day. We had set two anchors, one on a long chain and one on a rope because it is easier to pull up. We tried to pull the anchor, but the tall coral heads under the boat had ensnared the rope. Elmer went out in our dingy, *Limbo*, to gain a better grasp on the rope. When he started back he was rowing strongly but as I watched I saw that he was making no headway toward the boat. Finally, after a long, arduous pull, he was able to get back. He had pulled up the anchor but could not get the fifty-six pound anchor into the dingy so he was rowing with it over the stern, beating against a heavy wind. He had rowed so hard he had big blisters on his hands. The wind was piping up again, so we quickly motored out just as the tide was changing.

It took us a little over four hours to sail the twenty-two miles to Ahe against a ferocious current. We were more and more apprehensive about these atolls as we saw many sailboat skeletons on the outer reefs. When we arrived, there were sixteen yachts from various places in the world, anchored inside the tiny bay. We walked along the shore and enjoyed getting to know the people we had not met before. Mama Fana was the bread lady in this tiny village; she made the wonderful baguettes that the French are noted for. The bread was baked in big fifty-five gallon drums filled with coconut husks that were used for fuel. Her son, Hiti, had been an entertainer in Papeete, so they offered to have a feast and to play for us. We were all supposed to bring some food to add to the feast, so I baked a rice casserole and used up the last of the vegetables we had onboard.

Mama Fana was in charge of the feast and she provided delicious native food. We sat on the concrete pier and listened to the songs they sang while they played on the guitar and banjo. We enjoyed a gala evening, hearing the sea stories from the sailors who had come from Europe and Australia.

All of the atolls in the Tuamotu's have coconut palms and a few breadfruit trees growing on the coral. There is no real soil on the atolls, so no fresh vegetables were available until the supply boat arrived from Papeete. I was hungry for carrots and when the supply boat came in to port that next week, there was a big hemp bag full of carrots from New Zealand. We bought half of the bag and never had a carrot been so pleasing. I ate so many that I had no room for anything else.

The people who were still anchored in the bay got together for another evening of musical entertainment in Mama's little metal house. While we were inside the house, suddenly a torrential rain began pounding. We listened to the music as it blended in with the rain's rhythmic beating on the metal roof. Mama Fana moved to the door and hurried outside. When she came back she had a large tray of bottles to pass around. The bottles were full of chilled rainwater, something we had not experienced for years- cold water! We had some tapes onboard that Hiti wanted, so we agreed to exchange them for the wonderful entertainment that they provided. We recorded a lively cassette tape of the evening to add to our collection of local music.

After a week in Ahe I rowed ashore to sit on the edge of the reef at low tide, and watch a beautiful sunset and to say goodbye to the beautiful atoll. I observed a large crab walk along, slowly making his way down the dry reef in front of me. Just as it reached a spot several inches away from my legs, a big, black moray eel darted out from beneath where I sat and crunched the crab in between its powerful jaws. The repulsive looking eel turned his head sideways, either to look at me or to better fit the crab back into his hole, I could not tell. But the fright that took hold of me was startling. This was a graphic illustration of the fragile stability of life and how quickly it can come to an end.

We went ashore to say goodbye to Mama, Hiti, and his wife, Elena. I played the tape I had recorded of them singing several times while their two little girls giggled with glee. I gave Hiti my tape of Saturday Night Fever that he had asked for in trade and we had some gifts for the little girls. Sadly, we hugged and kissed Mama goodbye. The loving Polynesian people had quickly adopted the French custom of kissing on both cheeks. We enjoyed the contact of hugs and kisses, so we also made this part of our greeting and farewells.

All day the VHF radio had been buzzing with talk from Rangiroa, the biggest atoll in the group. Our friend, Mike Davidson, on *Starlight*, had arrived there along with many of other sailors we knew. We were eager to meet up with Mike, who was also from our area in Oregon, and partake in the excitement that we were hearing about on the radio. They told us that the Club Med Hotel had set aside one of its woven huts that usually rented for two-hundred dollars, at no cost for the visiting yachties. With the daily temperatures reaching eighty-eight degrees, it would be nice to have a shady place with a cool breeze drifting through, and to be able to renew acquaintances.

Sailing out of Ahe there was a thirty knot wind behind us, so we only put up a staysail. We did not want to proceed too rapidly in the pitch black of the night near these dangerous reefs. Rangiroa was visible at 8:30 a.m., and we made it to the Avatoru Pass at 9:30 a.m., just at slack tide. Entering these passes is not for the faint hearted, as the current is still tumultuous and very rough, even at the time it is changing. We sailed over to where our friends' visiting yachts were anchored in the sun-drenched white sand right in front of the hotel and dropped our anchor. We had a great time reconnecting with many friends whom we had not seen for a while. The Brazilians were there, along with Mike, from *Starlight*, chartering their boats to earn money. This suited the hotel manager as they could depend on experienced sailors showing their guests around the forty-five mile lagoon. Rangiroa's lagoon draws many tourists because it is the largest lagoon and motu atoll on earth. It is also the only place in the Tuamotu's where there is a city with all the amenities a tourist would require.

We walked the two miles to the store at the airport where they had fresh lettuce, tomatoes, cucumbers and cantaloupe that had been flown in. What a treat that was! In the evening we went to the hotel where Mike, the manager from England, invited us to join in with the tourists for an evening of music and dance. Mike and a lovely Polynesian girl performed an intricate Tahitian dance. The way he danced was very comical and extremely entertaining because his good-sized belly bounced around as he adeptly gyrated through the steps. We never tired of watching him; it was the highlight of each evening. This was a very difficult place to leave, as Mike enjoyed having the yachties entertain his diverse group of guests, and this made the whole experience luxurious for us. Every day, Carlos and Selso, from the yacht *Brazilerrino*, brought us a beautiful fresh fish that they caught while diving in the sparkling clear water of the lagoon. In return I supplied them with bread I made in the galley. We were having the time of our lives and forgot all of the unpleasant weather and dangerous trips of the past. We knew that it was time to leave because we wanted to be in Tahiti for the Bastille Day Celebration on July 14. We sadly left this South Pacific Paradise for a two-day sail across to Tahiti.

We spotted Tahiti at 1:00 a.m. in the moonlight, and since it looked so close, we took down some sail. At 6:30 a.m. we were still ten miles off, but the sun changed the solid dark silhouette to a deeply ridged, luxuriant green island. This was a welcome change after making our landfalls on the Tuomotu's atolls with a nine foot height. As we entered the harbor, several friends called over to show us where to pull in. There were hundreds of boats side by side, tied stern to shore with a bow anchor out in front. Thankfully, several friends came out in their dinghies to help us back into the narrow space, which was made more difficult by a beam wind blowing us sideways.

After we slid *Elysium* into place, we got into *Limbo* and rowed ashore. We then set out to explore Tahiti with our friends. The first thing they showed us was a place that blended the sweet fresh, golden pineapple, mango and papaya with ice for a very refreshing drink. Across the road from the fruit stand was a lady making leis out of the fragrant, vivid white and pink plumeria flowers. We bought some to have inside the boat, so the lovely odor permeated the warm, tropical air all around us. They showed us where the shower was on the main drive right below the highway into the city of Papeete. We could take showers and watch the traffic move along the road just above us. As we explored more of Tahiti, each time we walked along the road someone would stop to pick us up and take us where we wanted to go.

The Bastille Day celebration draws native Polynesians from many of the various islands in French Polynesia. There were colorful parades, and races for outrigger canoes and sailing craft. The beach behind the boats was strewn with ropes tying the big yachts to shore, and the children of the natives who were participating in the races strained to watch their parents out in the bay. One day I looked back and saw a darling little, dark-eyed coffee skinned girl standing near our rope. I smiled and tried a bit of my French with her. She quickly warmed to the conversation and climbed up the rope to the boat. We enjoyed having this lovely little girl aboard and took her to the bow to watch the outrigger race that her father was participating in. In the next few minutes our boat was filled with children of all ages, eager to watch the races. We let the oldest one use our binoculars and stressed to her how valuable they were to us and that it was necessary to always keep the strap around her neck. She took one look through them and laughed with delight to see how they magnified the racing boats. From then on, all the children wanted to look and she carefully instructed them about the care of the binoculars. Each of the following days, the deck was filled with boys and girls from morning till night, enjoying the view. It was great fun for us to have them aboard. They were extremely careful not to be in the way and were very polite and well-behaved.

The next day as we arrived ashore, a skipper from a German boat heatedly advised us that we had made a terrible mistake. "Those children will be all over the other boats in the bay, stealing things and causing all kinds of trouble." We were so surprised by his irritation that we didn't know how to reply, except to say, "The children caused us no difficulty at all while they were on our boat." His angry warning did not materialize. The children never approached any one of the hundreds of boats that were tied there.

One little girl particularly enjoyed teaching Elmer her language. She would carefully pronounce a French word, and when his elocution was faulty, she would pound her little fists on his chest exclaiming, "No, no masseur." Elmer liked to tease her, feigning ineptitude with the language. The delightful children added a lot to our enjoyment of the races because we could share their exhilaration as the swift rowing crews arrived.

When the celebration was over, we pulled anchor and sailed over to an anchorage in Moorea, where it wasn't so crowded. Our neighbors, Bill and Marcie on the yacht *Zephyr*, came along with us. As we entered

Elmer's French teacher

Moorea we were greeted with a magnificent sight: the contrasting turquoise greens of the surrounding barrier reef, the white sand, and the
dazzling foliage above were resplendent. We stopped where we could
see the anchor clearly set in thirty-five feet of water. When we arrived
on the shore, we were able to walk for miles along a small road without
ever seeing another soul.

The next day a young couple from Canada, Donna and Connell Ashby,
met us as we pulled the dingy up on to the shore. They had purchased
round-the-world airline tickets and were working in different countries
as they moved from one place to the next. Their little tent was filled
with vicious biting mosquitoes. Those pesky nuisances were ruining the
tranquility of their campsite. We invited them to come aboard *Elysium*
and have dinner with us. As we cooked dinner, Donna fit right into my
small galley space and we worked incredibly well together. Elmer and
I enjoyed having them onboard so much that we suggested that they
stay with us in order to avoid the mosquitoes. The following days we all
dove for shells, then we hiked many miles up the mountain roads, getting to know each other and weaving together an undying friendship.

When it came time for us to move on to the next islands we invited Donna and Connell to sail along with us. They were due to leave on a ship from Bora Bora in a few weeks and we were headed that way, so it worked out perfectly. We hadn't had people living on the boat with us before and because of the extreme heat we often did not wear clothes when we were sailing. Both Donna and Connell agreed that it would be no problem for them. They moved aboard that day and with our new crew we set sail for Huahine.

The sea was rough and sailing was very bumpy the first night out. Donna was seasick all night, sleeping up on deck close to the rail where she could throw-up overboard. The next morning we spotted Huahine at 4:30 a.m. When Donna woke bright and cheery, she said, "Someone has been sick around here"! Having such a rough trip, especially at night, is tough for anyone, especially for the first trip at sea. We sailed easily through the pass with Connell's help as he climbed up into the rigging to watch for coral. It was so nice to have these helpful young people onboard. Donna was happy to cook. She enjoyed making "chips," Canadian fried potatoes, and we often supplied a freshly caught fish.

Everyone went ashore and walked five miles around on Huahine. We met a man with a stalk of bananas who offered to sell them to us. Donna spoke French so she did the bartering. She wanted to use the two franks to purchase about twenty bananas, but the man handed us the whole stalk! He seemed delighted, but evidently he did not understand the French she had used to bargain. With our heavy bundle of bananas we headed back to *Elysium*. Now, at least, we had company to help eat them! We snorkeled in the clear water and picked up some shells. It was amazing how much help two added crew were. We saved time on chores and they were both very willing and insightful, seeing right away what needed to be done and pitching right in.

The next trip was easier for everyone. We sailed in the lee of the island chain with a good wind and a flat, protected sea to Riatea. The anchorages were all eighty-nine feet or deeper, so we decided to tie up to the dock beside the island trader ships. Being up against a dock was uncomfortable with the wind and current jerking the boat around, but it was better than pulling an anchor with a hand winch from that deep in the water. We went ashore and found lots of groceries at the store in town, so we stocked up with fresh fruit and vegetables and left the dock for the nearby island of Tahaa early the next day.

Connell was up in the rigging as we maneuvered through the coral heads and the pass. It took nearly the entire day to negotiate the channel to where we found a good anchorage. We dropped the anchor in a spot where the water was shallow, near a white sandy beach on an idyllic, palm-laden island, where we were eager to go ashore and swim. Bill and Marcie anchored next to us and we all set out for the uninhabited island of Tahaa. As we approached the spot, hungry mosquitoes smelling blood buzzed out to greet us. What could they have been eating before we arrived? We all dove quickly into the water and had to stay deeply submerged to keep from being eaten alive. When we returned to *Elysium*, we pulled anchor to get away from the little nuisances that were following behind us.

We had fine weather and a relaxed, easy day long sail to Bora Bora. We could clearly see the shimmering, light turquoise reef surrounding the main island from many miles away. This would be our last sail with our new crew and we would leave them with excellent memories of our South Pacific journey. We motored through the pass and anchored in a pure white sandy bottom that stretched out as far as we could see inside the lagoon. *Zephyr* and *Elysium* were the only two boats anchored in Bora Bora; everyone else had anchored near the Club Med resort. We could snorkel for miles and miles, skimming over calm protected water with a clear view of the stark white sand below. One thing we noticed were lots of big black rays darting swiftly across the lagoon. Donna and I got out our book of Polynesian sea life to check to see if these huge animals could be dangerous before we dove into the water. The book said they were afraid of people and would not be any harm to us.

The next morning we decided to snorkel to the outer reef where I saw several of the large black rays skirting around the lagoon. We remembered what the book had said about it being perfectly safe for us to be in the water with them. I put on my flippers and dove in. Each one of us chose a different direction to snorkel. The water was warm and crystal-clear and each of us was enjoying the vast expanse of white sand, diving to bring up a large assortment of perfect, brightly-colored cowries and other shells. I had just come up with a beautiful shell when I spotted a big, black shadow moving under me. As I looked down, an enormous ray was right beneath me, moving upward. I splashed my fins and arms furiously, but that just seemed to interest it even more. It was so close I could look into its eyes as it examined me. I started screaming frantically for help. Elmer heard me and swiftly came to my rescue. He had just seen a shark and was headed my way, so he was expecting to find that the shark was what the fuss was about. As he swam up, he spotted the ray just underneath me. He dove at it and the big animal quickly darted away. The only thing we could figure was that he thought I was another ray.

The next day we walked to the town to check in with the gendarme and receive our bond money that we had posted in Tahiti for our stay in French Polynesia. As we entered the office, a man with a New York accent was angrily shouting at the clerk. The man was demanding his money immediately. The clerk was trying to tell him that he had no American money until the Club Med, which was situated on the other side of the island, made their deposit. We hastily backed out of the office, thinking that this was not an opportune time to be Americans asking for anything. We decided we would wait several days before we tried again.

Donna and Connell went to the shipping office and were informed that their ship would be in port in a few days. We made the most of the rest of the time we had together. We walked all around the island and hiked high up on the central peak to look far out to the sea. This would be the last of French Polynesia for all of us. It had been a magical experience, never to be forgotten. To celebrate, we bought a half-gallon of ice cream. It had been such a long time since we had seen a store with ice cream. When we had eaten as much as we could, we spied two small children sitting on the side of the road. We offered the girl a spoon with ice cream in it; she quickly took the spoon and offered it to her brother. There was not a drop wasted; these two little children were able to finish every bite. As we left, the children waved and said goodbye again and again.

The next day we rented bicycles and shopped at all of the boutiques on the island. As we rode higher in the hills, there was a place with colored cloth laid out on the ground. The lady who lived there made tie-dye skirts, tops and bikinis. She laid them all out in the sunshine to set the dye permanently. These were just the items we wanted to remember our wonderful times by, so we purchased a bright yellow skirt set and a bikini painted with beautiful flowers. Coming down, we visited the Bora Bora Yacht Club and had wonderful showers, washing away the sweat and grime from our ride.

That night, as we all sat aboard *Elysium*, a fine mist settled down around the island. The moon was full and a huge moonbow formed over the pass, shining its muted colors for over an hour. We decided it was a good omen for us, as the next day Donna and Connell would board the ship for their next destination.

The next day we watched the big island trade ship enter the lagoon to dock. Donna and Connell climbed aboard after we tearfully said good-bye. We watched and waved as the ship pulled out and sailed off to Papeete. There they caught a plane back home and ended their two year trip.

Bill and Marcie came over with the sad news that the concrete yacht, *Aura*, which we had watched being built in Seattle several years before, had just hit a reef on Mopelia, a small island that was just a short way from where we were anchored. We had seen the skipper, Tom, several times while we were in the islands and he left Bora Bora just a day before we planned to depart. Bill had picked up his distress call on the radio and said they had just gotten off as the yacht sunk down, filled with water, and was out of reach for any salvage. Tom had many beautiful antiques onboard that he had added to the yacht after building *Aura*, but he was unable to retrieve anything from the yacht. His partner had left him sometime before, so he was sailing his yacht, the size of *Elysium*, all alone when he hit the reef in a squall at night. The holed yacht had stayed on the reef just long enough for him to get off before it plunged down into the deep water. The water police picked him up and took him to Bora Bora, where he planned to get a plane to fly back to Seattle. We all knew what he was feeling; we had faced the same possibility several times, in our imagination, when we were in trouble at night.

The next morning we went back to the immigration office to retrieve our bond money. We found the young man, Bengie, very friendly and eager to show us his children's pictures. We talked for some while before telling him what we were there for. He got our cash for us and didn't charge us a fee for the procedure. We went on our way, happy that the experience had been so positive. We had our visa for the next country we were planning to visit, the Kingdom of Tonga, also called the Friendly Islands. It would be a trip of ten to fifteen days and we were looking forward to catching up with friends who had arrived there a few days before.

The journey would take us to Vava'u, the northern most island group in the Kingdom of Tonga. We plotted a course that would take us past Palmerston Reef and planned a convenient rest stop at the island of Niue that was just four hundred miles east of Tonga. This would give us a rest after sailing for five or six days. The wind was strong when we left the protection of the last reef, and we were out in a heavy sea with a thirty-degree roll back and forth. It was now August, 1981, and our time in Polynesia had been very soothing, giving us a good rest in fairly protected waters since April 4, 1980. We had to relearn how rough and unkind the ocean could be. Cooking with the stove swinging violently back and forth was an art that I had to learn all over again.

The first six days, though rough, were ideal sailing. The wind vane, trailing generator and autopilot all worked well, and the seas were heavy but manageable. We were able to sleep with just one person on watch. We were getting close to the island of Niue and we looked forward to stopping for a rest and to explore the interesting island. Rolf, on *Califa*, was anchored there and told us by VHF radio about the beauty of the limestone cliffs and caves on the island. "The great variety of bird life and the large tropical forest are well worth stopping to see," Rolf told us.

Just as we were nearly in sight of the island, a big squall brought the wind around to the south and it surged up to thirty knots. If we were to head over to the island we would have to beat into huge seas and increasing wind for eighteen miles. This would be impossible for us with the daylight waning; the island was so close but too far away. We wistfully watched the lights from the island fall behind us as we sailed on to Tonga. We banged and slammed around, often rolling over forty degrees. The sloppy waves hit the side of the hull and broke clear across the steering station. Everything on deck was stiff with salt, which made the rust from the mild-steel bolts run freely over the deck. We moved along very swiftly and for the rest of the trip we had to tie ourselves down to sleep or sit. For dinner I cooked rice, but when Elmer poured milk and cinnamon on it, the plate flew out of his hand and we had sticky milk and rice all over the deck. Around noon on the ninth day we moved out of the heavy squall and the sky cleared enough for us get a noon shot. We only had seventy-five miles to go; we had to slow down so we would not reach Tonga in the dark. Even with just a small sail up, we were still moving ahead at six knots. We finally took all of the sails down at 9:30 p.m. to lay a-hull to wait until morning.

We lay down to rest as the waves and wind began to calm. We tried to estimate how close we were to the island and came up with an educated guess of fifteen miles from shore. At first light we saw the island silhouetted in the sky and we felt safe enough to go below to get breakfast. Just as we sat down to eat we heard a terrible sharp cracking sound along the hull. Elmer rushed up on deck, thinking we had hit a reef. Just as he reached the top of the ladder, a gigantic rogue wave broke over him and washed down the open hatch. Even though the huge wave engulfed us, we were both extremely relieved we had not holed the boat on a reef.

When we had everything in order again, we sailed around to the north end of the island and tried to start the motor to help us safely enter the bay. For the first time our faithful motor would not start, so we called on the radio so see who was inside the bay that could tell us what the conditions were for entering without power. The voice of our good friend, Mike Davidson, responded and gave us instructions to enter the anchorage. He said we would have no problem sailing into anchor. There were no submerged dangers and plenty of room to navigate. We beat into a twenty-five knot wind, moving carefully around the mushroom shaped little island motus. We dropped the Genoa sail and the anchor to come to a stop behind the protection of a large landmass. The wind calmed completely and we were glad to finally be at rest. Several friends sailed out to the bay to bring over fresh beef and vegetables. We fixed dinner together and caught up on where everyone had been and where they would be going from Tonga.

Mike helped Elmer look at the motor after dinner and found that the battery cable had completely corroded in the short time since we had last used the motor. The motor responded immediately after the cable had been cleaned, so we pulled anchor and followed our friends into the anchorage off the town of Neiafu with our quarantine flag up to notify the Chief of Police, Agriculture and Customs to come out. I completely forgot that I had put a fifty-dollar bill in my passport booklet while I was in French Polynesia. I remembered when the man from customs thanked me for the gift and everyone was so pleased to meet us. "Too late to get it back now," I thought.

A few days later we took *Elysium* to Pangaimotu, a small protected anchorage off of Ano Beach where there was to be a feast and handmade items for sale. The handmade baskets, tapas, woodcarvings in sandalwood, and a local black hardwood were unique and gorgeous. The feast was served on a long palm leaf and consisted of a great variety fruits, lamb flaps and many tasty seafood treats. The family that owned the Motu held this feast once a month for tourists and charged five dollars each in U.S. money for it. We really enjoyed the food and bought several beautiful carvings and baskets for our family at home.

The Tongan women wore long skirts and long sleeve dresses during the day. Some of them even wore a tapa wrapped around themselves on top of all of these clothes. It is very warm in Tonga, so I questioned a local lady who had lived in Neiafu for several years about their need for so many clothes. She told me that the missionaries had arrived in Tonga many years ago and told them that they needed to cover their bodies completely at all times. The country even made a law that men could not be seen in town without their upper bodies covered with a shirt.

When tourists visit they wear very skimpy shorts, tops and bathing suits when they go snorkeling. The Tongan people that we knew joked about their need to wear so many clothes and the fact that the same people that had proselytized them wore such skimpy ones. The Tongan women wear their long dresses even when swimming! Such is the way of these islands that were so completely converted by the religious ministers who first arrived.

There were many boats anchored in the bay and we all spent time together, visiting from one boat to another. Jim and Hutsuko from *Midpoint* came over to bring a present of hand-dried raisins and to say goodbye. We warned them that we were on the International Date Line and to be careful heading for the very dangerous reefed area of Fiji. They left that evening and we heard five days later that they had hit a reef and lost their beautiful yacht. After crossing the dateline they had failed to use the following day in the navigational books, which showed them sixty miles off of their dead reckoning, or DR, course. Any time a sailor is that far off of a DR course, they need to completely recheck their navigation. We were very sad for them as their journey ended with such a terrible loss.

Hans and Judy from *Claymore* came over and we spent a lot of time with them during the next week. They visited every day and shared stories about their time in Tonga. The year before, when they were leaving to sail to the Island of Tongatapu, where the capitol is, they took Aliki as crew. He was the eldest son of Hulu and Lisi of the Latavao clan that lived on Pangaimotu, a very well respected and loved part of the family. While they were in Tongatapu there was a very strong wind that knocked down a power pole. Aliki bent down to take the line off the road thinking a child could be hurt with it. Hans warned him it could be dangerous but Aliki thought holding it in one hand would be safe. He was killed instantly by a huge power surge. Hans and Judy took his body back to the family and there was grief and mourning all week. The family then adopted Hans as their son, as was the custom, and he was revered just as Aliki had been. Hans and Judy had stayed to help the family and take part in their rituals for another year. Now they told us it was time for them to sail on to Fiji and New Zealand. They planned to take another of the sons with them. Then they told us that they had told the family that their new son would be Elmer and we would be adopted into the family as they had been. We were very pleased to have this experience and went ashore to take part in the farewell Kava Party for Hans and Judy.

After that evening, the family became part of our everyday lives. Several weeks later we took them out to sea to fish in a part of the reef they could not reach with their small boats. The reef was situated out away from land and there were signs of wrecked boats on the outer part of the reef. Elmer was very careful to follow John Tavaki as he stood on the bowsprit to direct *Elysium* around the coral heads and reefs. When we anchored, the young men took another anchor in the dingy and hand set it around a coral head so we would be secure, as we had reefs all around us. That evening they all sat inside and sang and played the guitar before diving over

Elmer with lobster

into the sea to spend the night swimming through the water to fish. I asked them how they avoided the sharks that often visited these outer reefs? "If a shark kills one of us, that person has done something very bad," they replied somberly.

Evidently we had good men with us, because the next morning all the men returned safely with the dingy full of big lobster, a large sea turtle, and many colored fish. This was a good haul for them and would provide food for a very large feast and bring in much needed cash for the family. The largest lobster was a gift for us. Although we declined it, they insisted that we take it. We arrived safely back at our anchorage, exhilarated by the experience and the success of our trip.

Mike and Cornelia came out the next day to tell us that a young couple, Mel and Beth Boynton, had been left to camp on the beach when a yacht they were crewing on left without them. We invited them to come stay onboard with us as we had lots of room. They were an interesting young couple and we enjoyed having them aboard for the next month. We planned to fly to Portland and our Tongan family said they would watch the boat for us after Mel and Beth found a passage to New Zealand.

We flew from Tonga to Portland to visit our family and celebrate Christmas together in December 1981. We were able to visit with friends and see our respective parents. Donna and Connell flew down from Canada to visit us and meet our family. Howard Radke was planning to get married and wanted to spend his honeymoon on *Elysium* with us. That sounded like a great idea, so we completed making our plans for February, when it is so cold in Portland. We stayed over a month and enjoyed the respite very much.

When we arrived back in Tonga, we found that the boat was in perfect condition. Our family had scrubbed the deck and even scraped the bottom of the boat. Pangaimotu is four miles away from where we left *Elysium* anchored in Neiafu, but they had made that journey everyday to check on the boat and someone had often slept onboard. All was well on *Elysium* and we were happy to be back home.

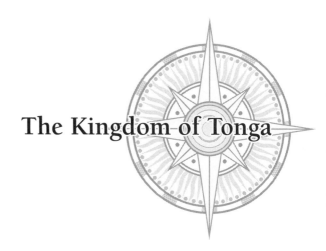

The Kingdom of Tonga

And could you keep your heart in wonder at the daily miracles of your life, your pain would not seem less wondrous than your joy.

– Kahlil Gibran

WE HAD BEEN in Tonga since September 1981, planning to stay seven months until the season to travel south to New Zealand arrived. On March 2, 1982, Hurricane Isaac altered our lives. Rousing ourselves from the near stupor from laying on the cement floor in Robin's house, we walked out into the now blustery wind and sunshine that comes with the aftermath of a hurricane. As we made our way down, we noticed that the Tongan couple had weathered the storm quite well and their house was still intact. They recognized immediately and the lady went to the cupboard and got my precious yellow bag for me. We were so grateful that they had saved our most valuable possessions for us: our passports, money, and address book. We told them that we had lost the thongs that they lent us and that we would come by later with new ones to replace them.

Walking on the road back toward *Elysium*, we came to the area where the rope we had used to pull the woman up the bank the night before was still attached to the tree. We were informed that the injured woman we had pulled up the bank during the storm had been evacuated to American Samoa. They had put her on a screen door on top of a Jeep to get her to the airport where she could be placed onboard South Pacific Airlines. She was treated for a broken pelvis and an injured hip. Later there was a very dramatic story of her ordeal in the National Enquirer.

We grabbed hold of the rope to belay down through the now up-rooted brush to see what was left of *Elysium*. We expected to see everything completely destroyed as Fuavai had described to us earlier in the morning. "I was down to look at the boat and it is very badly hurt everywhere," he told us.

Climbing down the slanted ladder into the main cabin we found that the interior was only damaged in a few places. In fact, the woodwork was completely unharmed. All of those layers of varnish and wax had protected it from the water. The items on the port side were soaked with seawater but everything was in its place and where we had left it.

The outside of *Elysium* looked terrible. On the starboard side of the hull, where the charter boat had slammed against us during the night, twenty-five square feet of the surface had been crushed. On the port side, where she was lying on the coral, there was a hole four-feet in diameter. In the stern of the boat there was another large hole caused by the rudder smashing on the coral head when we were still in eight feet of water. The rudder had pulled off and was nowhere to be seen. This hole in the stern let in the major force of the water so my books were soaked. I pulled some of them off the shelves and tried to separate the pages. The books that had glossy pages were impossible to open, but some of the others were not as bad, so I put them up on deck in the sunshine and carefully made my way back to the mid-section.

The bed was still dry and in good shape, but every hold on the port side was filled with seawater. We both felt that getting *Elysium* up on her keel would be the most helpful thing to do in order to further evaluate the damage. As we emerged, our Tongan family, who had taken such good care of us in the past, was wading in the water toward the boat, looking at the crushed starboard side. Our great friend, Matoto, had large tears in his eyes as he looked at our *Elysium*. All of his family members asked, "How could we work on it?" Elmer came up with a plan: if

Elysium propped up on coconut logs

they could find some palm logs, we could use them for braces to hold *Elysium* upright after we raised her onto the keel. Even though everyone had lost so much in their village, they set to work that night cutting down palm trees and floating them over to where we were. There was no power equipment on the island that would help us raise *Elysium*, so Elmer came up with the idea of using floor jacks.

The next day, with jacks from the public works, our winches, and a great deal of strength, we were able to raise *Elysium* about fifteen degrees and let the water gush out of the holes. By 2:39 p.m., on Saturday, our family, all-working together with great fortitude, had *Elysium* level and securely propped up on her keel with the coconut logs keeping her from falling over. Many people became deeply involved and everyone shared in the feelings of success. Kelepi's wife, Halatu'u, who had just had her seventh child a few days before, worked along with everyone else. An Australian teacher, other yacht skippers, and the wives of our Tongan family all worked together and fixed a huge meal in celebration of the success. Someone brought a propane stove along with green bananas and mutton flaps for a feast that everyone enjoyed.

For the next few days Elmer worked with our family to raise other yachts in the same manner we had used to raise *Elysium*. What started as a family helping us became a profitable endeavor for them, as they worked on seven other yachts. Happily, they earned some money for their needs at a difficult time. But, try as we would, they would never take a penny from us for all their work on *Elysium*.

Hurricane Isaac had blown seventeen yachts onto the coral and sunk all of the Tongan fishing boats in the harbor. We were interested to know how the skippers of the damaged yachts were reacting. The ones that had built their own yachts were quick to start repairs. Will and Judy, from *Adagio*, had survived the night afloat. The bumping that Will had thought was smashing against the hull turned out to be their dingy, which had sunk and was still attached, hitting the underside of the hull. *Red Hawk*, with Phil aboard, was pulled off the far sandy shore with no damage to the boat. Two other skippers drank so much alcohol that they were unable to cope with the conditions of their boats. Instead of working to repair them, they allowed them to deteriorate. It was helpful for us not to go to a hotel. Because we stayed onboard *Elysium*, we were able to begin work early in the morning and continue working during the day. The others had difficulty leaving a clean hotel room and facing

Yachts after hurricane

the chaos, mess, and stench of seawater on their boats. Several of them abandoned their boats and left Tonga, never to return.

Elysium was the most severely damaged yacht because of the holes inflicted on to her by the charter yacht. A Lloyd's of London insurance adjuster came to look at the boats for evaluation. He said that the boat that damaged *Elysium* was insured, and they were responsible for our damage. He told us to make an estimate and gave us the papers to fill out for the appraisal of the damage. When we submitted our estimate of fifteen thousand dollars, their reply was that the damage was an Act of God and we would not be covered. The Mormon insurance company that they were covered by was well aware of the fact that we would have had to go to Salt Lake City, hire a Utah lawyer and sue in order to receive compensation. The insurance company knew that the entire ordeal would cost us more than it was worth. With that information, we gave up the idea of pursuing any further action.

We could not have survived as comfortably as we did without the great support and friendship of our Tongan family. They were instrumental in motivating us to get started on the repairs. As *Elysium* was set on her keel, most of the water inside rushed out through the holes and we pumped out the rest. We pulled out everything washable, cleaned it and set it out to dry in the hot sunshine that followed the storm. We were sitting upright on a coral beach underneath the cliff so very little breeze drifted down to us. After a few days, we received a blessed heavy rain that helped us wash off the rest of the salt and allowed us catch plenty of fresh water.

Back in Portland, the news of Hurricane Isaac had reached all of our family and friends. Howard Radke and Beth had been married and planned to have their honeymoon on our boat, sailing and diving in the beautiful waters of Tonga. He was in a bus on his way to work when he spotted a headline on the paper held by the man in front of him. It stated that a terrible hurricane had wrecked many American yachts in Neiafu, Tonga. He said he grabbed the paper from the man in complete shock. He then called George and they tried to reach us by radio. He did not rest until he was able to contact a yacht and find out that we were not hurt, but that the boat was badly damaged. Ham radio operators are excellent at finding people in a disaster and relaying messages.

Our friend in Hawaii, Dick Latham, read the newspaper about the hurricane. He had a ham radio license that he had not used for several years. When he received the news of our loss, he purchased a ham radio and set up an antenna at his home in order to make radio contact with us. It was gratifying to hear from him by relay from another operator and be able to bring them up to date. They both wanted to know what they could send us to help our situation in Tonga. We both decided right away that the native people needed seeds to replant their gardens for food, as everything had been swept away by the force of the hurricane. Dick said he would go to the University of Hawaii and get seeds that would help provide the necessary vegetables to the Tongans as soon as possible. Howard and Beth planned a stop in Hawaii and they agreed to deliver the seeds to us. The seeds that he sent were ones suited to the tropical area and when planted promised a good food source for everyone. The Tongan recipients planted them immediately. The rich soil and abundant sunshine and moisture produced the bright green leaves of Butterhead lettuce within weeks. The lettuce plants lined the walkway up to Matoto and Ele's house and they brought the miracle of fresh green food to the feasts.

None of the electronics on the boat worked because salt spray had ruined everything. My treasured ham radio would not even turn on! We went to shore to call Howard to tell him to make other plans for their honeymoon because the boat was in such a dreadful state. He told us that both of them intended to come anyway. I warned them that our area was full of mosquitoes, rats, and cockroaches, but they persevered and offered to bring anything we needed to have replaced on the boat. We needed epoxy, a ham radio and electronics. Elmer's son, Steve, made new bearings for the rudder and they brought them to us.

I spent my days going through the drawers and storage places in *Elysium*. Methodically I took everything out and evaluated whether it was worth the job of refurbishing. Every day I washed monumental amounts of laundry, the boat was constantly covered with drying clothes and linens. All of our cushions were damp, so they had to be washed several times and dried. I made a pile of paper trash on the small coral beach to burn. When we had left home, friends of ours had given us Playboy Magazines for trading. But some were so descriptive I was embarrassed to use them for trade. The water had glued the pages together into one big lump so I put them at the bottom of the burning pile. Next I pulled out our supply of toilet paper that we had purchased in huge economy packages. Elmer had to hold my feet as I dove down into the bottom of the storage unit and pulled out the very heavy, water soaked packages. The toilet paper packages were set on top of the magazines. Books and papers were next. I only saved the books that the pages had not stuck together. The next morning everything in my burn pile was gone! The things thrown on shore were thought to be garbage that we didn't want so the Tongan people took them. We saw toilet paper set out to dry on bushes all around the town. I disliked the fact that those magazines were in someone's hands, but hoped that they were so wet they were unreadable!

One day as I was working in the interior, the entire boat began to violently shake. I started to climb up the ladder to get off the boat. Elmer shouted to me to stay down below. It was an earthquake and the boat could fall on me. The violent motion lasted four minutes, but *Elysium* stood strong on the palm logs throughout the whole terrifying experience. This was to be the very worst of the seven earthquakes we experienced while the boat was confined on the shore.

When we shopped at Morris Hedstrom's store in Neiafu, we met a lovely young girl named Primrose Broomfield working there. One day she introduced us to her mother Nan. Nan's husband was of Tongan and British descent, so they both spoke very good English. Nan had traveled more than most of the Tongan people and was very interested in our trip. We had spent many days having dinners together, enjoying long chats and becoming close friends. After the hurricane, Nan came to visit us to see how we were dealing with the challenges on the boat. "Are you having any problems with customs?" she asked. We had managed to locate a new sail that was to be delivered to us before we left Samoa, which should require no duty. The sail had not arrived before we left so we had it sent on to Tonga. We found out by radio that it was to arrive in Neiafu soon. We told Nan that this would give us some problem because the customs would charge us one hundred percent duty.

"Vai, the customs agent, is my nephew. I will talk to him," she promised. True to her word, when we went in to pick up the brilliant orange, yellow, and red headsail drifter, Vai wrote on the slip: "Sail sent home for cleaning, no charge." This was a great relief for us because the sail was expensive. The king had visited Neiafu after the cyclone and had promised that no duty was to be charged to the yachts for repair. He had not written that down for the customs officials, so it was left to Vai's discretion. Several other skippers came to us to ask us to speak to Vai about their incoming packages, but because they had not made any contact with the Tongan people, we could not help.

Elmer searched for materials to make *Elysium* like new again. He found New Zealand cement in the public works building. John Moa took him riding on horseback to visit a lady who had a chicken wire fence that could be used to repair the holes in the hull. Elmer paid the lady twenty dollars for the twenty foot length section of fence, and she was very pleased with the exchange. The next problem we had to solve was to find good sand to make the concrete mix. All the sand on the island was coral sand and was too soft for this application. I was able to contact George by ham radio and was telling him about our problem when an unknown voice broke into our conversation. Using no ham radio protocol, the voice said, "I can bring you sand." This was the voice of David, a pilot who flew for South Pacific Airlines. He then looked around and found a bag of #5 blasting sand in the hanger. He carried fifty pounds of this good sharp sand in the cockpit of the plane when he and his copilot, Kevin, made their next trip to Tonga.

The very things that we loved about Tonga, the remoteness and lack of commercial endeavors, were now detrimental as we faced the problems of repair. The great mental boost of the love and concern that were shown us by our Tongan family far surmounted the problems. As we started repair each day, they all arrived ready to work with us. The first job was to break out all of the concrete pieces in the damaged areas so we could have a clean space to bond to again. It took several days to repair the hole and make it ready for the concrete. The biggest problem was to get the rudder in place again. Matoto had spotted it out in the bay when the tide was out. It was not badly damaged, the one chunk out of the bottom was easily repaired.

We met the plane on which Howard and Beth arrived a few weeks after the hurricane. The boat was relatively clean, but the work on the hull was ongoing. We brought the settee cushions up on deck for them to sleep on because of the lack of fresh air below and the hot humid nights. They adapted well to the surroundings and after delivering the items we needed to complete the repair, our friends, Kelepi and Halatu'u, showed them around the island.

The rudder had to be welded in place again along with the new bearings that Howard brought for us. Installing the rudder was the biggest problem we faced because we did not know how to accomplish it without a welder. No arc welder was available and we had no electricity either. What would we do? We scouted around until we found acetylene and oxygen tanks at the road department. Two strong Tongan men brought the two tanks a long distance down to where we were on the reef. With these available, Elmer was able to weld everything into place. Now *Elysium* had a rudder again.

Tanganoa, Oniki, and Tomasi all helped Elmer plaster the concrete onto the new frame. Matoto mixed all of the concrete in a little wooden box and we filled our plastic wastebasket with the mix so it could be applied. The first hole that needed to be filled was the low one on the starboard side. Elmer sat in water up to his waist to fill this hole. He completed it just in time, as the next day the tide was much higher and the water would have filled the boat if that hole had not been repaired. We were aware that we needed to complete the work on the hull in time for the very high spring tide that would come in two and a half months. That was to be the highest tide for several months and would be our best chance to get off the coral.

Bill, on *Zephyr*, was in American Samoa and now was in contact by ham radio. He made arrangements to come down on the scavenger boat, *Debut Dick*, that was coming to Tonga to see if there was a chance to make money from the wrecked boats. The skipper had a pet ring-tailed cat onboard. Bill said this animal made the trip nearly unbearable for him. The wild ring-tailed cat would hide on the air ducks and jump

Tanganoa helping Elmer plaster the big hole

on his back and scratch him when he walked down the corridor to go to bed. He really disliked the animal intensely and evidently the feeling was reciprocated.

Bill brought us bottom paint, American food products, and items our Tongan family needed. Bill was a man of color and the Tongan family adopted him immediately, so he was also a member of the family. Bill stayed and helped with the entire repair. His wife, Marcie, had left for the states because she was terrified by a storm on their trip to Samoa. She was a dear friend and we were saddened by the news that she felt she could not face sailing anymore. Bill was now a single-hander looking for a crew.

Every night when we went to bed we would hear the loud murmurings of a local cat that would wait until the boat was quiet before boarding *Elysium* to steal our baked goods. I would bake bread or a cake and by morning most of it would be gone if the cat had found it accessible. One night I heard it in the galley and ran in to pounce on it. The cat ran up on deck and leapt the twelve feet to the ground. After that, it would hiss and growl at us from shore in the evenings. One night while I was lying naked and sweating on our bunk in the bow, a big three inch cockroach flew up into the hatch and landed on my chest. I woke up quickly, grabbed it, and flung it overboard. We tried to sleep on the coral one night because of the stifling heat in the boat. Just as we fell asleep, a hermit crab decided I could possibly be something to eat and soundly pinched my arm. When we turned on the flashlight we saw that the entire area was swarming with crabs, all scavenging for a morsel to eat. I did plant a small garden alongside the boat on the bank. We had some lettuce seed and I knew that the warm nights and the rich soil would quickly grow the lettuce that I had been craving. The seed did come up quickly and just as the leaves were getting large enough to pluck, some local pigs came rooting along and ate it all. The animal life was not friendly to us while we were stuck on shore!

Every day, all of the men from our Tongan family and Elmer worked on the big patch on the starboard side of the boat, immersed in water above their knees. One afternoon John Tavaki laid down his trowel and swiftly darted out further in the water. He quickly grabbed something in the water and brought it over to us. It was a stonefish, the most deadly of all sea creatures. The fish is almost indistinguishable from its environment in the water. Because it is the same grey color of its surroundings and has many loose and moving pieces attached to its skin, it looks invisible. We were awed by the fact that John could see it from where we were. If any one of us had stepped on it, we would have died in great pain from the poison emanating from the fins on top of this fish. John calmly took a knife, cut off the fins, and held it up for us to get a picture. The Tongan people have great knowledge of the sea, a quality inherited from many previous generations.

After two and a half months the plastering on the hull was completed. The rudder was in place and *Elysium* looked like a sailboat again. We used the bright red bottom paint that Bill had brought to complete the finish of the hull. We then began planning the work of getting her off the coral and back into her home in the water. A tourist had come by and asked us how we got our boat up that far on the reef to paint! When we told him that a hurricane had pushed us up and wrecked us there, he told us he didn't know they had storms like that in Tonga.

An Ex-Pat or, ex-patriot, who lived in Tonga, had a large pressure pump that Elmer used to sluice out as much of the sand and coral under the keel as he could. The family came to the rescue again with two logs, which they floated to us and that could be peeled to make a slick surface to slide the boat off the coral. We found out later that these trees had been growing in Pangaimotu for many years and were intended to be used as a new cookhouse for Matoto's wife, Ele. The logs were pushed under the keel into the holes made by the pressure pump. Next, we waited for the high tide to complete our plan.

The day arrived to make our move. Elmer had four anchors set out in the bay: one attached to the top of the main mast, one to be attached to each of the sheets and one to the anchor windless. He also had it set up so we had a four-fall block setup on each one. If a person pulled it by hand, they had a four-to-one purchase. However, when attached to the anchor windless and the sheet winches, it would give an eighty-to-one purchase. With three people cranking the winches and windless, we had two hundred and forty-to-three purchase. While the people worked the winches and windless industriously, *Elysium* slid very slowly down the peeled logs. We had a rope from the top of the mast tied to a tree on shore so we could slowly lay her over. Once she was tipped over, the men on the winches began their work. The purpose of having the line running to the top of the mast from the anchor and back to the winch was so that we could pull down on the mast to give the boat more buoyancy. However, we were able to move her without using that procedure, moving slowly into the deep water, sliding easily down the slick logs. The hull wasn't even scratched and we were floating without a problem. We were able to accomplish the entire launching using the equipment we had onboard: rope, pulleys and blocks.

It was an exciting morning for everyone. All of the family was there to watch the procedure. Someone had told Matoto that Elmer didn't know what he was doing and that his plan would never work. When *Elysium* started sliding down the logs, the whole family yelled with joy and jumped in the water in their suits and dresses to put a hand on her hull and give a push. The launching crew included Bill, the two pilots

Our Tongan family
back row: Fuavai, John Tavaki, Beth, Ele, Elmer, Matoto
front row: John Moa, Helen, Tanganoa, Fineola

from South Pacific Airlines, Kevin and David, John Moa, and Pierro from the yacht *O'Gigonia*. Elmer was directing and I was on the stern to help anyway I could. First they tipped *Elysium* over so far that I was nearly lying down on deck. Then it was not long before she moved and was floating freely in the water.

When we were out in the bay again, the family gathered on deck with our friends to play the guitar and sing to us. John Tavaki cried when he sang because he said in his song that now we would be leaving and we would never be back again. It was sweet sorrow for all of us. We were glad the hard work was finally over and felt sadness to be leaving the family that had endeared themselves so greatly to us.

We spent the next days making certain that the engine worked well and that everything was in its proper place. We took several people out sailing and to make sure there were no problems. There were a few bugs in the hydraulics that we had to take care of. I went into the head after one trip and that found all of my towels had turned bright red. They were soaked with hydraulic fluid from a leak in the line. The towels were very difficult to clean again, but it was good that we discovered this before setting sail for American Samoa.

When we were in contact again with George in Portland, he told us that our family and friends wanted to do something to help the Tongan people. Several friends sent money and I made arrangements with the elders of the church to start a fund to help needy parishioners. Matoto and Ele were very grateful as the Free Methodist church was the main gathering place in Pangaimotu and they assured me the money would be carefully spent.

Our daughter Donna, her husband Randy, and their two children, Chris and Wendy, came to visit before we left. They wanted to see Tonga and sail with us to Samoa where they could get a flight back to the States. The week before we left was filled with celebration. Matoto and Ele and the family had a huge farewell feast on Ano Beach. It was a gala affair with speeches by all of us. We also enjoyed singing with a kava party. Kava is a root that is grown in the islands; it is a very mild narcotic and is used by the people for a communal drink. The root is pounded into a powder and a young available girl places this powder into a carved wooden bowl of water, squeezing Kava from the bag she pounds it in. Then all of the men drink from a coconut shell cup passed around to everyone. After drinking, the men sing beautiful native songs. Each person who gave a speech cried, even Elmer. It was a very emotional time for all of us.

We planned to sail out the next morning. We invited the family to come to the boat for breakfast. The one stipulation we made was that the family was to bring no presents. We had several reasons for this request; there was no more room on the boat and we did not want to take gifts that they could sell at feasts to augment their incomes. As they arrived on the beach, we saw each person's head abounding with baskets of all sizes. When each of them arrived on *Elysium*, carried by *Limbo*, they presented us with these baskets filled with gifts of various kinds. The pride and joy of the presentation made it impossible for us to turn down such kind presents. We accepted them and returned the great love we felt for each of them.

Hulu, who was the head of the family, had told me that he wanted me

Elmer rebuilding bowsprit

to teach Lise, his wife, to make the pancakes we had often shared when they were aboard. He said that he thought that those pancakes were the things that made us so very strong. I made them with flour I ground and lots of eggs and milk. I also had canned butter and fruit jam from New Zealand aboard, which they applied liberally to each cake I turned out. The griddle was filled with pancakes cooking for over an hour as they all ate their fill. After breakfast, it was time for them to go ashore and for us to prepare to leave. The entire deck was filled with people, each one waiting for me to decide who was to go ashore in the dingy first. It was hard for me to have them leave and even more difficult to choose who had to disembark first. I am sure I kept the dearest of them for last, but finally it was time for John Moa, John Tavaki and Matoto to go. We all sobbed together and hugged. When the last of them were on shore, we loaded the dingy and began to pull anchor. Our family waved white cloths to us while we slowly sailed out to sea. We watched them for a long time, standing on Ano Beach, until they finally disappeared from our sight. We had been in Tonga eleven months, and seven months had passed since Hurricane Isaac.

Our sail to Samoa was an easy one as we had good winds and a crew to take some the watches. The only problem happened one night while I was asleep below. Elmer and his family were all on deck enjoying the evening sail. Suddenly I awoke with a start and went up above to ask, "What has happened?" No one had seen or heard anything, so I went back below. Listening carefully, I knew immediately what was wrong. I could not hear the sound of the propeller turning. It always turned freely while we were sailing. When morning light broke over the horizon, we found that the end of a sheet, which is rope from the sail, had slipped overboard and was now tightly wound around the propeller. Elmer had to go overboard and untangle as we sailed over the Mariana Trench, the deepest place in the ocean. He tied himself securely to dive down and he reported feeling very uneasy being in such a deep spot in the ocean.

Having arrived in Samoa after a two-day sail, we spent a week going to the airport every day early in the morning, trying to find a military flight for Randy, Donna and the children to fly back to the States. Each day the flights were full and the problem was that Randy had to be back on duty at a specific time. Finally, they had to give up the free flight and buy a ticket to Hawaii, where it was easier for servicemen to catch a military flight.

Elmer was able to find some very durable hardwood, similar to black walnut, for a very good price in American Samoa. He decided he would add a new deck for the bowsprit to replace the metal one that was now badly rusted. The paint had suffered several deep cracks in the hurricane and was impossible to repair. All American goods were available at this protectorate so we could get good varnish and we had 120-volt electricity to use our power tools. It took several weeks to finish the job, but the new bowsprit was a beautiful addition to *Elysium*, allowing us a larger walkway up to the end of the bow to lower the Genoa sail.

The anchorage was untenable and we often had to stay aboard to make sure that everything stayed in place with the strong wind and waves that invaded the bay. The shower on the dock was welcome as the humidity was nearly one hundred percent and the heat was always in the nineties. One day, as we returned to *Elysium* from taking a shower, we felt the anchor give way. The boat anchored close behind us belonged to Hal Holbrook and was lavishly finished. Luck was with us because we had just run the engine to charge the batteries before going to the dock to take a shower. The motor responded quickly when Elmer turned the key and we just missed damaging Holbrook's boat.

As soon as the bowsprit was completed, we applied for our visas for Fiji and New Zealand. *Elysium* was now equipped with a satellite navigation system that Howard and Beth had brought to us. We expected this system would be strategic in helping us to avoid the legendary reefs of Fiji and to allow us to get an exact position on the cloudy days when we could not get a sextant shot. We sailed out of Samoa confident that we could safely and securely enter Fiji.

The sail to Fiji was short and easy, but by the time we had gotten to the reef area, I had become what I called silicon junky. If we didn't get readout at least every few hours, I was anxious. Gone were the days when we were satisfied with daily shots to verify our DR. I now needed to know every few hours and watched the new electronic device constantly. Sometimes it was several hours before the Sat-Nav finally presented us with our exact location in the ocean. We decided to sail down to the island of Ovalau, through the reef-filled Koro Sea, relying entirely on the new Sat–Nav. We had no problems at all, but the fixes were not as forthcoming as I would have liked, especially at night, so we sailed slowly through the islands with just a headsail. In the morning we found the island of Ovalau and tied up to the fishing dock, glad to have arrived safely inside the reefs that surround the treacherous island chain.

Republic of Fiji and New Zealand

Security is mostly a superstition. It does not exist in nature. Life is either
a daring adventure or nothing.

– Helen Keller

WE FELT GREAT joy to be on the move again, to be able to explore the
Fiji Islands and to experience the mysteries of their existence. There are
so many reefs surrounding Fiji that European invaders did not overtake
the government as early as the other Pacific Islands. Our first anchorage
was at the island of Ovalau, where we raised our quarantine flag and
waited for the customs officer to come and check us in. Soon the official boat arrived carrying a sharp looking Indo-Fijian man who came
aboard. He was wearing the traditional British white shorts and knee
socks. His name was Mr. Sing and after stamping our passport books
and touring *Elysium* he cordially invited us to have dinner at his house
the next day. After checking us in he informed us that when we left our
last stop in Suva, we could not leave the boat again in Fiji. We accepted
his dinner invitation and bid him goodbye.

As he motored away we changed into our snorkeling gear and dove
overboard into the warm, clear, turquoise water. The tropical water and
our waning bottom paint had cultured huge barnacles that clung fiercely

to the entire bottom of the hull. We spent several hours snorkeling from bow to stern with the scraper, loosening a batch with each swipe. The local fish rushed over to feast on the crustaceans as they lazily drifted down towards the bottom of the sea. We always attracted many different varieties of fish as we stripped the bottom of the crustacean feeders. Some waited just outside the reach of our hands, boldly grabbing the succulent bits before another had a chance.

We were anchored outside of the small city of Levuka, where the first capitol of the island was based during the colonial times, when shipping was the main resource of Fiji. We were close to the dock where the huge tuna fish industry was located. This enterprise was started as a partnership with Japan's FAFCO fishing company. The dock was easily accessible for us to tie our dingy to and we were able to tour the facility and buy several cases of tuna fish. One variety was only nineteen cents a can, so we bought two big twenty-four can cases. We also bought two cases of the premium white tuna, which we bought for forty-five cents a can. Now, if we did not catch fish, we were still well-stocked for the future. The nineteen-cent variety contained some skin and was much preferred by the native people because of the higher fat content.

In the morning we followed Mr. Sing's directions to an expertly decorated little concrete home. Mrs. Sing had prepared a delicious lamb curry with a side dish of cabbage fried in garlic, which we gratefully scooped up inside the fresh, flour flat bread, *chapatis*, she had just fried. During dinner we noted that the family was living a life identical to the life they would lead if they actually lived in India. Mrs. Sing wore the traditional Indian Sari and, in their home, they both spoke English and Hindi. The television set had a movie playing the latest very violent Indian film. The entire house was decorated with wall hangings and brass depictions of the aspects of the Indian God, Rama. Mr. Sing told us that the British had brought the people from India to work in Fiji because they could not persuade the Fijian people to do the hard work on the sugar plantations. Now the Indo-Fijian population had grown to nearly equal that of the Fijian on this island. The original laws did not allow them to own any land, but they could lease the land for whatever they wanted to do, operate a store or farm a sugar plantation. We remarked that this was a situation that caused division between the people. They both agreed nodding their heads vigorously. We left a gift of a small lemon cake I had baked for them and we thanked them very much for their hospitality. We invited Mrs. Sing to come and visit us on *Elysium*.

The next day we visited the local Morris Hedstrom grocery store. There were no tourists on the island and very few of the population were in evidence on the streets. Every building was pristinely clean and freshly painted, and there was no litter on the walkways. The climate was always more pleasant with much lower humidity than we had experienced in Samoa. We came in contact with a man who spoke English and asked him where the points of interest were. He told us that Lovoni Valley would be an interesting place to visit. This valley was located inside the great caldera of the volcano that had originally formed Ovalau. He told us that the people who inhabited it were remarkable artisans and very colorful people. We walked over to where a trail started right at the shore and disappeared into the very dense tropical rainforest. We climbed up the trail and were immediately engulfed in the heavy foliage, where only moving spots of sunlight dappled through the large, deep-green leaves.

After climbing on the path for nearly an hour, we came across a crystal clear stream lazily moving down the hill. The weather was extremely warm and humid so we plunged into the fresh, clean, fragrant water pooled, for a swim. Just as we were emerging, a kava plantation owner came by, walking down the hill. We had learned the native greeting "Bula, Bula," to which he replied, smiling widely, showing his fine looking white teeth. We asked him if we were on the right road to Lovoni Village. He told us "Not too far," and pointed up the hill. All of the people we met in Fiji had some knowledge of the English language, which made communication much easier for us. After meeting this sociable fellow we asked each of the following people we encountered along the way the same question. Each time they assured us that we were coming to the village soon. They all were very friendly and eager to help. The men have the most amazing hair, very wiry and kinky, neatly carved into a cap-like-cut, which tops the cocoa-cream colored skin of the stunning Melanesian people.

We finally arrived at the top of the caldera and looked down on the bustling village below. There were many thatch-roofed *bure* huts that are the traditional Fijian's living spaces woven from palm fronds. There were many Melanesian people sitting on the grass weaving brilliantly colored mats and handicrafts. As we walked down into the village we were greeted with looks of surprise that eventually changed to smiles as we admired their work. By the interaction that we had with them, we discerned this was not a place many tourists visited. There was a winding stream snaking its way through the center of the village and we could see that it was well-planned for the activities of the people who lived there. Near the center stood a school where there were noisy children leaving for the day. The children spoke English and they interpreted for the adults who seemed shy about using the unfamiliar English language. As we sat and watched them weaving, they became more willing to communicate with us. We told them we had crossed a great sea to come and visit their land. It was a very difficult concept for them to imagine, thousands of miles of sea, as they had only experienced their village and its small surroundings. The fact that we had traveled the sea that made up the distance of many islands was amazing to the elders who had more of a grasp of distance. As we left, we were impressed by the fact that these people were completely unlike any we had met before in any of the islands. Their culture was still very unchanged and our communication with them offered us a unique experience.

Back in Levuka, we found a museum run by a local man who had been a teacher. We asked about Lovoni Village, where we had just visited. He told us that the people were a fiercely independent tribe and were descendents of the final inhabitants of Fiji to be subjugated to the Queen of England. He said that these people were the last of the cannibals of Fiji and had been reformed many years before. He was surprised that we had gone up there and were greeted by the inhabitants at all. "No tourists ever go up there" he told us. This was the reason for the unusual demeanor and we were doubly grateful that we had had this close encounter with them.

The next week we spent each day visiting the local waterfall and swimming hole at Tatoga creek. The water had the fresh smell of the green moss that lined the creek before it tumbled into a clear pool. There were long vines that the young boys grabbed to swing far out and drop into the deep water. The surrounding area was lush and green with tropical growth that made an idyllic spot to spend our afternoon hours. This became our daily stop to refresh ourselves and enjoy the contagious laughter of the children. The young people were not shy and took obvious pleasure in the interchange with us. Their lovely cocoa brown skin glistened in the sunlight and when they dove into the water their hair did not get wet, the water just formed small beads and rolled off.

While we were anchored we often had a visit from a young Fijian man, Napele, who claimed to be the heir of the original ruler of Fiji before the British made it a protectorate. He told us that the Fijian people were happily living a peaceful life of ease. They built their homes from the local palm trees, and found food easily from the rich land and the bounty of the sea. They enjoyed a very relaxing social life with kava parties and community gatherings. The culture of these people did not blend with the demands of the British colonizers. The people from India were very hard-working people and astute to the ways of the empire. They were judicious businessmen and labored very hard on the sugar plantations. The Indo-Fijians had never integrated with the dark Melanesian people, but kept their own language and customs. This made the division very pronounced and there was little communication between the divergent cultures.

One day when Napele was visiting, I mentioned the problem that was so apparent to us. He said to us, "Oh, yes, indeed, all of the people of Indian descent must go back to India. That is certain." We pointed out to him that these people were born in Fiji and had never known any other land. "It makes no difference, they are Indian and they must go," he stated emphatically. This conversation reflected the problems that we saw throughout Fiji between the two groups and gave us insight into the problems that were to occur in years to come.

There was still more cleaning to do on the hull of *Elysium*, so Elmer started to work while I puttered around putting more things away. I climbed down onto the wind vane rudder to put on my fins and help him. Unexpectedly, I saw a deadly sea snake very close to Elmer's head.

The bite of this variety of sea snake is instant death, but they seldom come near activity, as they are ordinarily quite shy. They have very small mouths so they can only bite into something like an ear or finger and are usually only aggressive during mating season, posing no threat to people. It was moving toward Elmer so I started yelling and slapping my fin on the water. The snake lifted its head in an arc out of the water and swam right toward me. Once I knew Elmer was safe, I slapped my fin at it and pushed forward toward it. It decided that this was too much activity for its liking and finally swam away. After that, I never entered the water without first checking the surroundings for a snake. The only other time I saw one was several days later; it was several feet long and swimming tail down in the water. I kept an eye on him and he finally slithered away, showing no interest in the boat or me. That was enough sea-snake experience for me to last a lifetime.

None of our friends with sailboats had stopped in Ovalau; everyone else had entered in through the large city of Suva and were sailing in the northern reefs. We heard them talking on the VHF radio and decided it would be fun to join them. We reluctantly departed and sailed down inside the inner reef toward Suva. After we left, we encountered very heavy fog and light rain. It was nearly impossible to see even the large buoys that just drifted in and out of sight, warning of immediate danger of reefs. When we finally spotted an island shrouded in the fog, we decided to drop anchor and wait out the weather. Several people came to shore and waved so we got the dingy down and rowed ashore. The people were all from Gothenburg, Sweden, attending an architect's convention on the island. They were very interested in our journey and asked to visit the boat, so we ferried them out a few at a time. When they learned that Elmer was of Swedish decent they were delighted. We were invited to visit them if we ever made to Europe and they gave us their addresses and phone numbers. It was a very pleasant encounter for us to find this group of warm and friendly Europeans.

We sailed on and anchored outside of the Suva Yacht Club, close to many of our friends. Will and Judy from *Adagio* were in the bay, preparing to have their yacht shipped to the United States. Judy's mother had become so worried about the coming baby and the possibility of another hurricane that she had persuaded them to accept their plane tickets and the shipping of *Adagio* back to the United States. It was not that unusual for young couples to have worried parents eager to pay for the shipping of their yacht to the safety of the United States.

Big cities like Suva never held our interest for long, but we always loved visiting the fresh vegetable markets. Entering the square we were met with vibrant colors and indescribable smells of the unusual displays of food. The brilliant purple eggplant, bright yellow squash and mounds of green leafy vegetables were laid out near a lady in a purple and gold sari. There was a table holding pieces of meat, animal heads, brains, kidneys, tongues, and other mysterious animal parts. In the next section were the multicolored fresh fish, octopus, squid and sea cucumbers. Around the corner were the tall, brilliantly colored cones of fragrant spices and pastes. As a customer came to buy, pieces of newsprint were torn into shapes and weighed out for sale, but no plastic bags or containers were used. We were surrounded with the mainstay culture of the islands, the food market, where all the people came to buy food fresh from the tiny garden farms in the area. The fruit market was filled with mangos, perfectly ripe at this time of year, lined up next to papayas and bananas of all colors and shapes. It was an exhilarating experience for us because we usually only found small areas to purchase food. Our icebox was filled with ice from the fisheries, so we could keep fresh foods for quite a while. We joyfully filled our backpacks to the brim. The next days we feasted on this abundant produce as we prepared to leave Fiji.

We hiked up to the Colo Forest Park with some of our friends. It was a two-mile hike up through a lush tropical forest, resplendent with fragrant red ginger plants. The trail was set with a stone path so we were able to easily cross the river several times. The lovely park had several pools and waterfalls in which to swim.

We knew that our approaching trip to New Zealand would be very challenging for us. Their weather is influenced by the warm winds of Fiji blending with the harsh cold winds originating from the South Pole. When the warm ocean meets the cool waters moving north, it causes rapid changes in the wind and wave motion. The common wisdom used for a trip to New Zealand is, "you will be hammered one way or another or both." This axiom had been heard for years and this is why some sailors decided to miss seeing these diverse southern islands.

After staying two months in Fiji we decided to take a bus ride across the top of the island of Viti Levu to visit the other shore. The bus was completely open with just a roof covering our heads. We sped along precarious dirt roads clinging to the edge of steep canyons with no side rails to keep us from plunging over the side.

As we arrived at the top, we saw giant sugar plantations still using oxen to pull cumbersome carts loaded with the tall sugar cane stalks. The sugar industry in Fiji is subsidized by Europe, so it remains an important crop. The entire inner part of the island was one land tenure of sugar plantation after another. Land tenure but not ownership of land is awarded to the Indian population by Fijian law. When we reached the other shore, we were in Lautoka. It was getting late so we rushed to find a place to stay. We found a very comfortable room and were amazed at the price of the beautiful little hostel. At 4:00 a.m. we were awakened by the Muslim call to prayer. The loudspeaker was just outside of our window, and the call was deafening. No wonder the room was so reasonable! By the time the lengthy call was finished, we were showered and ready to leave. We took a bus out to the reef area to observe the most beautiful coral and tropical fishes we had yet seen.

Another frightening trip on the bus brought us back to Suva to prepare *Elysium* for our voyage to New Zealand. The group that was to be traveling together had decided to have a race and the rules were set. There were sixteen yachts of all descriptions, including racing hulls and larger hulls of various mediums. The time any engine was run had to be taken off the total time, otherwise the winner was to be judged on the total time taken from Suva to the Bay of Islands in New Zealand. We were to begin our trip on Saturday morning, November 18, 1982, as the weather was reported to be fair with good winds and New Zealand was entering full summer.

We set out onto a very warm, brisk wind and a heavy sea. *Elysium* sailed very well in the thirty knot wind and we sailed on a good beam reach. Even *Danish Pastry* could not keep up with us. She was a racing boat with a large crew that had just won the transpack race from Hawaii the year before. As we approached the island of Kadavu we felt we had to cut sail. Helmut, who was the skipper of *Danish Pastry*, called us on the radio to see what the problem was. We told him we were getting tired and needed a rest, we were going to cut sail and let them pass. This was incredible to the racing crew; they never let someone pass them. Bill, on *Zephyr* called to us from ahead, telling us that the seas were getting worse and the wind was now forty knots. It was getting dark so we had to make a quick decision as to what we were going to do. We looked at the chart of Kadavu and decided that the hook of land that appeared on the east side would give us some protection.

We took our sails down and gingerly headed over, watching the depth sounder closely for any indication of reefs or shallows. As we approached the island we saw the native inhabitants gathering on the shore. As we watched, they took palm leaves and stalks to start a huge blaze. This, we felt, was showing us a safe spot to anchor. We approached very carefully and were soon out of the wind and in good protection. We were going to drop the anchor where it was still very deep when we spotted two men in a big blue, yellow and red wooden boat rowing out to meet us. They told us they would lead us in to a safe spot where we could anchor.

After racing along at nearly eight knots for hours, the calm anchorage was blissful. The men asked us to come ashore to their village. We told them that we had checked out of Fiji in Suva and were not allowed to leave the boat again. We found some corned beef, tee shirts, bright cloth and toys to send with them to show our appreciation for the fire beacon that lit the way in and their guidance to anchor. We added several tins of our newly purchased tuna fish that further delighted them. We told them we would be leaving very early the next morning so we would not see them again. These were people of the sea and we felt such a strong bond with them. They knew that their safe spot would be a welcome respite for us.

We both fell asleep immediately in the bunks in the main cabin by the window. Before sunrise, I heard something outside of the boat and rose to look out as the pink dawn was just lighting the water. There was the same boat with the men quietly holding themselves away from *Elysium* with their oars. We both hurried up on deck to bid them good morning. They had brought us fish and some cooked manioc to take with us on our journey to New Zealand. We had an instant camera so we took several pictures of them as they stood in their brightly painted boat. When the pictures developed enough to see their own forms, we handed them down as a gift. They were so excited to see their faces form on the film that they literally jumped with joy. I am sure they had never seen themselves in a picture before. We added a few cans of jam and some magazines for another gift. They said if we ever got back to Fiji, we were to come to Kadavu to stay with them.

We continued on for the next twelve days, finding the wind diminishing until we were becalmed completely. I had been taking my daily shower with Dove soap and a bucket of seawater. The seventh day out I was shocked as the warm tropical seawater had vanished and instead, in its place, was what felt like ice water. We had entered another sea current completely. With the boat sailing very comfortably in the rising wind, we drew several dolphins enjoying the currents with us. The weather was crisp and as clear as we had ever seen. As night approached we felt we would have a chance to see the green light. This is the light that appears just as the sun goes down. The green is the last color in the light spectrum to be seen at sunset where there is only the sea for a horizon and very clear weather. I had my camera ready as the sun disappeared from view. I did not see the light and turned to Elmer very disappointed just as he said, "There it is!" I missed it completely. It was the most beautiful night at sea I could remember, the half moon set at midnight and a beautiful, clear starry sky remained. No moisture was in the air so the salt on the deck made crystals I could sweep away.

We always seemed to make landfall at night. This did not change as we neared New Zealand. It was nearly midnight when we took sails down, fearing we were too close. Suddenly we encountered the unfamiliar and wonderful smell of pine trees. It was so strong, we were concerned that our fix from the Sat-Nav was wrong and we were closer than our fix had suggested, so we both stayed awake for the rest of the night to watch for the dark form of the shore.

Early the next morning we encountered a very strong west wind and could see the form of the island, so we began to tack into the wind for the shelter of the Bay of Islands. The more we tacked, the stronger the wind became. Bill, on *Zephyr*, was also beating toward shore. He finally called to tell us that he would wait until the wind dropped and was going to go to sleep for a while. We continued to beat into the now ferocious wind still finding a flat sea as the wind blew across the shelter of the island. We motored and sailed for twelve hours to cover the twelve miles into the lee of the island. The skippers of the small racing sailboats were out enjoying the fierce wind demonstrating great skill handling the small boats. We had resurrected all of our warm gear from the cedar bins in the front and wore sweaters, heavy pants and gloves, but we still could not get warm. We were tacking back and forth into a thirty-five knot headwind. It was such tough steering with the wind violently throwing the bow around that it was easy to lose way. Several times I was ready to join Bill and lay to until the wind eased a bit, but Elmer stubbornly forged ahead, undaunted.

When we finally arrived in Opua, we were directed by the harbor police to a spot where we could enter the country and have our passports checked and stamped. We put up the New Zealand flag I had made before we left Fiji and met the friendly customs agents. It took hours to check in, but the customs agents, Lew and Gordon, were such fun that it was not a problem. They stamped our passports and allowed us six months to stay in New Zealand.

We sailed over to Mathauai Bay near Russell in a twenty-five knot wind and anchored. What a joy it was to see all seven boats from Portland's Sauvie Island Yacht Club anchored nearby. Our dear friends dingied over to greet us and we spent the next five hours talking and catching up. We all had so much to recount as we had taken different routes to arrive in New Zealand. It was after seven o'clock in the evening before we could think of saying goodbye.

Late the next morning they all rowed over and brought ham, eggs, black bread and tea. We ate together and they told us about their experi-

Sauvie Island Yacht Club members in New Zealand
Dave, Jan, Elmer, Helen, Mike, Mary, and Tom

ences in New Zealand. Finally, at five o'clock, we decided to go to shore and explore the town of Russell. We had spent twelve hours catching up on the last few years with our friends. The joy we felt seeing them all again and getting such a good sleep could not be duplicated. After meeting George on the radio and telling him that we had arrived safely, we headed to the local Bistro for a night out.

The next morning we went ashore to wash all of our salty clothes in the local laundry area. We found hot showers that cost thirty cents for five minutes. We had not thought about a hot shower for years, but now in the colder climate, it was a real treat. It was December 1st, so we decided we would all be together for Christmas and would draw names to make gifts for each other. Elmer and I began making kites for our gifts.

That afternoon we heard a distress call from Bill. He had drifted around the top of the North Island and was now motoring out of the Tasman Sea in very rough weather. He needed fuel so Rolph volunteered to take it out to him. He did not arrive until late that evening and was relieved to be anchored in the bay.

More friends that we had not seen for a long time continued to arrive.

I ground some wheat, made a big batch of cinnamon rolls and invited all of the new arrivals to come over for tea. We got together to decide who had won the race, figuring we had sailed two hundred fifty-seven hours and motored fifty-four hours. We came in sixth, after the big race boats, which was not too bad for a heavy cruising boat. The winner was an eighty-five foot yacht with a crew to help the skipper.

Mike Davidson had hurt his back pulling up his anchor so we went over to use the "Touch For Health" technique that we had learned for muscle balancing. It worked very well and we were able to find the muscles that were out of balance, get them back in place and give him relief from the pain. Marina was also having a problem with her back so we balanced her muscles also. During the time we sailed, we found that the "Touch For Health" book that we had brought was extremely valuable because it pinpointed the spot where the muscle was in a spasm. With acupressure, kinesiology, and moving chi energy, we were usually able to provide relief to people who were suffering.

We found a tour bus that would take us to the mile-long beach on the west side of the North Island. We planned to eventually sail around this tip on the way to Australia, so we boarded the big bus for the tour. On the bus, we met Richard Bunting who had recently emigrated from England. Richard was an avid armchair sailor who had always wanted to experience cruising on a large sailing yacht. He felt he was physically too small to handle such an experience himself, so he listened with rapt attention when we answered his queries about our journey. The more we talked, the more interested he was in every small detail. We invited him to come to *Elysium* for dinner when we returned to Opua.

When he arrived on *Elysium* he could hardly sit still, moving around the boat, examining each station with obvious glee. The next day he was back to visit again. We spoke to him about the upcoming trip to Auckland in a week and invited him to come along with us. He accepted immediately, telling us that a friend would drive his car back to Auckland for him and that he had plenty of time to make the trip.

We had one repair job to do on *Elysium*, install a new toilet. The one we had was a constant problem and very dangerous. When we had guests aboard, children were especially drawn to it and used an abundant quantity of toilet paper to make it flush. This caused plugging in the exit pipes because when the seawater was turned on to flush, it did not send the contents into the sea. At this point the seawater flooded into the boat, covering the bathroom floor, and would eventually sink the boat if we did not correct the problem in time. There were many times Elmer took the complete toilet to the bow of the boat to clean out the mess of solid waste bound in toilet paper. We heard that a marine store had a "trouble free" toilet for sale, so we headed down to Whangarei where our friend, Brian Wintle, worked in the Kempthorne boatyard, near the Carter Marine store. Brian would be able to give us reliable advice about this most imperative item.

Arriving at the highway going south, we decided to hitchhike and stuck out our thumbs to catch the attention of the passing cars. Immediately a man stopped to pick us up. "We don't see old folks hitchhiking very often around here," he said to begin the conversation. We laughed at the disparaging remark and let it pass. He and his wife owned a steel sailboat called *Star*, anchored in Taranga, and he was completely rapt to meet someone who had sailed from the United States. He took us on to Whangarei, up to the door of the marine store. We found the toilet that Brian had recommended would be four hundred and forty dollars with a sixty-six dollar tax that would be returnable when we left New Zealand. We decided that any price would be agreeable to us at this point. Brian and his wife, Yoshiko, prepared dinner for us and invited us to stay the night. They picked sweet lemons, grapefruit, oranges and tangelos from their trees in the back yard to fill both of our backpacks. The next morning, Yoshiko walked with us to the highway where we could thumb a ride. Soon after we started, Sam, a Shell Oil salesman, stopped to pick us up. Sam was on vacation and on his way north to go fishing in Kawakawa. From Kawakawa to Auckland, a Maori couple took us across the ferry to Matauwhi Bay, where we could hike back to the dingy we had left on shore. We learned so much about New Zealand from these friendly motorists, as each one of them was from a diverse part of the culture.

On Christmas Day we all gathered again for the gifts we had been making and to part ways with our friends. We had a huge Christmas dinner together and shed lots of tears with the hugs goodbye. We were all going to be sailing off in different directions from this day forward. Most of our friends were going to go north, back into the tropics, and would not cross the dreaded Tasman Sea to Australia. LeAnn and Steve were coming to visit us in Australia with our two grandchildren. We were committed to the crossing, which now sounded more and more daunting to us. We heard stories daily about lost boats and the heavy storms that could be ahead of us.

On December 31st we picked up Richard and headed down the coast to Auckland. We were able to stop each night along the way in protected anchorages full of local sailboats enjoying the holidays. The sailors who were anchored in each bay were very keen to visit us and hear about our trip across the vast ocean. A very large percentage of people are sailors in New Zealand because the sailing and sea conditions are nearly ideal. Leaving the protection of the island and sailing into the Tasman Sea was not easily accomplished for their slim, fast boats.

Each bay we entered was lined with brilliant Phutakawa trees blooming with bright red flowers, as nature celebrated the coming of Christmas. We were able to dig large quantities of steamer clams for a meal each night. Richard was so thrilled to be on the boat that he seldom sat down, maintaining a watch on the sails and standing at the bow to watch *Elysium* slice through the clear turquoise water and send out white, frothy waves. He thrilled at the sight of dolphin playing in the waves, racing ahead to slide back and surge ahead again to urge us on.

When we arrived in Auckland, we tied the boat next to the dock at Marsden Wharf. It took over an hour to get the ropes all tied back and the fenders arranged so we wouldn't go under the dock, at low tide. We did not want to come up under the ledge of the dock, which would push the boat under the water five feet! *Elysium* was just long enough to stay outside of both pilings. We dug into the bins where our warm clothes were stored. The bins were all lined with Tennessee Red Cedar so there was no mold on anything. We had not worn most them since leaving California so they needed to be out in the air to get rid of musty smell.

Mike Davidson came by on *Starlight* and asked if he could raft to us, followed by five more boats that were too small to be against the dock. The people living on the rafted yachts were all very compatible and we formed a social group. Each morning they would hop from one boat to another, finally arriving on *Elysium*. We had the room for a get-together and usually spent several hours in conversation and drinking tea before we all climbed the steep ladder onto the dock to visit the city. There were people from Sweden, Japan, Denmark and Australia, plus the two of us from Oregon.

We visited the shop on the dock that sold sheepskin. The lady selling the wonderful smelling wool was Kim U'Ren. She told us that her husband, Merv, was especially interested in sailing vessels and invited us to their home for dinner. This was to be the beginning of a lifetime friendship. Merv was very ill with severe asthma and emphysema. He had great difficulty breathing but asked if he could visit the boat the next day. We told him that it was a long ladder descent down to the deck but he shrugged that problem off immediately.

The next morning he called down to us from the wharf and we invited him to the boat. He told us that being on our boat was the most wonderful thing he could imagine. If he could just come and sit on the boat each day, he would not disturb us. He would just be around if we needed anything at all. True to his word, he was with us every day he could spare. Kim, for her part, cooked hogget roasts and found produce for us. We became part of their lives like treasured family, loved and taken care of. Their son-in-law, Warwick, was in the sheepskin business so we decided it would be nice to cover our seats in the main cabin with sheepskin. He came down to measure the space and told us it would be a few weeks before they would be ready. We asked George to have our accountant, Dean, send money to the New Zealand bank in Auckland. The money would cover the cost of the sheepskin, the toilet and give us plenty to tour the South Island. We would have enough to get us to Australia, when we would have LeAnn and her family bring us more. We usually carried enough cash to keep us for six months at a time, as we had few expenses, mostly bottom paint and repair to the autopilot. During this time we had monthly living expenses of about three hundred dollars.

Richard came to tell us that he had vacation coming up and wanted to take us camping on the South Island. "The South Island is like visiting the best places in Europe," he told us enthusiastically. "There are fjords, glaciers, hot springs and the beautiful Mt. Cook. We can visit them all" he continued. A young man named Curt, who worked on barges, and was a friend of Merv's, agreed to stay on *Elysium* while we were gone. We dug out our little pup tent and the warmest Oregon clothes we still had onboard. Soon we were off for a great adventure, camping and visiting the remarkable places along the coast of the South Island. We traveled with Richard for seventeen days and each stop was like visiting a new country. We crossed on the ferry from Wellington after visiting Tim and Wendell, whom we had met in Acapulco, Mexico. They had a beautiful big ranch house and a thousand acres of grassland on which to graze their sheep. Watching Tim's dog round up the sheep and run them into another paddock was great fun. They had many acres in peas so we picked and ate peas till we could hold no more.

We then went from one sight-seeing spot to another, never finding big crowds although it was the end of January and the warmest time of year. We walked on glaciers that came right down to the sea, trekked on well-marked trails in Milford Sound, and enjoyed calling to the seals that lined the bay. The bright green hills and deep fjord lakes from Dunedin to Queenstown had an unbelievable amount of fluffy white sheep grazing on them. We were able view Mt. Cook on a sunny day and enjoyed the fields of many-colored lupines that surrounded the mountain. We drove up the west side of the island, an area that was much less traveled, and viewed the mighty Tasman Sea, whose waves constantly gnawed at the coastline. We returned to Auckland on the tenth of February with perfect timing, as the weather was turning wet and very cold. The sunshine had stayed with us for the entire trip. We left Richard with great sadness as we had become close friends throughout the blissful and carefree trip.

The six months we were allowed to stay were coming to an end and it was time to prepare for our trip to Australia. We told Kim and Merv that we were soon going to leave for the Bay of Islands again. Merv said he would very much like to go with us and that Kim would be glad to pick him up. Curt also wanted come along, so we had a crew for our sail north. Richard lived in Auckland and was on hand whenever we needed to have a repair done. We bought the toilet and installed it, throwing the old one down into the water under Marsden wharf. We never heard the end of this from Merv, as he would write and tell us about a diver who found a toilet under the wharf. Richard, Merv and Curt helped us get all of our gear in order. We got the autopilot working, the satellite navigation, or Sat-Nav, fixed, and all of the woodwork varnished and mended. We built a big boom gallows to contain the heavy timber that held the main sail, and installed a Bimini, or cover for the helm, to protect us from the weather.

We had several meals together to say goodbye to the many friends that we had met during our stay. Among these were the Wharfie, or the official who works on the wharf, who brought us a bottle of milk each morning, and Johnny, who operated the tug, bringing in the ships and moving them out again.

The Wharfie hooked up a hose for us to fill our tanks and wash off the boat. What a joy to use all the water we needed to scrub and get rid of the grit and dirt from the exhaust of the ships and the dust from the city. Richard came by to see if we needed any more trips to town because he had a car for two more days. We went to town and picked up our money to pay Warwick for our gorgeous sheep skins and found that they had just devaluated the money nearly twenty percent on the United States dollar. We paid all our bills and had a lot more money than we expected. We took *Elysium* over to Westhaven, where they had a free slip for big boats, to put on bottom paint. There was a hose and brush available to scrub the bottom. We painted as soon as it was dry, counting on our luck to keep away the daily rain. We replaced the zincs and put a shine on our brass propeller. The job was well done, but we could not get to the very bottom before the tide rose again. Hiro and Midori from *Puka Puka* worked with us the entire day. Richard came by to see that the last things were taken care of. We said a very heart rending, last goodbye to our dear friend, knowing that we would probably never see him again.

We provisioned with plenty of ice because Kim had shopped for fruit, vegetables and lamb. The boat was literally stuffed with food in every available spot. We would have big hearty meals on the trip up the coast. Now we were waiting for the north wind to turn and we would be off. Everyone was eagerly waiting for the trip. When the wind finally turned to the west, Merv was down to the dock at 7:00 a.m. to join us. Everyone climbed aboard while I dashed around, stowing everything that was left out of place. We sailed out of Auckland with a perfect wind moving along at nearly seven knots. It was easy sailing and the crew was eager to take the wheel. This gave me time in the galley, so when we anchored in Mansion House Bay, I had roast leg of lamb, potatoes and apple pie baked. Everyone was starved and quickly finished the entire meal.

Last Sail with Lynn, Curt, Helen, and Merv

The next morning I woke up before dawn to make pancakes. We had to sail nearly fifty miles. Merv was enjoying the sail and was now looking much more healthy. He had regained much of his health just by coming down to the boat and helping Elmer with the daily chores. He was exhilarated as we sailed along making an average of eight knots. We arrived into the anchorage at about 4:00 p.m., giving us time to row ashore for a hike up the hill to look out to sea. I prepared a dinner of stuffed wiener schnitzel and pork. Our crew had prodigious appetites and finished every scrap, including the left over apple pie. The sun shone brightly for the next few days and we were able to put up our orange, red, and yellow jenniker so we could sail smoothly in the wind.

The last day we had to get to Red Head to enter Russell on the flood tide. We anchored in Matawi Bay and soon Kim and her Dutch friend were at the dingy dock. Merv and Curt rowed ashore at about 3:00 p.m. and we ate at the Bistro, enjoying their specialty of snapper. Saying goodbye to Merv, Kim and Curt was almost unbearable for us as they had been our companions for much of our stay in New Zealand. We were again filled with tears and promises to visit one day in the future. Merv looked like a different man, head held high, breathing well, with color in his cheeks. We would never forget these wonderful people as long as we lived. Back on the boat we experienced the empty feeling that always accompanied leaving people who we had come to love, but we looked forward to a new land where we would meet new people.

The very next day we started an exercise program, step-ups and hiking six miles up a hill, keeping track of our pulse and going as fast as we could. We increased our speed each day, knowing that we would need lots of stamina for facing the Tasman Sea. Several yachts were waiting for good weather to signal the time to leave. I had met John, who lived on Norfolk Island, on the ham radio. He told me that he would watch the barometer and predict when we could safely leave. He and his mother invited us to visit them on Norfolk Island, so that was our first destination, just seven hundred miles away. Groups of us were gathering, uneasily looking at the sky, watching the barometer and doing our exercises daily waiting for a break in the weather, which we hoped would last the entire nine days. That was the time we planned to take to reach Australia. Customs had given us an OK to leave when the weather was settled. Lew told us that they would not force us to leave just because our time was up.

Finally on April 16, 1983, we checked out of New Zealand. John, on Norfolk Island, gave us a route analysis from North Cape to Norfolk. It would be calm with little wind. We encountered the wind as we rounded the top of Cavalli Island and we headed out onto the tumultuous Tasman Sea.

The Tasman Sea to Australia

...the nature of man. We are born free, like nomads. But step-by-step we insist upon crawling into little prisons on little streets in mean little villages. We must destroy these prisons and restore the nomad spirit.

– James Mitchner

WE SAILED OUT of the Bay of Islands on Saturday, April 16, 1983, with Geoff and Deidre on the yacht, *Moonchild*. We spoke to John on the ham radio on Norfolk Island and told him that we planned to arrive there Tuesday, April 19. At least that was our plan. We enjoyed good weather as we powered against the strong current coming into the Bay of Islands. Then, as we rounded the light at Cavalli Island we encountered uncomfortable conditions. We experienced heavy wind, torrential rain, and fog for the next three days. We took every sail down but the Yankee and still moved forward, being forced along by forty knot winds.

By April 19th we were still several days away. The sun came out for a brief time and we were able to get a good radio signal to George at home and to John on Norfolk. John cautioned us that a front was coming our way and to be prepared. We looked out onto the sea ahead and observed a very heavy swell forming. As the sun was sinking out of sight, the storm hit hard. Elmer started up the ladder, telling me "You stay below, I can take this small staysail down by myself." I objected, as it sounded like the storm was in full force. He tied himself to the lifeline and disappeared into the darkness above. When he came back down he was bleeding badly and said that he had gotten his right index finger caught in the winch. The fingernail was severed in two and the flesh was hanging off both sides of the bone. We quickly retrieved the first aid kit and put finger splints on both sides, squeezing the damaged flesh back together. I tuned into Tony's ham radio net and asked if there was a doctor listening. Werner, a Danish doctor we knew, was sailing in New Zealand. He told us we needed to keep the finger dry, especially from salt water, and watch closely for infection. If it was not infected in three days, we would be fine. We found some plastic with which cover the bandage and kept it protected from the salt spray.

The front carried a strong wind, or "fresh," as John had predicted. We dropped all of our sails and climbed down the ladder to get some rest in our bunk while the boat rolled heavily throughout the night. In the morning we were able to put up some sails because the wind calmed to twenty knots. Tony, on the ham radio net from New Zealand, now met us every day to see how Elmer was doing. We were able to change the bandage each day and never saw any sign of infection. Just as the sun emerged again at midday, a huge flock of swallows came out of the sky and landed on the boat. *Elysium* was covered with tired birds resting on every surface that they could find. To give them energy, I made up a drink of honey and water, but many of the exhausted little birds still died. They had flown through the storm as they started their yearly migration from New Zealand to Norfolk. At sunset, the wind calmed further and they bravely took flight again for their journey to the island, where they could benefit from a well-deserved rest before resuming their flight to Australia.

The wind was now in our favor and we sailed into what John called "mostly fine" weather, sailing along at six knots on the same tack. When we saw the two red lights far ahead on the island, we dropped the sails and decided to sleep until morning. The morning dawned with a beautiful sunrise, revealing the dazzling emerald green of Norfolk Island.

There is no real harbor on Norfolk Island, only a loading jetty in Cascade Bay. As we approached the bay, a brightly painted white and red launch came out to show us exactly where to anchor. The skipper, Byron Barrel, told us, "This is a deep, sandy spot and your anchor will hold well." We were both uneasy after experiencing the quickly shifting weather, but Byron assured us he would stay nearby and watch *Elysium* while we visited onshore.

As I jumped down onto the launch, I noted that it had a long heavy rubber bumper on the bow and wondered to myself what it was used for. I was soon to find out! As we reached the jetty, immense waves were washing over the bright green seaweed on the cement landing block. Several people who had come to greet us were standing on the step above the block. Byron stationed me on the bow of the launch and just as a big wave washed heavily over the block, the bumper hit the bottom riser of the step. "Now jump," they all yelled at me, and I flew forward. The group on the step grabbed my arms and pulled me to safety. Elmer made the jump easily and we were both warmly welcomed to Norfolk Island.

John was a great host and took us all around the thirteen mile, historical island. He had been born on the Norfolk Island and was an extremely knowledgeable tourist guide, telling us the history of the largest population that lived there. The local people were descendents of Fletcher Christian, who had mutinied the *HMAV Bounty* many years before. Fletcher Christian, his crew, and many captured Tahitian women had first landed on Pitcairn Island. When the population outgrew the limited space and resources on the small, isolated island, many of them had been resettled on Norfolk Island. He also showed us the terrible dungeons where Australians had brought prisoners many years before. Many unfortunate people had been imprisoned there simply because they had the skills that were needed to build the vast prison complex. Throughout the time we were visiting, I kept thinking about myself jumping back onto the launch to get back to *Elysium*. This concern dampened some of my delight because I could see the rough ocean surging onto the island from the vantage points we visited.

John's wife, Florence, and his mother, Katherine, fixed us a big lunch.

As we enjoyed the meal together, we learned more about our friend John, who we had spoken with on the radio for years. It was time for Tony's net in New Zealand. Tony opens radio discussion every day so operators can meet each other and discuss technical radio problems and, in our case, the weather. All of the people enjoyed the QSO chat with him and eagerly traded cards in remembrance of meeting a new ham radio friend.

After lunch we drove over to see the largest Norfolk pine in the world, towering over two hundred feet tall. The island is named for these beautiful evergreen trees that cover the island. The amazing thing about them is that they are never misshapen or damaged by the constant wind and salt spray. We hiked to another vantage point where the lovely, white fairy terns nesting in huge quantities completely covered the craggy cliffs. We visited the golf course where the lush, green grass grew plentifully and the cows grazed side by side with the golfers.

When it came time to leave, we were saddened to say goodbye to these extremely hospitable people. We returned to the dock and found, to my tremendous delight, that the launch had been raised high, level to the step by dual winches. All we were required to do was to step aboard and be lowered down into the water. I could see that my apprehension had served no purpose and had just created useless anxiety.

Byron, John, and several other men took us back to *Elysium* in the launch. They came aboard and were especially interested in learning how the boat was built and in hearing about our voyage across the Pacific Ocean. They left us gifts of pineapple, capsicum, and pumpkin, and then returned to the jetty where I noted they were again winched up onto the step as the launch was taken up for the night. We went to sleep at 7:00 p.m. and slept soundly for twelve hours, only waking a few times to check that the anchor was holding well.

We set out again, refreshed and ready for what we thought would be a six-day trip to Australia. The sun shone in clear bright blue skies and the water was only disturbed by a fifteen knot wind as we sailed off toward the west again. For two days we enjoyed ideal sailing, and we were just congratulating ourselves, believing that we had been through the worst of the weather, when we received a call from Tony in New Zealand on the ham radio. John came on the band informing us that another front had developed in the south, and that it would hit us within twenty-four to forty-eight hours. Sure enough, just as dark of night descended, the conditions indicated that the front was arriving. We immediately dropped all of our sails and thought we were ready for the storm. How bad could it be? I went below and happened to glance at the barometer. It was falling rapidly. Not good. By morning, the ocean was rolling with huge sea comers breaking on top of the boat. We were pounding so hard into the waves that we could hardly hold ourselves in place. Everything on the boat jumped out of its place, even where the bunji cords in the past had held them securely. Drawers suddenly flew out and spilled onto the floor as the boat lifted and slammed down on the water. This was the worst night we had yet experienced. When morning arrived, the seas rose up even larger, with waves over thirty feet high. We still had four hundred and sixty miles to cover and the enormous waves breaking into the bow were holding us back, so headway was minimal. We had black and blue bruises all over our bodies from being slammed around inside the boat, even as we tried to move carefully. Cooking was doubly hard for me, with the boat not only swinging from side to side, but also jerking back and forth as the huge waves hit us. I opted for chicken vegetable soup and crackers several times each day. I could hold one pot on the stove with the clamps and when it was hot I immediately transferred it down into the deep sink. Then I covered it with insulating towels to keep it warm while we sipped out of our mugs.

The next evening the full moon rose large and red in the clouds. Even though the saying goes, "Red sky at night sailors delight," the vision gave us an ominous feeling. The barometer was rising and we were hopeful that the front had passed. It seemed that the sea was easing a bit, so we each took two-hour watches as the other slept. The morning brought heavy wind and tremendous rain from the east. The rain was so heavy that it helped flatten the enormous waves. The radio was reporting extremely adverse conditions, so we dropped the sails to wait until all of the squalls had passed. As we looked out beside the boat, we spotted a huge albatross flying just above the height of the cabin, almost within reach of us. The colossal bird was so close that we could see its eyes staring back at us. We were exhausted, so we just sat on the lounges in the cabin, under the shelter of the tent, watching the rain and sea, thrilling at the sight of the bird. It did not move its wings at all, but drifted along in the strong wind, staying in the shelter of the boat. We felt that this bird had bonded with us; it felt like a good omen.

On the ninth day out of Norfolk Island, the sky turned as black as night. We endured several squalls that brought with them strong wind and thundershowers, slamming into us one after another. John called us on the radio to tell us that we were just reaching the worst of the trough. As we concluded our contact, the most dreadful storm we had ever experienced hit us. The anemometer read sixty-five knots of wind, hurricane force, and brought with it incredibly torrential rain. It was as if we were under a waterfall. The fierceness of the storm left us exhausted so we dropped all of the sails again and went into the lowest passageway in the boat, near our bunks, and let *Elysium* be tossed by the sea with no navigation. We placed every pillow and any padding we could find on the floor and wedged ourselves in tightly together. We were so fatigued that we slept soundly for the rest of the night. In the morning, we looked out and found that the conditions had slightly improved. We checked the log and found that our night's rest had pushed us forty miles back toward Norfolk Island. We still had one hundred miles to go before reaching Brisbane. Meeting John on the radio he said, "Things should be getting better soon. The storm is passing." In that instant, vicious thunder and lightning began. I was helping Elmer drop the main sail when my finger got caught and snapped near the knuckle. Now both of us had a damaged finger. It was still raining very hard when a heavy wave hit the back of the boat. The rigging on the wind vane snarled and broke all of the cords that held it together. We had to get out the emergency tiller in order to steer. I was despairing, wondering what more could happen on this ill-fated trip?

We began the morning of the tenth day with another squall hitting the boat. Then, unexpectedly, a fifty knot gust came from nowhere and tore the staysail winch off the mast. It hit with such force that the winch swung around and entrapped all of the foreword rigging and the ham antenna. A huge wave came with it and rolled the boat way over, ripping out the clew of the Yankee sail. Because of this, the jib halyard was completely unusable. Just then the weather lifted a bit and we spotted the light on Morton Bay, Australia. What a dilemma we were in. We could not sail because we had no headsails and motoring into the heavy wind and rain coming off the shore would barely give us four knots. We decided to call for help on the VHF, or very high frequency radio. There was an immediate call back from the water police. They were working on a boat wreck on an island near Morton Bay and had sent the *MMBowe* out to pick up the stranded people. They said that they would lead us into the bay. This area of Morton Bay is very dangerous; there is no shipping channel and many unmarked reefs. If the rescue boat had not been there, we would have had to motor with our crippled rig for at least three days to get to the mouth of the river in order to enter where the shipping channel is located. The police led us through the unmarked channel, often moving out of sight. They would then wait for us to catch up. When we were finally in open water again, we motored the rest of the day to get to the quarantine anchorage at Mud Island. We gratefully dropped our anchor in heavy fog and rain and took down what sails we could. The radio signal was very good when George and Tony called to see how we were faring. Because we had lost the radio antenna, all I could do was send Morse code telling them, "We are OK," over and over again.

The next morning dawned unbelievably clear without a cloud in sight. We had slept for fifteen hours and were ready to face the wreck of our sails and mast on the deck. Elmer took me up in the bosun's chair to untangle the halyard winch from the tack pennant and antenna. I was up sixty feet above the boat when the wind began to blow, making it very difficult for me to get all of the pieces together, but I carefully retrieved everything. We were lucky our antenna was not damaged and we had not lost any of our rigging.

We called the customs agent and he told us to come up the river at noon when we had the tide with us. We fried up a huge batch of potatoes and eggs and ravenously devoured them, our first big meal for many days. A big river barge came by and offered to lead us up the river when the time came. Several other barges and a dredge called us on the VHF to tell us that they had been listening to our distress calls and they wanted to welcome us to Australia. Because our VHF radio in the United States uses different channels than Australia uses, we stayed on the busy contact channel for the entire time. The contact channel is available to everyone for reaching their party only, and then they must choose another channel for their message. George and Donna in Portland had been very worried so they called on the ham radio to see if he could find a ham operator nearby us. They found Wendy Davies who lived in Buderim near Mooloolaba. We now had a new contact nearby in Australia.

Arriving at the customs dock, we found that Sylvia and Roy, our friends from Canada, had immigrated to Australia. Being ex-sailors, they kept a VHF radio in their home and often listened for new arrivals to find out if someone they knew was arriving. When they heard our voices, they brought fresh vegetables and fruit to us at the customs dock. The customs agent who questioned us about the purpose of our visit was very nice. We told him that *Elysium* had been badly damaged in a hurricane and we needed to do some further repairs in Australia. We asked him for permission to stay in Australia for two years so we could see the country and finish our boat repairs. He told us when our year was up to come back and see him and he would give us another year. After checking in, we moved on to the local guest dock to rest a few days before sailing north to Mooloolaba, which was only a short sail away.

When we arrived at the Mooloolaba Yacht Club we were amazed to find Bobby on the dock to meet us. We had met him when we were crossing the equator. He was crewing on the delivery yacht, *Acushla*, and had promised us a spot in the Yacht Club when arrived in Australia. We would never have expected to be able to find him so quickly. He made arrangements for us to have a very convenient slip at the Yacht Club for as long as we needed it. We had a great deal of boat work to do, as our quick patching in Tonga needed some final refinishing. When *Elysium* pitched heavily into the seas on the way to Australia, the unforgiving waves had broken our new, wooden bowsprit in several places. With our new slip, we could easily access the boat-yard building, which would give us the opportunity to take down the masts and have shelter inside to refinish them. We also needed to build new spreaders because the relentless beating they had endured had left them bare and weakened.

The day we brought *Elysium* into our slip, a group of eighteen Boy Scouts were visiting the coast from Roma, which is one day's drive to the west coast. When we saw the boys walking down the dock, we invited them to come aboard for a visit. These young boys had never been to the coast before and were entranced by the boat. Each boy found the perfect spot that fit him and snuggled in. They did not want to leave when Janet, the scoutmaster, called to them. This experience started a lifelong friendship for us with Janet, her sister Josie and family, and their parents, Les and Ivy, who lived in Roma.

The luxury of being tied up at the dock gave us electricity, access to a washing machine, a dryer, and a hot shower. LeAnn, Steve, and the children would arrive soon from the states and we had an ideal place for them to visit us. At this time Mooloolaba was a quaint little fishing town. We had access to a great variety of fish in the market where Josie's daughter worked. There was also ice available so we could keep everything fresh. The beaches were beautiful and devoid of the deadly box jellyfish and crocodiles that plagued the areas further north. There was a shark net that was patrolled by overhead helicopters. They kept watch for sharks that came through into the swimming area. A loud alarm sounded if a shark broke through. Fortunately, no one was ever bitten by a shark in the two years that we were there.

Walking along the dock we met a man named John, who was planning to leave Australia and crew on with an American yacht. He owned an old Toyota Corolla, which he wanted to sell for five hundred dollars. "I'm an auto mechanic and know everything that needs work on this car," he told us. He said he would introduce us to his friend who had a small auto repair business and that he would be able to repair the problems and give us a car that would take us safely wherever we needed to go. We met the mechanic and immediately felt confident in the friendly, young man. After driving around to get what parts we needed, we left our new vehicle with the mechanic. He overhauled the engine, installed new tires, and fixed the clutch. When we drove out of the shop, we were entirely satisfied. Now we had a way to show LeAnn and Steve the sights of Australia. All we needed to do was to learn to drive on the left side of the road. We had to be at the airport by 5:30 a.m. to meet them, so we could practice our driving on all of the nearly empty highways.

We picked the family up at the airport and did a bit of sightseeing, then had dinner aboard *Elysium*. The next morning after a good sleep with all onboard, we set off to Lone Pine, where our grandsons, Josh and Justin, enjoyed seeing the extraordinary animals of Australia. They could walk around and touch the tame kangaroos, hold Koala bears and look through into an aquarium where duckbilled platypuses were swimming. We enjoyed a picnic under a tree where a kookaburra serenaded us with its addicting laugh. We took them to a place called the Big Pineapple, a huge replica of a pineapple where there was a display and diorama educating people about their famous pineapple. We were able to sample the delicious fruits and the macadamia nuts that grow nearby. We then made plans to sail north the next day to let them experience the coral reefs. We wanted to keep moving because they only had two weeks to see what they could of this massive and extraordinary country. They took the train to Brisbane to see the sights while we readied the boat for the trip.

We sailed out with a stiff wind into the rough and unprotected ocean. We hadn't gone far when Steve and Josh became very seasick. LeAnn and Justin were enjoying the sail on deck with Elmer. I exchanged buckets for the seasick victims below and tried acupressure and ginger to help them recover. All of us thought they would soon become accustomed to the swell and be able to come up to join us on deck. Instead, Steve began to experience severe stomach cramps and was not even able to hold down a small sip of water. When Steve's face turned an even more alarming yellowish green, I asked him if he could possibly climb up on deck into the fresh air. He said "I have never been so miserable in my entire life. Do you think it would be possible to go back to shore?" he asked meekly.

We had been sailing for a few hours with the wind and returning, we would be beating into a very rough sea. Elmer came down to evaluate the situation and decided that we needed to take him back. We spent the rest of the day beating into the wind and rough sea to get back into the safety of the port. Steve remained very ill for the rest of the evening, and we now knew that sailing would be out of the question for the rest of their visit. Steve would probably never sail again.

When we were docked again, Bobby came down to see what had happened. He told us that we could take his Datsun van so the boys could sleep inside and we could camp. We drove north and it rained for the entire day. When we arrived at the campsite in Bundaberg, we decided to rent a small camp trailer, or what the Australians call a caravan, to make cooking dinner in the rain a little bit easier. When we arrived at the Barrier Reef, we were able to rent a powerboat so we could take the family to see the beautiful coral and vivid fishes. The reef protects the sea so there was no rough water for Steve to endure.

We had just returned to the yacht club when we were told that a hurricane was expected to hit Mooloolaba very soon. Just as our visiting family was back aboard, the hurricane hit. We had to vacate *Elysium* and transfer the two sleeping boys to the safety of the club building. We watched in distress as the fierce storm hit the little bay. Because of the brutal wind, a large dredge broke loose and swept down the river, crashing onto the yacht club boat ramp and slips. One section after another buckled and crushed the yachts as the burden of the storm surge of the river battered them. Rescue boats were out to clear the debris before more damage could be done. A man fell off of the dock and was quickly swept out of sight into the river. The small power rescue boat plucked him out of the water just as he came out of the heavy current to the surface. It was a very dramatic rescue by a very capable woman in command. *Elysium* was incredibly lucky this time because we were docked safely in the very last slip downriver, which remained untouched.

As Steve watched this violent scene, he said "We would have been out in that storm if I hadn't gotten sick!" The worst of the wind from the hurricane lasted only four hours, so by evening we were able to climb back onboard to spend the night.

It was necessary to take the family to the airport the next morning, so we set out in the extremely heavy, driving rain that followed the hurricane. We had to drive our little Toyota through two large rain-filled lakes on the road. Just as we reached the deepest water on the road, the motor died, and we had to push the car ahead, walking in water above our knees. I remember Justin looking out the rearview window with such a puzzled look on his face as the three of us pushed the car through the water. It would be a trip he would not soon forget.

The next day, after the family left, we set to work putting the boat up on the ways, taking down the masts, and beginning the long, tedious process of refinishing them. In the following months we replaced everything that was broken, torn, or smashed. We installed new windows that were made of thick glass throughout the entire boat because the lexan ones had become cloudy and difficult to see through. We varnished and repainted every surface on the entire boat. All of our bins needed to be emptied and washed and repainted. After five months, we had finally taken everything out of the boat, cleaned each area and restocked. The very last job before re-stepping the masts was to sand the entire outer surface of *Elysium* and to spray on epoxy and new bottom paint. I sanded and painted the bottom a bright dark red. The next day I was very sick to my stomach and lost consciousness several times. We decided that the toxic bottom paint I sanded had remained on my skin for too long. To take a break from the hard work, we swam every day in the warm ocean, often walked our six miles, and socialized with the increasing number of visitors who came to the boat. One man said, "You people do nothing but work on that boat all of the time!" Indeed, we had spent many months working every day.

We had arrived in Australia the first of May, the beginning of the Australian winter. We had worked almost all winter on *Elysium*. Finally we felt that she was back in ship shape, so we could sail the Australian coast when the fall came again. *Elysium* was secure in the slip, and well looked after so we decided to take our little car out to see the outback of Australia. We packed camping and emergency gear, gas cans, and water jugs.

"What do you want to see that area for? There is nothing out there," asked our friends in Australia.

"Have you ever crossed an ocean?" Elmer replied.

Our many friends who came to the boat offered to watch *Elysium* while we were gone. They enjoyed coming down to the yacht basin and sitting on deck so it was no problem for us to leave.

The first leg of our trip was to visit the town of Roma and see our friends, Les and Ivy, their daughter Janet, and her husband Rod. Rod and Janet took us to their sheep ranch, Carinya, where they raised sorghum, barley and wheat. They drove us back to their fence line where we were thrilled to watch about two hundred and fifty kangaroos, or "roos" as they called them, bounding along. Driving further, we spotted a group of emus running along, maintaining a speed of twenty miles per hour. We also saw large flocks of the pink and grey galahs, which filled the bright blue skies. This was our introduction to the incredible variety of animals in this great country.

Ivy had a leg of mutton waiting for us for "afternoon tea." The custom in Australia is to have tea in the morning, then morning tea–tea that is breakfast, afternoon tea–tea that is lunch, and finally, tea that is dinner. Even the dogs and cats get tea in the evening. We drank lots of tea while we were in Australia, as that is their treasured social time together. We made the error of inviting a new friend to the boat for tea, thinking to have a cup of tea and some snacks. I put tea and snacks on the table, but definitely got the feeling that more was expected. As I served them more snacks, they politely nibbled and said nothing. Later I learned that they had expected to be served dinner and that the word tea sometimes means dinner! Soon after, they returned the favor and invited us for tea. They served the same, thinking it was an American custom to serve snacks for dinner or "tea!"

Les and Ivy took us to view all of the interesting sights nearby. Because they had not experienced a drought recently, everything was green and the bores, or what they call wells, were filled with water. We went to Walleroo, where the Fernsides had a seventy thousand acre station. They took us out to see where the aborigines had chewed ochre and sprayed what was in their mouth around their hands on to the wall inside a cave. The prints were still clearly visible.

We sat on a log and sampled the smoky tasting billey tea that is made by boiling tea in a can of water over a fire. The boiling tea is stirred with eucalyptus branches. A little later we had "smoko," which consists of more tea accompanied by a sandwich. I never understood the difference between smoko and afternoon tea. The Australians have an endearing language of great sayings that sound foreign until they gradually become familiar over time.

We said a sad farewell to our wonderful new friends in Roma and drove south to Bourke. We saw trees full of scarlet, deep blue and brilliant green parrots along the Darling River. The weather was very hot, over one hundred degrees in the afternoon, while we were looking for a suitable campsite. Just as we completed setting up the tent, clouds formed and electrical storms with cooling rain broke out all around us.

We drove on to Cobar, which looked like the flattest land in the world, much like the ocean. We picked a spot and set up camp. Later we were walking across the bridge nearby that led to an Aboriginal settlement. As we approached, a native man sitting at the edge of the road called out to us, "Will you shout me a beer?" I told him, "I have no money." "Oh you have lots of money," he said. "You have lots more money than I have. You are rich, really rich," he almost taunted me. "I'll bet you have three hundred dollars!" As I walked, on I thought to myself that he had been right. I did have three hundred dollars and he had just made me rich.

Our next campsite, near Burra, had a beautiful stream running through it on which black swans were swimming. There were beautiful abandoned farmhouses built from quarried red stone. At the camp, we met David and Margaret Morton from Alice Springs. David told us that the farmers who were veterans from the war had been given land to develop by the government. They had abandoned the farmhouses years later when the severe drought came and the arid land became untenable. We spent several days with David and Margaret and their three beautiful little blonde daughters. When we parted, we exchanged addresses and invited them to come and see us in Mooloolaba and stay on the boat. They, in turn, invited us to stay with them if we were ever able to visit Alice Springs in the future.

We ended our trip on the coast by visiting Granite Island where fairy penguins live in little dugouts near the sea. We enjoyed watching them as they marched in a line, up out of the sea and ducked into their homes. On the island there were also many little tame, grey wallabies that ate from our hand.

We drove from Granite Island, down the great ocean road where the white frothy waves broke out of a turquoise sea, carving shapes out of the yellow, orange and red rock of the shore. We saw many more of the enormous variety of brightly colored birds for which Australia is noted. We visited the William Ricketts Sanctuary, where the artist has created clay figures of aboriginal people over the moss-covered rocks. We were most fortunate to meet Mr. Ricketts himself and hear the story of how he began his immense and compelling work when he came from England and moved onto the reservation for eight years to live with the aboriginal people. He felt that they had essential information to give the world and this was his attempt to transfer that information onto the rocks in the rain forest. We spent the day in the reserve and felt inspired by the artist's message.

We drove back to Mooloolaba by way of the coast, starting in Melbourne and driving on up to Sydney. We stopped and visited with many of the people we had sailed with during our trip. Bobby told us that Peter, who was part of the crew, was staying in Umbagumbi, near Bermagui. We called him on the phone and he met us in town and led us out to where he was living. We stayed a few days catching up with Peter, learning about the other members of *Acushla's* crew. We headed back to Mooloolaba up the beautiful eastern coast. During the trip, I listed eighty-six species of sea and land birds in my diary that we had never seen before. We arrived back in Mooloolaba on January 10, 1984. Now we were ready to prepare *Elysium* to sail north to explore the islands and the coast.

By this time we had numerous visitors each day on *Elysium*. Steven Driver, who was just sixteen, marveled at stories that Elmer told him about navigation and the places we had visited. Steven had first been quite angry about the fact that "you Americans stole the America's Cup Race"! We did not defend the American racing sailors because we knew nothing about it. When we accepted his views, he accepted us com-

Loading the Land Rover for the outback trip

pletely and became a daily visitor after school.

Rae Fry and her parents, Josie and David, also became very dear friends. Josie is Les and Ivy's daughter and Janet's sister. One day David said to us, "we're taking off for a look see into the outback for a month or so and we'd like to take you along to show you some of Australia that you would never see as a tourist." We were thrilled to be invited and pledged to buy the gasoline for the expedition. David and Josie had a Land Cruiser that was perfectly fitted for their many excursions and had plenty of room for our baggage and us.

Indeed, we did visit places a tourist never would be able to see: we traveled the red sandy dunes and explored the tiny towns in outback Australia; we visited little stations that had not seen rain for eight years; we visited stations where the owner's house was forty-five miles in from the entrance; we saw the bores where the water rose up from the ground, boiling hot; we visited and climbed Ayers Rock and the Olgas; we drove up a perilous, rocky creek bed to visit billabongs that were surrounded by lush green cycads, a prehistoric plant found nowhere else on earth. David and Josie were the best tour guides one could wish

Trappey

for. We camped at night beside the two-track road in the sand and never saw another car.

We visited the famous little station of Birdsville, where there are more birds than people. In the evening the tree branches turn white as they fill with cockatoos and parrots. In Birdsville, we were able to meet Trappy, who was an Aboriginal that worked at the station to rescue people who become lost in the outback. He was a wizened old man and related many stories to us about the perils of the outback. He even allowed us to take a picture of him, which is usually forbidden by Aboriginals.

Finally, it was time to head for Alice Springs to look up David, Margaret and their girls. Margaret was teaching school where she taught transitional Aboriginal students of all ages. Students attended school when it was convenient, when they were not on "walkabout" or hunting with their parents. She had Elmer and me speak to them about crossing the ocean to visit Australia. The room was full of striking looking young people with deeply set, dark brown eyes listening intently to our story. They asked how we secured enough water and food for such a long trip? They felt that we had experienced life much like they did in their outback home, foraging for food and water. They drew and painted pictures of us as we spoke to them, but would they not give even one up for us to take as a memento of the occasion. Margaret had taken pictures of us talking to them, but as often happens with these indigenous people, not one photograph developed showing their faces. The only aboriginal picture that I took that turned out was the one taken with Trappy.

David Morton and his friend, an anthropologist, were planning a trip out into the desert in an uncharted area to study Aboriginals who had not been in contact with white people. They were planning to use a sextant to find their way across. He invited us to go with them on a short trial run, and we quickly agreed. We drove over brick red sand dunes where the deep sand changed to light tan and back to red again. We drove along the Darling River and saw many species of birds and animals that David's friend identified for us. We did not see a road or another person for the entire week we spent on this trip. This was, indeed, a completely new experience in our lives. When we returned to Alice Springs, we invited David and Margaret and their girls to come to the boat for Christmas in return for the time they had spent with us.

Our trip took us through many northern towns on the way back to Mooloolaba and we arrived just as winter was again setting in and it was time to renew our visa. We had received permission to spend another year in Australia from our friend at customs, so we prepared *Elysium* to sail north into the warm tropical waters and into the protection of the Great Barrier Reef.

At the Yacht Club there were several new yachts getting ready to sail north. Audrey and John on *Judy*, and Lynn and Warwick on *Barefoot Bound* were close to us and we soon became good friends. They had made the trip north several times and were most willing to show us the best spots. Audrey and John were from Tasmania, and John had built his big steel yacht many years before. Audrey had everything a woman could want for easy cruising: a washing machine, a dryer, and a microwave oven. I was very envious! Warwick had built his fifty-eight foot yacht in Sydney and they were on their third trip north. As we sailed up the coast, Lynn confided in me that she was pregnant. She had never wanted to marry Warwick, though they had been together for many years. Now they decided that their coming child needed two parents and they asked us if we would stand with them and speak at their wedding. We had become very close to this couple and were glad to be part of their marital plans.

After the wedding we all sailed north to spend the winter on the white sandy beaches of the Whitsundy Islands, which are part of the nine hundred islands protected by the Great Barrier Reef. The warm winds and water draw many tourists to the area, but we were able to cruise into isolated bays rimmed with high promontories where the shores were thickly covered with countless green-lipped mussels. Small tropical fish also provided tasty meals, so we only needed to visit the stores when our vegetables bins were bare. We were not always alone. Occasionally, an Australian cruiser would find its way into our anchorages and would share time with us.

When we landed on the island beaches, we always had to contend with big waves that curled and crashed onto the shore. Our landing procedure was to row the dingy vigorously with its stern to the shore. When we hit the sand on shore between waves, I would jump out and aggressively pull *Limbo* high onto the beach with the help of the next big wave. Because of the grating of the coral and sharp sand, the keel of the dingy was wearing very thin, so Elmer attached a piece of stainless steel sail track all along the bottom. We thought that the next time we entered the shore we would have a smooth sliding keel, but we did not take into consideration the effect it could have on me standing in the big waves. On a particularly rough beach where the waves were breaking heavily, I jumped out to pull the back of the dingy up, but the sail track caught the nail on my big toe and tore it completely loose. There was just the one side where it stayed flapping in the wave. I howled like a banshee as the salt water and sand hit the raw area. Elmer quickly helped me back into the dingy and when we got back to *Elysium*, he poured iodine over the whole area, holding my foot in a vise-like grip as I writhed in pain. It seemed to me that he had no sympathy at all. "We have got to stop the possibility of infection," he said.

For a couple of weeks I wore a boot at all times and Elmer dressed the wound twice daily. I could not enter the salt water for the rest of our stay in the islands.

We spent the next few weeks exploring Lindeman Island. As the sun set over the island, the flying fox population covered the sky as they moved out of the thick forest on the nearby island. It is hard to imagine the amount of fruit and flowers necessary to feed this enormous foraging flight of animals. The flying fox is a fruit bat, which is twenty inches long and has a wingspan of five feet. They weigh over two pounds and have voracious appetites.

We often visited the tourist spot on Lindeman Island to chat with the people who were visiting the resort. One day, a lady who we had often seen asked me "…would you mind telling me how you lost your leg?" I had never thought that my boot looked like a missing limb, but I assured her that my toe was the only thing that the boot protected.

When spring arrived, we knew that our time in Australia would soon come to an end and we still had many things to accomplish before leaving. The countries we were planning to visit next would not be able to supply the great advantages that we had enjoyed in Australia. We had planned to sail to Bali in Indonesia to observe the culture and many art forms that we had read about. Unfortunately, the latest news from the cruisers was that yachts were no longer welcome on the island and some on the radio had told us that they had been turned away and not allowed to come to shore at the port of Denpesar. With this information, we changed our plans and decided that our next port of call would be the Solomon Islands.

Our Australian friends told us that the flight to Bali was very inexpensive and included a stay at a luxury hotel. We learned that we could fly there, spend two weeks enjoying the culture of the island and leave *Elysium* at our slip in Mooloolaba. We made arrangements with our friends to keep an eye on *Elysium* and we boarded a bus for Sydney, where Warwick and Lynn were home and back to work. They picked us up and we spent the night with them. At 6:00 a.m., Warwick woke up to take us to the airport to catch a flight on Indonesian Airline to Bali. We set a time for our return and they promised to be there to pick us up.

It is hard to describe the experience of arriving in Bali. It is unbelievably warm and humid and all the arriving tourists are packed together into very small buses. The bus careens through the crowded streets at a reckless speed, honking at everyone. We arrived at our four star hotel at Kuta Beach, glad to be inside our room and to turn on a fan. Now that my toe was healed, we decided to cool off in the surf that was washing up onto the smooth white sand beach in front of the hotel. The temperature of the water was even warmer than the air! The beach was filled with nude bathers receiving massages and people bargaining for sarongs and clothes with the local women.

After exploring the town, we decided to rent two bicycles and find a spot that had more of a local population. As we rode to the north on Legion Beach Road, past the brilliant green rice patties, we were out of the tourist area right away. We found a small village where people stopped and stared at me, a woman riding a bicycle, but smiled when we waved and smiled at them. We stopped at a small food stand to eat our breakfast. The owner, Putu, and his wife, Wyanne, had some benches inside to protect us from the hot sun. They had two of the most charming, gorgeous little girls we had ever seen. Putu spoke English and served us a delicious meal of Nasi Goring. This became our favorite spot for our meals from that day forward. Every day we rode to the little eating-place and the little girls would shout out, "Here comes Eskimo," as they spotted Elmer's white hair gleaming in the sun.

We stayed in town and were thrilled to hear the Gamelan music that the musicians played on their ancient hand carved instruments. We saw the Hindu Epic of Barong, which is the most violent and dramatic of the Balinese dances. The two demonic characters of Barong and Rangda are used as an exorcism depicting good and evil. The dance is done by olive-skinned muscular men who use the Kris to stab their chest as the dance ends. The Kris is a very sharp, double-edged dagger with a blade that has curved waves down to the tip. We were sitting close to the men and could not see any evidence of pierced flesh. The legendary Kris is a very important religious object for the people of Bali and each family inherits the important artifact for its magical protection.

We were telling Putu that it was our desire to see the other parts of

Tranquility in Bali

the island where there were no tourists. "I can take you anywhere," he told us excitedly. We followed him to the back of the stall where a long curtain separated the eating area from their living space, and he showed us a car that was parked behind the curtain. "This car was my inheritance," he told us. I will show you all of the island places that no one else sees," he promised.

True to his word, Putu drove us to the black sand beaches where the people lived in stilted houses. These people scraped the sand each day to provide the people of the island with mineral salt. We drove to the two active volcanoes, Mt. Batur and Mt. Agung, which are ringed with the green stocks of rice irrigated by artistically sculptured rills flowing down the mountainside. We found Bali to be very beautiful with gigantic stone sculptures, intricate painting, batik and Ikat cloth, wooden carvings and metalwork. Their artwork could not be surpassed.

Each day we viewed ancient works of art and parts of the preserved Balinese-Hindu culture. We felt there would never be enough time to take in all of the wonders that exist on this gem of an island. When Nehru was Prime Minister of India, he called Bali, "the morning of the world" and that is the best phrase to describe the pristine quality of the island and the tranquility of the people.

When the time came to leave, we had one last amazing experience, a cremation on the beach. It was a colorful and joyful occasion and we were all engaged in the spirit. Beautiful paper mache animals were set on fire and sent out on the waves from the beach. No one minded the tourists sharing the occasion because the ceremony reflected so much of their culture. When the family has no money for an expensive cremation, the body is buried until the time when the family can afford to exhume the body and cremate it properly.

Every day we filled ourselves with pineapple, mangosteen, durian, rambutan and other exotic fruits. We had viewed amazing carvings, visited the homes of local people, and taken part in the rice festival. Putu had made our visit so meaningful and unique that we were sad to part with this warm and loving family.

In mid-December we arrived back in Australia. Now it was time to prepare *Elysium* and get ready for our next adventure. Margaret, David, and the girls were to arrive for Christmas. When the "white princess," as they called their Land Cruiser, arrived, there was mud covering both sides and the top of the vehicle. It had obviously been a very difficult trip. The car drew lots of attention as it sat dripping mud in the parking lot of the yacht club.

When they were settled on *Elysium*, we took them out sailing and gave them an experience they had not had before, seasickness. The girls had not visited the coast, so every day was a new adventure. One day the water around *Elysium* was full of tiny baby turtles that had just hatched on the nearby shore. The two little girls were so thrilled to see the little creatures paddling around in the water that it doubled our pleasure to watch this new generation being hatched. On the shore, there was the daily dance of the ghost crab who emerged from their little holes to roll sand into thousands of perfectly shaped balls. The design they make as they sift the sand for food and roll the waste into balls is like a lacy drawing on the beach. We enjoyed visiting with our good friends whom we would not see again.

By January 1985, we were listing the jobs we needed to do before sailing north by April. We put the boat on the ways and applied two coats of bottom paint, varnished all of the outside britework, put in a new shaft and repaired the rudder shaft. We also bought solar panels and a new alternator. During this time we had so many daily visitors that the main cabin was often crowded. We had been in Australia for two years and knew that we would miss our dear friends with whom we had enjoyed such a fantastic time.

When the day came to leave our Mooloolaba moorage, the dock was crowded with people who had come to bid us goodbye. Audrey and John filled a stainless steel urinal with wine. The urinal was engraved with, "From the pisspots of Australia." All of the sadness and love expressed by our friends made us feel much like we were leaving Sauvie Island all over again.

We sailed north to Bundaberg to meet Rod, Karen, and little Levi on the steel yacht, *Sunburn*. Rod had built the thirty-eight foot yacht several years before and the two of them planned to sail north to the Solomon Islands. When their son Levi was born, they decided to wait until he was eight months old. When we met them, they had asked us if we would sail with them and stay in sight to be sure they were not in danger. We agreed to sail with them, but we knew that staying in sight would be extremely unlikely. We said we would sail nearby and keep in radio contact. We did not tell them that in rough seas there is not much one yacht can do to help another, except to pick up survivors.

We left Australia together on May 7, for Lady Musgrove Atoll, located several miles out from the coast. We anchored for a rest and when we all felt we were ready to tackle the intimidating Coral Sea, we pulled anchor and sailed out into the darkening sky and rolling ocean waters.

The Solomon Island Chain

If one advances confidently, in the direction of his own dreams and endeavors, to lead the life, which he has imagined, he will meet with success unexpected in common hours.

– Henry David Thoreau

THE FIRST TWO days as we sailed away from Australia with Rod and Karen on *Sunburn*, the wind was "fresh" but not unbearable. Chesterfield Atoll was located a few days sail ahead and we planned to stop inside the protection of the atoll to rest. When we were a half of a day away, a very strong thirty-five knot wind, on the beam, churned the shallow waters. The sea responded quickly with giant waves cresting high in the air with foamy tops. When we came into sight of the reef surrounding the atoll, we could see there were enormous waves nearly breaching the coral near the narrow entrance. We called to Rod on *Sunburn* and warned them that it would be too dangerous to go any nearer because the wind was blowing the seas toward the reef. When Rod called back, he let us know that they were dreadfully tired, and that Karen, in particular, needed to stop for a rest. He said that they were still intending to find out if they could possibly sail in through the entrance into the protection of the atoll. We felt very apprehensive because if they had any trouble near the reef there would be nothing we could do to help them.

We informed him of our decision and told them these conditions would put *Elysium* in extreme danger.

We were very relieved when Rod called and told us that they found that the reef was too dangerous to enter and that they would be catching up with us as soon as they could. We continued to sail along on a beam reach that sank us down into dreadfully deep troughs in the waves. We rode high on a cresting wave and then slid heavily down into the trench. At times we could see the entire bottom of Sunburn as the yacht was tossed off of the top of the huge waves. Karen said that when she put little Levi down on the bed he was immediately rolled up like a sausage in his blanket. She was terrified and prayed that the weld joints in the bottom of the hull would not split open as the heavy seas pounded on the boat.

I was gazing out the stern of *Elysium*, watching the familiar sight of towering waves that were following us, when I just happened to glance down into the water. Just as a heavy wave hit the wind vane sideways the sturdy shaft holding the rudder broke off completely and began to rise up to the surface. We both were barely able to seize the rope that was holding it together and drag the whole apparatus onboard. Now we had no more wind vane steering, but it was a stroke of luck that we were able to retrieve it from the heavy sea. Because of the deep troughs hitting the side of the boat, the sails were also being yanked viciously, tearing at the stitching. Every sail we had was torn out during this sixteen-day trip. Our aging sailcloth had succumbed to the bright sunlight and heavy whipping on the stitching. We were planning to purchase new ones when we reached Hong Kong, where the original sails had been made.

With the sails torn we headed for the closest land, which was Port Mary on Santa Ana Island. Technically we were supposed to check into the Solomons at the main island in Honiara on Guadalcanal, but with the heavy weather we wanted refuge, especially for Rod, Karen, and Levi. They were emotionally and physically exhausted and we knew that they were in dire need of shelter and rest.

The anchorage at Port Mary was protected and easy to enter. We had traveled eleven hundred miles and were delighted to find refuge and rest at last. We put up our green and blue Solomon Island Flag and waited for someone to come to greet us. Soon *Sunburn* joined us and they gratefully dropped their anchor into the clear, peaceful turquoise water. When no one came to the boat we decided to go to shore to see if we could stop for a rest and to repair our sails. The island people greeted us with happy shouts and the chief in a purple shirt gave us permission to stay as long as we needed to. There was also a local policeman there and he granted us shelter to finish the repairs.

Santa Ana was a paradise for us. It had a big freshwater lake in the center of the island where we could swim every day. We were accompanied there by all of the beautiful, almond colored, curly-haired children. They especially loved to carry Levi; he was blond and very white skinned who looked like a bright light against their dark skin. The inhabitants offered us a bounty of fruit and locally caught fish.

When we were revived, we set to work on mending our sails. As a respite from our chores, we hiked into the lush green forests that covered the interior of the island. We watched the fishermen carve their hooks from bone and fashion a unique and imaginative wooden fishing float to hold them at the right length into the sea as they drifted out.

It took us a week to repair our sails and prepare to sail on to Honiara. On the way there we stopped each night and anchored in the well-protected bays we found in the island chains. For this part of the trip, we enjoyed restful day sailing and good weather. We found the people of the Solomon Islands spoke excellent English and were extremely friendly. They produced excellent, burnished dark hardwood woodcarvings inlaid with nautilus shell. These carvers brought their wares to the boat hoping to sell some of them to us.

Before we got to Honiara, we anchored in Marau Sound on the tip of Guadalcanal. An old man visited us as he sailed by, using a big palm leaf to push his little dugout canoe downwind. He related his memories to us about the airplanes that came during the Second World War and dropped bombs nearby the villages. "We had no idea what was happening, but we all vacated our villages and ran up into the hills. The noise

Our coast watcher friend with palm leaf sail

was terrifying and we were afraid to go back to get food. So we ate what we could find in the jungle," he told us.

He became a coast watcher for the American army so he could report the movement of the Japanese soldiers. Hearing his story brought back many memories of the war for us as he related his tale with vivid descriptions of the terrible tragedy that prevails with war. When he left we sat quietly and looked at the lush palm growth that was evident now, and thought about the terrible waste of war.

That evening we were able to contact a ham radio operator who offered to run a phone patch for us to anyone we wanted to reach. We decided to try calling Ralph Carver, a good friend who had fought on Guadalcanal during the Second World War. In our haste reach him, we neglected to consider what time it would be in Oregon. Unfortunately it turned out to be 2:30 a.m. and a very sleepy voice answered. Just wakened at this hour, Ralph could not understand how I could call him from the Solomon Islands! When we ended the conversation, he woke up and called the man back and asked him to run the patch again for another contact. This time we had a lively conversation about Guadalcanal. He told us about the devastation of the island and about the many battles that were fought in this now peaceful place. Guadalcanal was the first major battle that the American troops fought against a Japanese held island. He said that when he had been here the complete coastline was burned and not a green thing was left standing in the rainforest. He related the story we had heard so many times about Red Beach colored with the blood of the soldiers who were killed there. The entire war became more real for us as we realized the energy that was left behind on this whole island chain. The bay where we were anchored is called Iron Bottom Sound because there were so many large war vessels sunk there.

We checked in at the immigration office in Honiara and were given a three-month visa. When our time was up, we would be able to check out in Gizo, which is the last island to the west on the island chain. We toured Guadalcanal for a short time and saw the enormous assortment of rusting American tanks, trucks and other various types of war equipment that was left on the islands after the war. This spectacle was a grim reminder of the appalling bloodshed and the needless waste that war creates. Deep down in the crystal clear water there were fighter planes and bombers still evident with their equipment deteriorating inside. Passive fishes lazily swam throughout this rusting equipment that once brought death and destruction to the islands. The airport on Henderson field that was built by the Japanese in 1942 is still being used as an airport today by the government of the Solomon Islands.

The one thousand Solomon Islands were declared independent in 1976. Since that time, there has been much instability because of ethnic violence and crime running rampant throughout the islands. We were warned that cruising the Solomon Islands could be dangerous, so we were cautious and avoided the problem areas that we had heard about from other sailors. The voracious blood-loving mosquitoes that carried malaria were the other grave danger that existed. Two kinds of mosquitoes thrived in the climate of extremely heavy rainfall and very warm temperatures. To protect ourselves from the disease we always wore clothes that covered all of our bare skin when going ashore and took large quantities of vitamin B. We also covered ourselves with a mixture of citronella, cedar, eucalyptus, and geranium essential oils. The Anopheles mosquito is particularly virulent as she carries a malaria parasite that is very difficult to treat and often leaves the victim in a deadly coma and fever. The Anopheles mosquito enters the area quietly and rests until nightfall when she senses her victim is asleep. Then she swiftly draws the blood and leaves the parasite that resides in her maxillary gland in the blood of her victim. That parasite invades the liver and breeds there, causing the malaria. We were very fortunate that we never contracted malaria in our travels.

We sailed the short distance to the small island of Gavutu Ngila. Gavutu Island had been purchased by a multi-national company to use as a lavish resort, with plans to build a large main hotel surrounded with small grass huts. Unfortunately, the company had gone into bankruptcy so all that remained on the island were the cement foundations of the buildings. The island was very beautiful with tall palm trees lining a white sand beach. The proximity to Guadalcanal would have enabled tourists to arrive and depart easily. As we dropped anchor we could see the sleek brown body of a young man swimming under the water nearby. He came up to the surface and flashed a big grin at us while rubbing his eyes that were stinging from the salt water. One of the gifts that we carried onboard was a goggle to protect the eyes when swimming underwater. We held a pair out to him and showed him how to cover his eyes. This time when he dove again he speared a fish and broke the surface with surprise and joy at being able to see clearly underwater. He dove again and brought us two tasty fish for dinner.

The young man's name was Gabriel and he lived on this little island with his clan of a small family group. Gabriel visited us every morning and brought us fruit from the family trees and played our guitar for us. It was surprising he was able to learn to play so well, as he had no guitar of his own. I had been trying to learn to play for years and never reached the ability that he demonstrated.

One day we told Gabriel that we would like to meet his family. We asked if he would bring them out to the boat, emphasizing that we wanted to meet the women also, as we usually only met the men and children. The problem for the women on the islands was that they had no western style clothes to wear and they could not speak English. They only wore a grass band covering the front of their genitals. We assured him that it would be no problem for us, so he went ashore and we brought the family aboard a few at a time in the dingy. So they would not be uncomfortable, I put on a topless sarong and went out to meet them.

The women were very shy but we could tell by their bright smiles that they were excited to be onboard a yacht. One woman was pregnant and she looked like she would give birth very soon. They all climbed down the ladder into the boat and looked with awe at the furnishings inside. As they walked through the bunk area where our mirrored wall is located, they gasped as they stared at the full-length reflection of themselves. We were certain that the four women had never seen themselves before except in the reflection of the water. They giggled excitedly and stood watching themselves for a long time. It would have been the picture taking opportunity of a lifetime, but I couldn't bear to invade the privacy of their nearly nude bodies.

Gabriel spoke very good English and spoke of the customs and communal village life, which we enjoyed hearing about. He told us that the Solomon Islands were not yet set up for the tourist trade, partly because of government unrest and lack of facilities for tourists. The people all lived in small huts along the coastline and moved around in the wooden dugouts that they made from the large trees in the rainforest. The few little stores that could provide food only carried a fat-filled, disgusting canned corned beef and a very miniscule amount of daily necessities.

The Seventh Day Adventist Church has been extremely influential in converting the people on the islands. They instructed them that the bible says that no one should eat any sea animal without fins. Because the islands abound with lobster and other shellfish we were able to trade from our stash of clothes, fish hooks, saw blades and diving goggles for a lobster every day.

The church also encouraged the people to refine their ability to carve the abundant hardwood and to inlay nautilus shells in the carvings. In the past, the people of the Solomon's were cannibals and headhunters. Their art form, called *Noosa Noosa*, is a replica of an exaggerated

Melanesian head that they affixed on the bow of their carved dugouts. The *Noosa Noosa* form held a person's decapitated head under its chin. When the church taught the people that it was wrong to kill and eat other human beings, they changed the head and carved a dove of peace in its place. We heard stories about the last of the cannibal activities from a young man named Richard who came aboard one day. He told us the Australians, who came to "blackbird" or kidnap and enslave the people to work in the sugar cane, tricked them by dressing like priests to lure them onto the ships, convincing them that they were representatives of the church. The last time they tried this, the chief was aware of their evil work and cooked the large man in a pot. Richard told us this story just as it has been passed down through the years. We could understand why there is still distrust of white people among these natives.

We heard that there was a man from New Zealand on the island of Tulagi teaching the native people how to build concrete fishing boats. We sailed over to see if he would be willing to repair our broken wind vane rudder. Seascape Boat Building was started by New Zealand to help the people on the island build an industry and to promote self-sufficiency. When we arrived we saw a giant concrete hull just being finished. Allen Mills was the friendly blond "Kiwi" who looked at our rudder and said, "Sure mate I can fix that." We spoke to him about the problems we experienced with the steering in heavy seas, so he and Elmer engineered a "perfect" rudder for all occasions, a rudder that would be extremely strong. When the rudder was repaired we sailed off to visit the rest of the Solomon's to take advantage of the four weeks we had left on our visa.

We stopped at Ugi Island to anchor overnight and get a good sleep. We did not know there was a school on the island and were surprised by a visit from a young man from New Zealand who was teaching young boys there. The children arrived in their own small dugouts, paddling several hours to be able to go to school. The school building was spacious and had a roof to protect the students from the daily torrential rain. The temperature is usually eighty degrees or higher in the daytime, which often made teaching challenging, but the two teachers and the students were very dedicated. Often the children arrived with only a piece of coconut for their afternoon meal. I could not imagine children in the United States accepting such a parsimonious meal and being as motivated as these children seemed to be.

We left in the evening to sail across the New Georgia Strait with a wind of a perfect eighteen knots behind the beam and smooth seas. The wind vane was doing all of the steering so we lay on the warm deck and looked up at the stars. Then suddenly a most unusual phenomenon occurred. Bright lightning flashed across the sky without a cloud in sight; it was the beginning of a spectacular firework display that continued the entire night.

We sailed around Mboli Island, which was positioned in a place that guarded the southeastern entrance to Morovo Lagoon. When we arrived inside we stopped at Telina where John Wayne, the most progressive master carver of the islands, lives. We were sure that his name furthered his fame and popularity. The distinct prominence of the Seventh Day Adventist religion is evident in the carvings that the villagers do. One day while we sat and talked with John, he picked up a small stick of hardwood and carved an intricate knife that had a *Noosa Noosa* head on the handle for me. His small grass house had numerous gorgeous carvings that had been commissioned by people on yachts and the museum in Honiara. He also taught carving skills to many other young men, allowing them a way to earn a living. While we were anchored in the cove, many other carvers came aboard to show us their wares. The highly polished, black ebony woodcarvings were perfectly inlaid with nautilus shell. These outstanding carvings were the best example of what is possible to create out of the extremely hard wood. Because of the limited space we had on *Elysium*, we bought mostly small pieces we planned to use as gifts to friends on our next trip home.

Our guests brought many interesting stories aboard when they came. One day Horace, who visited us often, asked in a low voice, "Do you have any cigarettes"? "Horace" I exclaimed, "You're a Seventh Day Adventist! Do they allow you to smoke?" "No" he said ruefully, and then brightened up, "but I am a backslider" he said proudly. Horace carved us a wonderful crocodile in just two hours as he sat on the boat. It was impeccable and a true work of art. Horace told that us he was not originally from the Solomon Islands. "We lived on a very beautiful island in the north," he said. "Someone bought our island because it had lots of phosphate for fertilizer and we all had to move," he related with deep sadness. This was a heartbreaking story for me to listen to, but it is true of many of the islands where the government, and not the native people, has control over the land.

We visited the beautiful Viru Harbor, motoring carefully over the pass as the water funneled in swiftly with the tide. The sparkling clear water magnified the brilliantly colored coral and grains of sand and it looked to us as if we would be grounded in the pass, which was hundreds of miles from any assistance. We had read in a pamphlet that there was enough water for us to enter, but if we had looked at the pass first, we would never have believed it. We both breathed a sigh of relief as we cleared the coral and glided swiftly into the lagoon.

As soon as we were anchored, the children emerged in their small dugouts and happily clambered aboard to examine *Elysium*. They stayed all day, just sitting contentedly on deck and giggling among themselves as their other friends joined them. Later in the afternoon I got out my largest cooking pot and prepared a big pot of rice. When this was finished, I added canned tuna fish and bits of dried vegetables that I had onboard. By the time I got up on deck, there were many small dugouts tied off to *Elysium*. When I put the big pot of food down with some small plastic bowls, they came, helped themselves to a portion, and scurried back and quickly devoured the food. Finally, there was not a grain of rice left in the pot. We told them we were going ashore so they all scrambled into their little boats and followed behind *Limbo*. The meal of rice and fish was repeated many times as we visited these lush green islands. We made the dish for the visiting children and found them always hungry and eager to eat whatever we provided. The eating customs of the native people of the islands are that the adults eat first and the children receive what is left over. This is because the adults do the heavy work and are responsible for the survival of the family, so they need to have the bulk of the protein that is available. The children often only have a bit of breadfruit and coconut to eat. Once they found that we provided a meal onboard, we were visited daily until we pulled

Snake bean gifts from the children aboard Elysium

anchor and left. They often brought gifts of snake beans or shellfish to compliment our meal.

The lagoon was carpeted with flame-colored, spiked coral that was unlike any we had seen before. The untouched reefs were a sanctuary for brilliantly colored blue, green and scarlet fish that darted about freely among the coral's sharp spears. As we snorkeled along, skimming over the tops, we spotted a Zebra fish below us. We were quite shallow and could have easily touched its poisonous spines. Fortunately we were very well schooled about all of the deadly fish that lived in these reefs. We spent days thrilling at the spectacular diving, feeling exhilarated by the abundance of species that we had never seen before. We also scooped up many colorful shells to add to our collection. The annual rainfall in the Solomon Islands is over one hundred and twenty inches a year, but there was no cloudiness in the reef or signs of damage from the village's sewerage. The small population and lack of tourism had left the entire reef healthy, vibrant, and beautiful.

One night a very fine looking, ebony-colored man came aboard with a large oval shaped bowl. He wanted to sell it to us for fifty dollars in

U.S. money. We knew he expected us to bargain him down to twenty because that was the price for this type of work. He had scooped out the shape with his tools to perfection and inlaid the shell around the edges. His name was Penne Sage Kalena and he was the leader in the village. He told us that very few yachts ever came into the harbor and that the village was without the funds needed for supplies. We decided that the price of the bowl would be utilized for many things in the village, so we agreed to pay it. Several days later, Penne came back with the most beautiful carving of a dolphin jumping out of the water. He said it was a gift and suggested that we paid way too much for the bowl. We thought this was an interesting case of conscience and we assured him that we wanted to help the village. We told him that we knew he would do the best thing for his people. His bright eyes glistened when we told him how much we valued his work and his honesty. The good feelings that we kept from this interchange stayed with us every time we saw our beautiful bowl.

A man named Radio Vaghi visited us. His mother had heard the radio for the first time when he was born, so that was what she chose to name him. He had a very painful boil on his foot and asked if we had a way to heal it. I got out the Domboro and hot water and began the long process of drawing out the puss and embedded shell that was inside. After several hours the heel was ready to be opened. He did not flinch when Elmer took a sterile knife and released the build up of puss and flushed out the piece of shell. We put antibiotic ointment on it and bandaged it carefully so dirt would not penetrate it, as the flip-flop shoes he wore invited contaminants that lived in the soil. We instructed Radio to come back to the boat every day so we could watch for infection and put on new dressing. He came out regularly and also brought other villagers who had real or imagined wounds to be looked at. One day Radio told Elmer that a lady named Mary was suffering from a very swollen knee and asked if he could and look at it. Elmer went ashore with his liniment to see what he could do. As he worked on the knee, her friends looked on admiringly, chatting and laughing throughout the entire experience. Elmer and I enjoyed this interchange very much, as the people were childlike, vying for his attention. The day we left, the deck of the boat was filled with sad faces of the people that came to say goodbye.

Our visa was running out of time, so we made our way to Gizo to check out of the country. Gizo was one of the few places that had supplies for tourists. Besides being a port of entry, it also supplied diesel, fresh water, and many different kinds of food, including fresh meat. Although the town was unkempt, and the buildings were in disrepair, it had a certain charm. The buildings were built for the people during the Second World War and there were several vestiges of the war still apparent. After filling our tanks with fuel and water, we set out for Bougainville, an island that was still part of the Solomon chain, but restructured after the war to become part of Papua New Guinea.

Bill Jones, from *Zephyr*, who we had met in Polynesia, had found employment at the copper mine in Bougainville and we planned to meet him there at the port of entry. We had not seen Bill since he left us in New Zealand. Our friend Marcie, who had been his wife, had left the boat, deciding she could no longer tolerate the difficult life of sailing. When his divorce was final, Bill married Ginny, an Australian girl who worked at the mine. When we met Bill on the beach, we had many tales to catch up on as our travels had taken us different routes.

Bill introduced us to his co-workers who formed a real community of sailors from around the world. They were living in the town of Panguna, built to house the people who worked in the mine. There were two types of paid workers. The white people of Panguna who were on the gold roll, and the black people from New Guinea who were on what they called the silver roll. The silver roll was paid much less for the same work than the gold roll, which caused a big rift between the working people.

The group welcomed us and we became part of the group's social circle. One couple, Jeff and Pat Tite, were building their own sailboat. It was a hefty steel hulled sailor that they planned to use when Jeff left the mine. We had only installed a hand crank anchor windless on *Elysium*. When Elmer saw Jeff's beautiful hydraulic windless, he said he wished we had installed one on our boat.

"Take mine and order me another one from New Zealand," Jeff offered.

"That sounds like a great deal to me," Elmer accepted.

Now we had the windless and planned to install it when we arrived in the Philippines.

After touring the mine and spending time enjoying the social life on the island, we were getting ready to sail on. Jeff asked us if we would consider taking Pat and him along with us to get a taste of sailing. We agreed and prepared *Elysium* for two guests as we readied to leave. We had replaced some rusty pipes on the hydraulic system and replaced the entire gunk-filled fuel filters. The autopilot and the Sat-Nav were not working so they were shipped out again and would be returned to us when we reached Madang. We were ready to sail toward Rabaul, still continuing in the islands of the Solomon Island Chain.

For the first days of the sail, we were in waters protected by the islands so the seas were quite calm. We had taken the precaution of giving Jeff a scopolamine patch to keep him from getting seasick. On the third day he said, "I don't need this thing. I'm not feeling seasick at all." We cautioned him that we would be in much rougher seas, but he chose to go without the patch. When we left our anchorage, we hit a very rough patch of sea with a squirrelly wind that jerked us around a great deal. I had just gone below to cook dinner and when I came up the hatch and saw that Jeff was the same color as the yellow slicker he had on. He dashed past me over to the side of the boat and wretched miserably, finishing with the horrible dry heaves. I went over to help him straighten up and to mop his brow a bit. When I saw his face, it had changed grotesquely.

"What has happened to you?" I asked in disbelief.

"I lost all my teeth overboard just now" he told me miserably.

Jeff was only forty-six so I had never thought that he could have dentures. We were still several days out of Rabaul. "What in the world will I feed him?" I thought to myself.

The next days were difficult for all of us. Finding soft food for Jeff in our stores was difficult and his gums grew sores. We were very glad to enter the anchorage in Rabaul, New Britain. We had a map and had to be careful anchoring because of all of the sunken ships on the bay floor that could foul our anchor. The area was inside of an old caldera of a volcano that provided us with total protection from the wind. Jeff and Pat were off *Elysium* as quickly as possible and on a plane headed back to Bougainville. Both of them decided that they would put the hull that Jeff had worked so hard on up for sale, as the trip had shown them that sailing was not as comfortable or easy as it had appeared to be.

We went ashore to explore Rabaul and found a huge market with everything one could want–vegetables, fish and meat. We also toured the caves that Rabaul was famous for. The Japanese had built a huge underground system during the WWII. We found the caves very claustrophobic, as we could not even stand up straight in them. We tried to imagine being down in the dark caves with bombs falling everywhere. Rabaul was the area that endured the most bombing of all the islands during the war.

The next morning the water around *Elysium* was all grey and strange looking. I dipped down a bucket to see what it was and found the entire anchorage was filled with pumice! We knew that Rabaul was built on an active volcano but did not realize that it was this active. We decided to leave the next day. Rabaul remained the capital with a large population until it was later destroyed completely by the volcano. Not a place for us, we decided.

We sailed on, stopping at the small islands along the way to spend the night and then to set sail the next morning. On Put Put Island we were able to tie up to a long dock. Just as we were getting all of our gear situated a young man ran up to the boat. "You must come with me," he panted, urgently. At a near run, we followed him down the small palm-lined dirt road for over a mile. Soon we came to a small grass hut where the young man hurried up to the door. He brought out a tiny white-haired woman who peered up at us with obvious delight. The young man told us that she was the oldest woman on the islands and wanted to meet the people who had sailed the big boat up to the dock. The young man had seen our American Flag and told her that we had come from the other side of the world. She reached out to touch us with her tiny withered hand. It was an unforgettable experience for both of us. Walking back to *Elysium*, we thought about what the woman's life had been like, living all her years on this tiny island. The young man had told us she was over one hundred years old and looking at her tiny, frail body we could believe that it was true.

One particularly beautiful place was Garove Island. It was another caldera of a volcano, but so tranquil that the reflection of the lush greenery lining the shore made a perfect picture on the water. A young boy came by to take us snorkeling and to show us where a Japanese submarine was still sitting on the bottom nearby. The tiny submarine was lined with copper and still in good shape. It had become a tourist attraction for the people of the island who enjoyed diving for old war mementos. We stayed a day enjoying the beauty of this island and the colorful Catholic mission that was located on it.

From Garove, we would head for the big island of New Guinea. We set out midday with blue skies, a light wind, and bright sunshine, heading over to anchor at an island that had a big cinder cone, looking for fresh water. Suddenly, when we were about ten miles away, the cone belched smoke and erupted high into the sky. As we sailed by, a fierce storm hit us, brought on by the explosive heat of the volcano. The clear blue sky turned dark and a strong wind developed, bringing with it torrential rain. We sailed on to Madang on the big island to provision and prepare *Elysium* for our next journey to the Philippines, where we were told there would be pirates. We wondered how we would know a pirate from anyone else.

Papua New Guinea

Nothing great is ever achieved without enthusiasm.

– Emerson

NEAR THE END of October we arrived in Madang, which is located on the southern side of large island of New Guinea. It was a safe and secure harbor so it drew many sailboats to anchor there and it was an excellent place to gather information about cruising. We met Rod and Barbara Noble, an Australian couple, who were stationed there as political emissaries. They planned to cruise in their yacht, *Talio*, when their tour of duty ended the next year. They lived in a comfortable little house that faced a small, protected seashore spot called Nagada. They invited us to come and anchor in front of their dock and use their shower and laundry facilities. As we stayed with this couple we enjoyed all of the amenities of home. The natives came by every day with fresh papaya, pineapple and other fruits charging a very small fee and we could walk to a nearby market for other food. Barbara had several refrigerators so she allowed me to store some perishables there.

After becoming acquainted with this great couple, they asked us if we would like to ride in their car to the highlands since Rod would be traveling through that area on business. He suggested that we stay in Mt. Hagen for the time that they were gone and then on the way back they would pick us up. This would give us ample time to explore the highlands and see the local handwork. We immediately agreed, delighted to have the opportunity to travel on land because sailors usually had no opportunity to leave the coastline. We had good friends anchored nearby *Elysium*, so we were able to leave her in their care while we traveled. We packed our backpacks with hiking gear and set out together on this new adventure with great enthusiasm.

When we reached Mt. Hagen we were amazed to find barbwire surrounding the hotels and churches, and men with machine guns guarded the entrances. The Baptist Church was the only place that was open and welcoming, so we stopped to see if there was a guesthouse we could rent. We knocked on the parish door and a lovely, gray-haired woman opened it saying, "Come on in." The little home was filled with artifacts from many countries, the floor was covered with a big zebra skin and pictures of native people covered the walls. We asked her where she had been stationed recently and she told us she had come from Assam. I told her my friend in Portland had been stationed there and wondered if she possibly could have known her. "Yes, indeed, I knew Dorothy very well!" she exclaimed. Imagine meeting someone in this far away place who knew someone we did! The common friendship promoted a warm feeling between us so we sat and enjoyed chatting together for several hours. Our new friend told us that we could rent the guesthouse for six dollars a day. A kitchen was provided so we could cook our own meals, an ideal situation for us because we enjoyed cooking local food.

We walked into the town and found the Mt. Hagen Market, filled with a complete selection of fresh fruit, vegetables, frozen kangaroo meat, and local handcrafts. The patrons were dressed with startling variety, some in western clothes and others in the local "ass grass," literally, grass that covered the behind and tied with a string in front. The bright string bilums or woven bags covered their hair and also carried babies, pigs or firewood. The market covered at least five acres and was filled with people who had traveled from many of the provinces to bring their produce and handicrafts and to trade for goods. It was a bustling hub of humanity. I stopped at one place where a lady had a heap of brilliant white cauliflower, bright orange carrots and many types of greens. "Where do you come from?" she asked in perfect English. We told her that we had sailed in our boat from the United States. She was extremely interested in every detail and asked many questions. Her name was Martha and she asked us to come see her again when we came to the market. We bought a bilum and filled it with vegetables and fruit. It was an amazing carrier as it kept expanding and accommodated everything we put into it.

The next day we decided to explore the area visible to us further down the mountain. There was a flatbed truck with an orange tarp over it that served as a bus, so we followed some local people onto it to go exploring. Outside the city, the flora turned into thick rainforest with small dirt roads branching out in many directions. We jumped down off of the bus at a stop and began our hike down one of the unmarked paths. As we were admiring the beauty of the lush forest, two men rushed down the path from above us. "What are you doing here?" they demanded. "It is not safe for strangers to be in this area. Someone has been killed and there is a council meeting now in the village at the top of the hill. You could be used as a payback." We didn't know what they meant, but we took their advice and went back with them to catch the bus to town.

When we went to the market the next day we asked Martha what a "payback" was and explained about our experience in the forest. "You must never go there without someone local to guide you. I have a nephew who will take you to see the local areas and he will know where there is a safe place to take you," she said sternly. "The payback is when the elders decide who must pay for the life that has been taken recently and the family could have abducted you to use instead of one of their members. This is a very serious situation here in our area so you must be aware of what is happening at all times," she said earnestly. She called out to a group of boys standing nearby. "This is Douglas, and his friends Lenney and Richard. They will take you to see some of the villages," she offered.

I invited the boys to come to our cabin at the Baptist mission before we went for our tour. They were very pleased to be invited and ate the kangaroo and vegetable stew I fixed with great pleasure. The three of them spoke English as they had attended school at the Baptist mission. They were filled with questions about the United States and where we had traveled. It was hard for them to imagine the many years at sea we had experienced and the many people and languages used in the places we had visited. After the meal Douglas said to me, "I know you are very unlike other people that have visited here because we have never entered a white person's house before. Other white people are afraid of us" he confided. We decided he must be correct, as the barb wire and machine gun guards suggested that people visiting felt danger in this area.

We all set off on a tour to the village where a relative of Douglas' lived. We called Richard by the name of Muscle, because that was printed on his faded red sweatshirt and it pleased him. We saw the beautiful, finely-woven grass huts in the village and were able to find his relative at home. The native man showed us the inside of his home and a bow and arrow that he had just finished making. There were the most amazing-looking pigs everywhere; their large tusks curved up over the top of their snouts. When I mentioned these to Douglas, he took me to the woman's house where the woman cared for the piglets along with their own children. The families prized the piglets and if their tusks grew in a circle, it was a sign of wealth and was worn as a bracelet. He told us that one of his relative's neighbors had just had a pig die. The neighbor was trying to decide which family's spirit had been responsible for the death. We learned about the spiritualistic religion that these people practice. It is their belief that unpleasant things are either caused by the displeasure of someone or a voodoo type of spell, bringing illness or death to an animal or individual.

We spent every day of the next week with our three young friends, eating together and visiting Martha and her family. We hiked high up into beautiful spots where brightly colored birds made musical sounds that echoed in the forest. We were able to spot a tree kangaroo running along the branches of a tree. Douglas said that these animals were highly prized for their fur and because of this they were very wary of people. Later, at the market, we noticed many hats made from the soft and lustrous kangaroo fur.

Helen with Douglas and friends on a tour of the village

The four of us spent a lot of time in worldly discussion. Douglas was exceptionally bright and very interested in technology and geography. He and Elmer were discussing what had happened in New Guinea during World War II, when he mentioned that the Japanese were making a movie about the Kakota Trail they used during the war.

"They are hiring local people to be in the movie right now," he said.

"Are you boys going to be in the movie?" I asked.

"Oh no! If they put a red mark by your name you have to die," Douglas exclaimed.

They all looked very serious and nodded their heads.

"Douglas! You don't really die in the movie. You just pretend to," I said emphatically.

The three of them looked shocked.

"You Americans are certainly tricky," he said.

In my mind I pictured these boys watching a violent American movie and thinking about all the people that were being killed and wondered how many other people thought the same thing. That is the culture of New Guinea: death is not unusual there.

When the time came for Rod to pick us up, we had become such fast friends with these boys that they were like our family. As we packed the car with the artifacts we had purchased and the food we were taking back to the boat, I hugged each boy and placed a kiss on each cheek. They had been so good to us, arriving to take us sightseeing every day, and we felt so grateful to have learned so much about the culture and the life in the highlands. Douglas looked at me and said with great sadness, "Now I know that you are my true mother." After leaving New Guinea, I received letters from him for a long time, begging us to let him come live with us. I pictured how difficult it would be for him to adapt to life on the boat and I knew it was impossible, but we remained very close friends for many years.

When we returned to *Elysium* anchored at Nagada, we were just unloading and getting things in place when Rod rowed out to tell us that the *Melanesian Discoverer* was about to leave for a trip up the Sepic River. The owners were friends of Rod and Barbara and had just come to tell them they had one berth that was not filled. They asked if Rod wanted to go with them for a very low price, but he could not go and instead came out to see if we were interested. The Sepic River has the largest flow of all the rivers in the world. It is a swift flowing river that winds snakelike down from the mountains into the sea near Wewak. The area is known for the most creative carvings and cultural treasures in all of the area. We would never be able to navigate *Elysium* up into the area so we were extremely eager to take part in the tour.

Rod and Barbara employed a native lady, Dumop, to clean and take care of their house. We hired Dumop to care for *Elysium* because we would be gone for an undetermined time and she needed some care. She was happy to stay aboard and clean everything, so Rod drove us down to the dock where the *Discoverer* was berthed. She was an old Island Trader that an enterprising couple renovated to make eighteen berths, each with toilet facilities and comfortable bunks. We jumped aboard just as they were getting ready to leave for the tour.

We had not been around Americans for several years so we were excited to meet the people signed up for the tour. They were from different parts of the United States and were interested in meeting people who had traveled to New Guinea by boat. One man knew a lot about rivers and told us about what was transpiring as we worked our way up the water flow and into the immense grassland reserve. There were giant grass islands that had been ripped free from the shoreline by the swiftly flowing river and were headed downstream, where they would eventually reattach to land. The entire river washes out to sea with such force that no delta forms at the mouth. It is said that people can constantly find fresh water, miles out from shore.

We enjoyed the luxury of having meals served to us and conversing with English-speaking people. The ship stopped at each available spot to observe the culture of the people. We saw the men's house, or Haus Tambaran, where the spirits live. This building is where the men go to contemplate life and carve the large canoes with crocodile bodies and heads. Each pillar of the building is an ancient carving of an ancestor, intricately fashioned from dark hardwood. We were able to enjoy visiting the huge building during a meeting as they accepted the visiting tourists. The front had a log that was notched out for a ladder and was made so it could be pulled up if a visitor was not invited. While we were visiting one meeting house, there was a musician playing a long, native horn that reached down to the ground. Another man, laden with heavy recording equipment, was transcribing the sounds made by the horn and the people imitating birds. This was not part of our tour but it was very interesting for us to hear.

The ship stopped at one village that was built entirely on the water, so we anchored nearby. We had a local native man, James, crewing aboard who explained the culture of every village. We became friends with this native New Guinean man and learned about the culture we might otherwise have missed completely. The village was built on water in order to avoid the hordes of mosquitoes that swarmed hungrily over each person as they arrived on land. Here there were none. There were pigs, dogs and children swimming out to greet us. As Elmer and I stood on the little motorboat that had brought us to the village, a young man rowed up on a long, flat, plank-like dugout. He walked easily across the boat and asked Elmer if he could take me for a ride. Elmer nodded enthusiastically, but I was a bit uneasy balancing on the flat surface of the boat. However, it was a great experience to ride over and meet the people in the stilted houses. I knew I could swim if I were clumsy enough to fall overboard. The young man then took me back to where he had picked me up and thanked Elmer and left. Why I was chosen to have this experience out of all the people there was a mystery, but I was very pleased to have the opportunity.

The next village had a long, log-walkway to traverse across to the land. The area was lush and green with beautiful woven houses lining the river. Each house was woven from different colored grasses and housed several families who gathered out in front to offer carvings and weavings for sale. We only had backpacks so we could not buy large items. I bought a pig woven from the heavy twine made from trees that grew there and a mask built on a turtle shell. The masks and carvings that were for sale were incredibly well done with features just like the people who lived there. It was fortunate that I had little room because it would have been tempting to buy many items.

In the next village we visited, the men had covered their bodies in brightly colored paint, grass and feathers. They had woven seashells into coverings for their genitals and the costumes were amazing to behold. The intricately carved instruments they wielded must have been passed down for several generations. They danced for us and performed some native rituals that brought laughs and shrieks of joy from the children who watched.

We arrived at area where a small plane was to pick up the tour passengers and take them back to their departure point in Madang. Unfortunately, there had been a torrential rain in this area for several days and the landing strip was soaked and muddy, making the landing impossible. We were told we would have to wait several days for it to dry out before the plane could land. The tourists were extremely upset with this change in plans. They had tickets that had to be used, people they needed to meet and plans that had to be carried out. We were so used to being flexible that the distress of the tourists was amazing to us. Instead of relaxing and enjoying the extra time, they were nervous, pacing the deck with obvious disgust. We talked with our friend, James, who told us it would be an interesting adventure for us to take a local boat down the river and go cross-country back to Wewak. He said that the owner of the dugout was a friend of his and that he would arrange for us to have a ride back to the coast. The owners of the cruise told us it would be extremely dangerous to try to return this way because most of the country was swampland and there was no good route except for the river. Now we had to decide whether to take our good friend James' information or stay with the ship. When we met his friend with the dugout we decided to take a chance and go with him. We could see that the tour passengers were certain we had signed our death warrant as we jumped aboard the dugout filled with the native passengers.

The man in the dugout was traveling to the coffee plantations where he would buy coffee to take downriver for trade. Our plan was to go with them to a place where we would meet a truck that would take us to an area where we could get a bus to Wewak. As we paddled down the swiftly flowing river, the man steering the dugout suddenly veered the dugout over to a plank landing. The inhabitants stepped out onto the planks and motioned for us to follow them. We were a bit hesitant as this was not part of what we understood to be the plan. Perhaps they were going to kill us after all. We followed them into the jungle and then came to an opening where the ground was covered with huge, dark-green watermelon growing on the ground. "You take one," our guide told us. So we gathered up one of the huge melons and followed everyone back to the dugout. We cut it open and we all feasted on the bright-red, juicy flesh. We then continued down to the place where we were supposed to meet the truck. We walked down through the jungle on a well used path to a screened-in council house. We entered and sat down to wait and see what would happen next. We did not know where we were and there was not a living soul around. Several hours went by and darkness was descending, so we arranged our backpacks so we could lie down on a table, wondering how we were going to find our way out of this deserted area. About ten o'clock in the evening someone came in and woke us up, a small jeep pick-up or, Ute, as they call them, was parked outside. They helped us up into the back to get seated first

Meetinghouse – Sepic Haus Tamberan

and then the long line of twenty people who were waiting climbed in to fill the entire space left. There were three men inside driving and drinking beer. As we looked through the back window, we could see where the headlights shone on thick brush and tall grass. We could not discern that there was a road at all. One of the men sitting with us in the truck knew the owner of the dugout and James. He told us that we were going to the coffee plantation where he worked and we would spend the rest of the night in his hut when we arrived.

After several hours of very rough driving, we arrived at the clearing where the people lived, and were shown to a very small room that had a makeshift bed on the floor. The people of New Guinea sleep on mats, which they pullout into the sun during the daytime. This room had been supplied with a piece of cloth-covered foam rubber, which had not been cared for. The room was extremely hot, over eighty-seven degrees, with no ventilation and the sweat stained bed had evidently been in use for a long time. We both laid down on the single piece of foam and fell immediately asleep. When one of us turned over, the stench that rose up between us was dreadful. We were grateful, however, to have our keeper sitting right outside of the door, as there was a lot of drinking and a loud party going on outside.

In the morning our benefactor came in and told us that his friend was ready to take us to the place where we could catch the bus to Wewak. I asked if we could use the bathroom. He showed me to a room that had a toilet, but I noticed when I used it that it was not hooked up and the contents only seeped slowly into the ground underneath. At any rate, all of our needs had been met and we were grateful to have had the protection that had been given to us.

The friend who came to the plantation greeted us in English and said he would walk through the bush with us to the place to catch the bus. He had been a police officer at one time, before returning to work on the coffee plantation. He told us that growing coffee was very good for the area and that they were able to sell it for a good price. We saw the large flatbed truck that served as a bus come to a stop to pick us up. It had some benches on the back and was covered with corrugated iron on posts. We asked the driver, in the presence of the man who had come with us, how much money it would be to get to Wewak. He told us the amount and we got out that much money with the help of our officer-guide. The vehicle was empty until the next stop, where we were joined by people with huge bags of peanuts, pigs and other items that were going to be sold in the capital, Wewak. We stopped at many times until the bus was extremely crowded and we were pressed tightly into a corner. We rode for a long time before the bus suddenly stopped and the driver asked for the fare. He asked for a much larger sum than we had been told, but we just smiled and handed him what he had originally asked for. All of the people stared at us as the man demanded that we pay him more. We just smiled and pretended we did not understand what he wanted. Finally, he gave up in disgust at our obvious stupidity and drove us on through the jungle until we arrived at Wewak. We were very fortunate that he did not throw us off the bus, as it was a long way into town.

We found a very nice motel in Wewak and immediately dashed into the large shower for a long soak. We had not been able to wash for many days and I don't believe I have ever enjoyed a shower and slipping into the fresh clean sheets in a bed as much as I did that evening.

The next morning we were famished, as we had not eaten for an entire day. We went into the little restaurant and ordered a huge breakfast. Next to us was the man we had seen recording the native music up the Sepic River. We went over to ask him how he had been able to record the sacred music. He told us he was a composer from England and had asked the governor if he could catalog the music of Papua New Guinea. He promised them that if they would give him a letter of introduction to each village with a request to allow him to record the ritual music, he would give a copy to the New Guinea National Library. The sacred ritual music is never played for anyone but the men in the village and had never been recorded before. He was also going to use it for what he called "Sounds of the South Pacific." I mentioned that I had a similar recording that someone had made in Africa, called "African Sanctus." He said that was also his composition. We had a great time listening to stories about the places he had been.

We learned that there would be a ship leaving the next morning at 9:00 a.m. for Madang. This would be the only passage available until the next week. We arrived at the wharf at 6:00 a.m. and scrambled aboard as soon as the wire gate opened to allow us passage onto the ramp. When it was completely filled up at 7:45 a.m., the crew cast off and we left the pier. We had been very fortunate to arrive early or we would have been in Wewak for another week. The inside had double bunks filled with people who were resting for the trip; we found a bunk and lay down for the trip to Madang. When the man came for the ticket, we told him that we had sailed a boat from the United States to arrive here. He told the captain and we were requested to join him at the helm. We were able to see the coastline and watch him navigate the rest of the way to Madang. It was a great trip and we enjoyed the conversation with the captain very much. We were very glad to arrive back home on *Elysium* and were thrilled with our unique adventure.

Rod, Barbara, and several other friends were planning to leave in a few weeks for the Philippines. We planned to sail with them, stopping first in the Hermit Islands, located about four hundred and fifty miles north of Madang. These islands are part of New Guinea, but very isolated, so we decided it would be a very interesting rest stop. We did a lot of provisioning and finally received our repaired autopilot and Sat-Nav. We heard from George that our friend, Harold Eilts, who had built his boat at the same time as we built *Elysium*, wanted his son, Scott, to join us for the trip. We told them that we would be leaving soon so we would meet him at the airport in one week. Scott arrived on the 31st of December, so we all celebrated the New Year and our upcoming trip together and decided on a good time to leave. We had met many people stationed in New Guinea, including the missionaries from Ukaraumpa. They all came down to have a final meal on the boat and say goodbye. Goodbyes were always both a happy and sad part of our life.

Scott told us he would clean the bottom of the boat, which left us free to check out of New Guinea. We filled the boat with ice and all the succulent fruits and fresh vegetables that we could hold. We sailed out on January 18th with several friends motoring out to see us off. The weather was very good and we would have a short trip to Bagabag Island for an overnight stop. The three yachts sailing with us had not been out to sea before and they relished short hops to get their sea legs before making the long stretch to the Hermit Islands. We stayed another day to make sure we would have fine weather and to have a chance to snorkel along the apricot colored soft coral in the beautiful clear water. The reef was alive with brilliant blue and black reef fish. Scott made a spear and brought us some fish for dinner.

We left Bagabag to motor sail in bright sunshine to the Island of Karkar where there was an old German Plantation that had been given to the Australians. John and Anna lived there and invited us in for dinner and cold drinks. The day was blustery and it was not a good anchorage for us. Scott swam along the reef and caught a few more fish. We elected to leave in the evening as the wind had calmed for good sailing, stopping at Laing Island at 10:00 a.m. the next morning. We enjoyed a restful sleep before going ashore to see the Belgium Biological Station, which had a lush forest with brush turkeys and flying foxes filling the branches of the trees. We took off again for the two-day trip to the Hermit Islands. We followed Rod and Barbara on *Talio* for a while and noticed an oil slick on the water. We called them and told them that they were leaking diesel. Rod said he knew he was losing a small amount, but thought it just coming from his bilge and was no problem.

Sailing north, the wind was on the nose with a strong eastern current against us. Scott was seasick and quite miserable, not eating or taking an interest, even when we went through a large pod of humpback whales. One whale came right up to the boat and looked us over. Finally, turning on the motor we sailed thirty degrees off the wind to move the boat ahead five knots and were able to catch a big Wahoo just as we arrived at the Hermit Island Atoll. Sleep came to us quickly, although the anchor chain rumbled noisily over the coral.

Visitors from Hermit Island

Our friends were very tired when they arrived and wanted to rest for the remainder of the day. When we returned to *Elysium* there were three native boys, one of whom had a very bad infection in the lymph gland in his groin. I knew that this was a dangerous infection but I did not dare give him penicillin because of the possibility of allergy, so I gave him tetracycline, as it was a much safer antibiotic to use. I told him to apply heat to the swelling and take the pills that I doled out to him in separate packages. I hoped that he would survive this infection and that it had not advanced too far for the antibiotic cure it.

The next morning we were awakened by loud shouts at the stern of the boat. As I looked out, I saw a deer swimming furiously toward the boat with swimmers close behind brandishing clubs. As I watched, the water became red with blood as they bludgeoned the terrified animal to death. The whole thing left me feeling a bit ill.

The next morning we met a group of local natives who were cutting copra. One lady had a small fawn that she planned to keep for a pet. The group offered us the leg of a deer for meat and we accepted it with smiles and thanks. We took it aboard, cooked it in the pressure cooker for a deer stew and invited the crew of the other yachts to join us. We had asked the group where the fresh water was and they pointed to an area uphill from where we were. After a short search we found the spring shooting out of a length of bamboo and gratefully filled our water jugs. We bathed in the fresh sweet water and planned to come back and do a washing later in the day. Just as we boarded *Elysium*, a small native, gaff-rigged sailboat came by. The native man introduced himself as Namu and welcomed us to the Island group. He invited Scott and Elmer to go sailing with him. When they were gone I took the dingy ashore and met Helena and Rose, two women who live in the little hut there. I gave them some dresses I brought from Madang, which delighted them.

When I returned to *Elysium*, a man named Noah brought me some more deer meat. I cut it in strips and made jerky so it would not have to be refrigerated. He also brought a huge coconut crab and killed it on the deck of the boat. The meat of the huge crab tastes like coconut and was a delicious treat. We also cut some small palm trees with Noah's permission and ate the tender hearts of palm for a salad. This island provided wonderful meals for us.

Early the next afternoon, a native woman brought a very sick young girl named Aldine to us. I took her temperature and gave her Tylenol. I sent another three for her to take hoping it was not something serious and that she would recover before we left. No one had visited the island for over a year and during that time they had received no medical help. Fortunately, all the medical treatments we used to help them were successful. The young man that Namu brought out with the infection had recovered completely in a few days. I think the fact that they believed we could help them worked miracles. The next patient was a woman with a severe swollen, bright red machete slash on her leg. I applied packs of a drawing liquid called Domboro to her leg for several hours and she recovered nicely. We also left some of our medical supplies with them to treat things that could come up, instructing Namu on how to use them. We carried a very large medical kit and we could easily share band-aids, iodine, Tylenol, and salves.

We met a woman named Nem who invited us to hike up to the garden with them. It was a very steep climb and the view of the sparkling, turquoise sea and the island-causeway below was breathtaking. Nem showed us how the children rubbed the flowers together to keep the plants producing. She said that they had bees at one time, but they all disappeared in a storm. It was incredible, that they had figured out that they needed to pollinate the plants when the bees were gone. Nem said that they once had tomatoes, but they had lost the seed.

The people in the village wanted us to take them for a sail so we loaded twenty-one people on board and sailed for two hours in a fifteen knot wind. We stopped at an outer reef where two boys took the dingy and collected sea-gull eggs for us for breakfast. They were a bit fishy tasting but we enjoyed the color of the very bright yellow yolks filled with lots of vitamins. One of the boys gave me an alligator tooth he had around his neck as a gift.

We were listening to the radio when we heard that typhoon Judy had crossed just above us along the track we would have taken to Koror, Palau. The ham radio was not picking up a signal as we seemed to be in a depressed area. We were making plans to leave but Rod and Barbara, on *Talio*, had lost their entire supply of diesel and could not go any further. We tried by radio to see if a supply boat would take diesel to them as we didn't want to leave them without supplies.

In the morning I made a large batch of cinnamon rolls and invited everyone aboard for tea and rolls. Barbara and Rod could not believe I could make them in this isolated spot. We had a grain grinder aboard so I could grind the wheat, and with yeast, honey, raisins and cinnamon, they were delicious and everyone enjoyed the treat. The natives brought paw paw, squash, guava and a big stalk of bananas for us. We were still trying to find out about the supply boat for *Talio*, as we wanted to be sailing on to Palau while the weather was good.

When we finally received a radio contact, we heard that our friends on *Innocent Bystander* were sunk at anchor in the Gulf of Oman. They were between ships that had been firing at each other and had taken a direct hit. They dove off their yacht and swam to the safety of another yacht there. When we were together in Australia, we had planned at one time to sail with them up into that area and then changed our minds. It was a real shock to hear about their loss. We did speak to George and found that he had sent some of our supplies to Palau. Two Australian yachts, *Senang* and *Bon Temps*, carrying friends of Rod and Barbara's, were now anchored at the island. They had been in contact with a supply ship that would bring diesel to them, giving us an opportunity to leave. We said goodbye to our friends on the island where we had lived a month, and Namu sailed his boat with us out of the harbor to wave goodbye until we were out of sight.

We sailed north in light winds and crossed the equator the next morning. That afternoon dark clouds formed very suddenly; the weather looked very threatening. Just as I was taking down the sail, a very dark shaft shot down from the dark cloud into the sea and pulled up a huge dish of water around the bottom. It was a waterspout, which is a tornado at sea. All we could do was watch helplessly as it visibly spun around, not even a mile away from us. If it came in our direction it would strip everything on deck and we would be wrecked. Finally, it began to rise again into the black cloud it had come from and was gone. We breathed a sigh of relief, safe from the danger.

The next morning a sudden, strong wind tore our mainsail across the stitching again. Without this sail we had to use our old, torn sail that had been mended many times and hoped it would hold together until we arrived at Koror. We called back on the radio to see if Rod and Barbara had received fuel yet and we found that the supply boat, called the *Sepic*, had left Madang with fuel for them and would arrive in a few days. That was a relief as we had been hesitant to leave them behind. We slogged along with very little wind, motoring off and on for nine days before we finally spotted some sea birds, a sign that land was near. Late in the evening we saw lights, so we took the sails down to wait, reaching Malakal Harbor in Koror by early morning.

Palau, the Philippines, and India

The proper function of man is to live, not to exist. I shall not waste my
days in trying to prolong them. I shall use my time to live.

– Jack London

WHEN WE LEFT the Hermit Islands we sailed into the American territory of Palau to stock up and see the sights before sailing on to the Philippines, just five hundred miles further. Palau is the farthest west island
of the Micronesian Islands of the Pacific. There are both Melanesian
and Asian people inhabiting the small island of Koror. The Asian influ-
ence is apparent, as it is a busy, bustling town. As soon as we docked in
Malakal Harbor, an American couple came over to say hello. Russ and
Julie Lloyd from the state of Washington spotted our American flag and
were eager to meet us. Russ had been a bush pilot in Alaska when the
President of Palau hired him to as a personal pilot. Russ really loved the
scenic change to these beautiful islands, but Julie experienced "island
fever." She could not adjust to living in a space that was only four or five
miles in length and width. Koror is the only island that is inhabited, and
there was no other place nearby to visit.

Russ and Julie escorted us everywhere on the island by car, sightseeing and helping us gather the available American goods. As we were

preparing to leave, Russ came to the boat and earnestly asked, "Would you consider taking Julie with you to the Philippines. She's very unhappy these days and the depression is beginning to worry me a great deal," he confided. I asked him if she would be willing to leave her two children, Angela and Andrew, and he replied that she was desperate. We told him we would be glad to have her sail with us. The trip would only be five or six days if we had favorable wind behind us. We planned to visit the beautiful Apurashokoru Island and do some diving, so we told him we would return for her in a few days.

When the tide was low, we worked our way through the reefs in the Rock Islands and found a perfect isolated spot in the aquamarine waters. To our amazement there were trees up to thirty feet tall covering the limestone islands. The lush growth along the shore was covered with trailing orchids and cup shaped flowers that drew insects into their bowls of nectar. The completely surrounded bay formed by the islands contained pristinely clear water, filled with a wealth of marine reef fish nurseries around each outcropping. Scattered along the bottom of the bay were many of the largest bivalve in the world, the tridactna, also known as the giant clam. These huge clams have dinoflagalates lining the mantle of their mouth reflecting deep blues and greens so that the algae can photosynthesize and provide food for the clam. The land locked lake was a diver's paradise, with no sharks inside. We had to carefully gauge the tides when we left so as not to become a permanent visitor!

Returning to Koror on March 22, 1986, we found Julie was ready to come aboard for her sail with us to the Philippines. Immediately upon leaving the protection of the reef, the sea became extremely rough with a thirty-knot wind behind us. Julie said to us as we sailed out, "Please take me back. I had no idea it would be so rough out here." Unfortunately we were sailing away from the island and going back would have taken all-day or longer and been much rougher on everyone. I told her that she would get her sea legs eventually, but unfortunately she never did. She lay on the chaise lounge and vomited onto the deck for the five days it took to enter the protection of the Philippines. She lost ten pounds during that time, which was pleasing to her when we were in calmer water.

Before leaving Australia we had read a frightening article in a sailing magazine that was written by a Swedish sailor who was traveling in the waters of the Philippines. This story was printed again in our notes to sailboats, reporting areas that could be dangerous to sailors. The warning concerned a French boat anchored in Palawan, the farthest island in the Philippines. A speedboat with several men aboard approached Pier Tangvald and his wife while they were anchored there to escape a storm in the South China Sea. His wife stayed in the hatch and held a gun on the men as they came alongside their boat. When they spotted her they shot and killed her and then turned the gun Pier as he stood at the helm with his young son holding onto his knees crying in terror. When these men looked down at the small boy they turned their boat around and left. This warning traveled the sailing circuit and quickly spread to all sailors planning to sail near the area. As with any circumstance like this, news quickly spread to all of the sailing yachts.

Elmer had spoken to a sailor who had left the area recently. He said we could enter safely through the Hinatuan Passage, north of Mindanao and south of the smaller island of Bucas Grande. He gave us compass headings for the passage and told us to be extremely cautious because of the vast number of coral outcroppings. We started in with good sunlight and were confident we would see where the channel led us. As we sailed near the island, there were fishing boats with men onboard wearing white hoods covering their heads. They looked very threatening to us, but we leaned out and waved to them and they all waved back in a friendly manner. We learned later that they take white tee shirts and cut out holes for their eyes to protect themselves from the sun, making them look like bandits. As we neared the most difficult spot, the sun went behind a cloud and *Elysium* went hard aground on the coral. We watched helplessly as the tide rushed past us leaving us in a foot of water. *Elysium* lay over forty-five degrees on the coral, hard aground so we couldn't do anything thing until the tide came back in. Because the high tide was not due until late at night, Elmer decided it was time for a nap on the lounge. Several small boats came by to offer us fish or coconuts to drink! Later we learned that a recent drought had diminished the supply of coconuts, so their gift was even more appreciated.

The channel was barely visible and quite narrow so we hoped that a full moon would give us the ability to navigate through the heavy coral. A young man came by in a small dugout and told us his name was Maximo Cudillo from Surigao City. He said the tide would change late at night, and that he would return when it was dark to guide us through the channel. We gave him a small sail from our dingy for his boat, because the one he had was very tattered and was made from the plastic sacking in which rice is shipped. He was pleased to have the sail and hanked it onto his mast and sailed easily away with the light breeze.

Stuck on the coral

When the tide rose it became very dark and clouds covered the moon. Elmer couldn't see anything in the water and wondered if we would be able to navigate the small channel, even with a compass course. When we were becoming more concerned, Maximo returned. He came aboard and told Elmer exactly where he had to motor to follow the channel. He carefully pointed either left or right, steering for five hours, and finally told us we could drop the anchor. We were in seventy feet of water so we did as he directed. How he was able to navigate us through that coral reef was a complete mystery to us. We could see nothing in the blackness of that night. He said he needed to go home and accepted our deepest gratitude. We never saw him again and I believe that he was an angel sent to help us.

Maximo, our night guide

When morning dawned we found we were anchored safely at Talavera Island in front of a big village. Soon a small dug-out with Cenon and his family came out to greet us. Cenon was from the United States and had returned to the island to build a church for his mother. We invited him and his friends to come out and have pancakes with us to celebrate our safe arrival. There were thirty people from the island eating with us and many of them spoke excellent English, as they often traveled to other countries. We truly enjoyed the company of these friendly people. Cenon told us that we would still have to follow a channel to get through the coral ahead, but that the sunshine would allow us to see any dangers.

The morning was cloudy and Elmer again had difficulty seeing the channel from the ratlines. We were just getting ready to leave when Cenon came out in a motorboat. " I will lead you out safely," he promised. This was an enormous relief, not to have to weave through the coral again. We noted that he had a mast on one of the larger boats, but no sail. He told us that they had not been able to make a sail, so we retrieved an extra sail that we thought would fit perfectly on their mast. When Cenon turned to go back, we thanked him and offered him the sail. He was overcome with joy and said that the gift would enable them to go farther out to sea to fish without using the motor on the boat. When we parted we felt great happiness that the exchange had been so favorable for all of us. We cast out any doubt about further problems in the Philippines.

From Talavera we sailed through another narrow pass and anchored at San Jose. That evening we had visits from many fishermen who had spent long days at sea and were glad to be invited aboard for a cookies and tea. They told us it would be safe for us to anchor in Ipul, Mindanao. Mindanao was questionable, but the men told us we would have a safe place there and we did not have to worry. We successfully made the journey through the final part of the narrow Hinatuan Passage with very few navigational aids. Next we stopped in Maasin, Leyte, where we were safe from the perils of the reefs, and could proceed with more speed.

Our next spot was to find Jau Island, where we were informed that we could dock the boat safely and leave *Elysium* if we desired to visit the United States again. We found the area managed by a German man named Heinz. He told us we would be welcome any time and that he had a lagoon that was completely protected by mangrove trees and was typhoon safe. There were several yachts moored there that had been left in his care. We had a good meal at his little resort and stayed a few days to rest.

Julie was anxious to purchase a ticket in Cebu and return to her family. It was an easy trip over to Pooc, Cebu, where we entered the country and were given our visas. Because Julie was a Seventh Day Adventist, she visited the Resurriccion Plaza Seventh Day Adventist Mission and was welcomed royally. When they learned she had arrived by yacht, they all begged to visit the next day. I hurried back to *Elysium* to make her presentable for visitors after our rough passage. The mission had been closed down for the day and at least thirty people came aboard. They were most interested in the yacht and asked questions about every detail of our trip. In return, we were invited to the mission for dinner. We spent several days with these friendly people in Cebu while we waited for a flight for Julie.

It was nearing the end of April and we were eager to visit the United States again to check on the health of Elmer's mother and meet some of our new grandchildren. Within just a few months we were able to get *Elysium* situated at Jau Island and find a flight to Hong Kong where a ham radio friend, Tony Lough, invited us to stay with him. In Hong Kong we could find an inexpensive ticket to the United States, so we stayed with Tony in his beautiful apartment overlooking Deepwater Bay for a month. Tony was a pilot for British Airways and his apartment was vacant when he was away on flights, allowing us to explore wonders of Hong Kong. We bought inexpensive tickets to the United States and visited our family for a few months. When we were about to fly back to *Elysium*, Steve and Anjali told us they were going to visit Anjali's family in India in December and invited us to accompany them for a three-month tour. With *Elysium* in a secure moorage, we felt we could leave her without concern. We returned to Hong Kong to secure our tickets to Delhi and agreed to meet Steve and Anjali.

Traveling in India is unlike visiting anywhere else on earth. With a huge population and different social mores, we enjoyed a completely different lifestyle. We met Anjali's mother in Bogpur. While we were there we visited nearby Dehra Dun where Gordon Taylor had built a children's home in 1945. There were three hundred and eighty children from homes whose parents were lepers. The home allowed the parents to see their children once a year and the children were not put up for adoption. These children would have otherwise been begging on the streets, so they adjusted easily to the support of the people in the home. While we were visiting, a dentist from Pennsylvania was donating his time repairing children's teeth. Many professional people from the United States supported the work in the home by visiting to ensure the health of the children. We met several boys and girls who had graduated from the home and who had obtained a good education and ability to secure employment.

We visited Anjali's sisters, who were very hospitable, even giving up their bedrooms to honor us. While we were there, we were able to visit many of the ancient buildings that were carved from red sandstone. There was nothing in our experience to compare with these amazing works of art that date back many centuries. These buildings are now falling into disrepair, as India does not have the finances to maintain them. Anjali's brother-in-law was the manager of Radio India in Gorakpur, a village near the Nepal border. We mentioned that we hoped to meet a yogi while we were in India, as we had just read *The Autobiography of a Yogi*. When we were at his radio station, a group of four cars arrived to pick us up. Ravi, the driver, told us they were going to take us out to see a yogi, or a saint as they are called, and they would also broadcast it on the station. We drove through the village honking our horn at men on bicycles and carts full of sugar cane. It seemed that people flowed along the highway like water, filling every void. As we neared the excitement grew. We had to arrive before sunset because it is fabled that the saint entered the river at sundown and would not reappear until sunrise. We stopped at a stand and bought apples and bananas for a donation. When we arrived, the crew set up the taping for the station and Ravi got down and touched the ground with his lips in front of the saint to show his devotion. The saint had long strands of hair that circled his naked body. It was very cold and we were in heavy sweaters, but he sat there showing no sign of discomfort. He blessed us and then passed out many baskets of fruit to everyone who had arrived in the meantime. We brought only one basket of fruit, but when they passed it out, there was fruit for everyone. Radio India taped their broadcast and we experienced something we would never forget. Ravi then told us that his grandfather had been a disciple of this saint back when he was a boy, which would have made the saint over ninety years old.

On Christmas Day we boarded a train to visit Corbett National Park, which is a national tiger reserve located in the foothills of the Himalayas. While on the way, we were told that we probably would not be able to locate accommodations or secure an elephant to ride because the park was an extremely popular retreat for the local people in the Christmas season. We spoke with the taxi driver taking us to the park and luckily he said he would personally arrange lodgings for us. The next morning it was extremely cold, but we woke up early to see what chance we would have to hire an elephant. First we were told that no elephants were available, but after an hour the mahout, the man in charge of the elephants, called to inform us that the people who had hired his elephant were put

Elmer with baby elephant

off by the cold weather and we could go with him. We had a magical ride out into the park in the early morning mist that was rising from the river. As the huge animal tromped out into the tall elephant grass and sal forest we came close to sambar, wild boar, and huge lizards, but we just missed the elusive tiger. We only saw footprints which showed us that he had just recently been there. We crossed a river looking down at crocodiles on the banks from the elephant's back. When we arrived back in the village we passed a tiny baby elephant tied to a tree. Our mahout, Mr. Mahalie, told us that it had been found in the forest and left behind by the herd because it had been injured. This little fellow took a great liking to Elmer, wrapping its trunk around his arm and holding on tightly. Mr. Mahalie invited us to come to his place for Christmas dinner and to meet his family.

His home was only a piece of corrugated iron covering some wooden walls, but inside it was cozy and warm. We were served a sumptuous meal of mutton cutlet, rice and dhal, eating even before his family of twelve children. The experience was a treasured time because Anjali was able to speak the Hindi language, enabling us to communicate with everyone. It was a Christmas dinner to be remembered and we appreciated the effort this family put forth.

After Steve and Anjali left us, we hired a car to travel across India to Jaisalmer, Rajasthan, a walled city of carved stone buildings. We secured a room in a castle that had three balconies where we could look out to see the beautiful sunset over the desert. After a meal we hired two camels from a man named Jasma to take us out into the barren sand-duned desert, where we followed the route that had once been used to trade with Egypt. We rode for four hours to view a deserted city where people had lived two hundred and twenty years ago. There were carved sandstone Jain temples and fantastic structures demonstrating the erosion from the sand storms which left them sinking down in ruins. As we returned, the view of the fort of Jaisalmer high on the desert was a beautiful sight because riding a camel is very uncomfortable and we were relieved to finally set foot on the ground again.

The entire road trip took us over a month. We experienced untenable single lane road conditions and difficulty with chaotic traffic. Everyone drove into any space available. If a vehicle breaks down, it is often left in the road with huge rocks around it to keep cars from crashing into it. When we came upon one of these vehicles we had to pull out into the desert to move around them. There were many very serious accidents on the road, all of which had to be sorted out before we could pass. Once we were stopped by a herd of over five hundred camels that passed across the road in front of us. There were camels pulling carts, returning from delivering a load. The driver sleeps on the cart while the camel finds the way back again, making the road difficult for other vehicles to maneuver. The car and driver we hired did return us safely to the guesthouse in Delhi, for which we were grateful.

In January, 1987, we left Delhi and flew back to Hong Kong for a rest in Tony's beautiful apartment and secured tickets back to the Philippines and *Elysium*. It took us more than a month to accomplish the usual boat chores, removing mold from the ceiling, wiping it down with Clorox, and going over the side. We spent a week removing the growth from the bottom of *Elysium*. We sanded and varnished all of the bright work and restored *Elysium* closer to her original condition. We stayed until July, enjoying the small resort, making trips to Cebu to secure the repair parts and spending time with friends there. We made the trips to Cebu on the small ferryboats that were always packed with people. We always chose a place as close to the open windows as possible because of the many reports of ferries sinking. Most of the Philippino people do not swim well, so many people were lost when these ferries sank. One night as we slept someone was able to steal our backpacks full of repair parts for *Elysium*, plus several packs of books. When the ferry docked at Bohol, we went to the police station to report our loss. Inside the station the entire wall was lined with dead bodies that were covered with blood. We decided we would not press our charges since the police were extremely busy bringing in more of the dead. When the boat came for us from Jau Island we asked Renaldo what had happened, thinking that some sort of war had started and a massacre had ensued. He said that too many people had embarked on a ferry that was bringing large drums of fuel to the island and when heavy weather had struck, all the people hurried to one side of the ferry. This displaced the heavy drums, which then slid over on top of the people, smashing and overturning the boat. It was a horrifying spectacle for us and remained in our consciousness whenever we embarked on a ferry for a trip to the mainland.

When our work was done we sailed over to Liloan, Cebu, where most of the other yachts in the area were anchored. For us, it was a daily celebration with barbecues on the beach and sailboat races as we lounged on the warm sandy beaches. Six times we had to stop our recreation and rush up into Carmen, located on the north side of Cebu, to retreat from a passing typhoon. Carmen has a mud bottom with lots of mangrove trees outside the lagoon, so each time we were able to escape any damage. While we were anchored in Carmen, we became close friends with Oscar and Lorie Pinot. This couple was born in the tiny village and was very helpful to us, offering to watch *Elysium* as we made day trips to visit a friend, Nan, who had contracted cancer. Oscar introduced us to Nardo and Rosalinda Villamor, who were looking for work on a yacht. Usually the people who owned yachts only hired people who had a reference from someone that they had worked for in the past. We hired the couple on Oscar's recommendation and they helped us finish the much needed upkeep on *Elysium*. The going rate of pay for workers in the Philippines was eighty cents U.S. a day. They both worked so diligently that we paid a dollar. We suggested that they take a rest once in a while. Soon *Elysium* was polished from one end to the other, including the bilge. They had four children, three boys and a girl. We found that the boys were able to go to school, but there was no money for the girl, who would likely become a prostitute to support herself if she did not marry. We told Nardo that we would pay her school fees so she could continue her education. We were able to send money for this to Nardo's grandmother for several years until she completed high school.

Nardo and Rosalinda were able to stay onboard while we flew down to Zamboanga, Mindanao. Zamboanga was reported to be a very interesting place, but sailboats were not allowed there because the National People's Army had caused problems in the area. We found an agency that assured us that it would be safe for us to fly there and we would be safe if we stayed at the hotel. When we arrived, we found that we were among just a handful of people staying there. We received royal treatment from the staff and the meals were excellent. We did wander out into an Islam settlement to look at their beautiful handwork, but felt some hostility from the people there so we hurried back to the hotel. Later, we read about some tourists being kidnapped and held for ransom, so we were lucky to be able to have a positive experience.

Zamboanga is located on the southeastern tip of the peninsula near the fabled Sulu Archipelago. It was chartered in 1635, one of the first chartered cities of the country, and an important port since the early days of discovery of the Philippines. From our hotel window we could see the indigenous population of the Sulu Islands living aboard long, thin outrigger canoe-like boats. They are known to sail the shallow waters of the reef that no one else can navigate. They are called the Sulu pirates, as they are reported to smuggle goods between Mindanao and Malaysia, just across the Sibutu Passage. They also are able to navigate the vast area of shallow reefs to pick up the beautiful shells only found in this area, highly prized by collectors. This area is considered off-limits to anyone but this tribe of people and it is reported that boats that venture into the area sometimes disappear, never to be seen again.

We saw these remarkable people slide their longboats up onto the beach and let the small children jump off and frolic onshore while dinner was being cooked in the rear area of the boat. We saw as many as six people living onboard, walking easily back and forth doing laundry and eating together. Soon the signal went out and the little ones hurried back and jumped onboard. The only times they were able to leave their canoes was when they returned to their houses on stilts, where they store their supplies. It is a unique lifestyle and we felt fortunate to be able to observe these people from the safety of our hotel.

When we returned to *Elysium*, we found that our friend Helmut Geisner had just arrived on his yacht, *Svetlana*. Helmut had offered to install the hydraulic windless that we had purchased in New Guinea. When it was installed Elmer found that our chain, which was American standard, did not fit the wildcat, which was metric. What a dilemma this presented: after all the expense and work we were not able to use it. Then someone suggested that we might be able get a wildcat cast in the foundry in downtown Cebu. To our amazement they were able to cast and mill it in a few days, out of bronze, for only fifty dollars. We were always amazed at the ingenuity of these enterprising people. After the new wildcat was installed, the hydraulic winch worked perfectly and made our anchoring effortless.

During the three months we were working on this project we became close friends with the Dutch couple, Nanda and Jacob Bakker, from the charter yacht, *Esperanza*. Nan had just learned that she had cancer, so we were helping her choose a healthful diet and researching the things she could to improve her condition. Our friend Tony, the British Air pilot who lived in Hong Kong, brought books on healing from Holland, where Nan was born. These books gave us insight into the procedure a Dutch doctor, named Hans Neiper, used for cancer patients. To help her manage her fear and pain, Elmer used hypnosis and guided relaxation. We were anchored in Carmen because of the constant threat of typhoons, so we had to flag a tricycle every day to make the trip down to where she was staying. Nan had been a very strong, large person at the beginning of her challenge, but had lost nearly seventy pounds and was very thin when we visited her. She did regain much of her strength with the love of friends and a good diet, so she was walking daily on the beach and swimming in the warm, tropical waters. The end of the year was approaching and we wanted to sail through the many beautiful islands and move on toward Borneo. Leaving Nan was very difficult for us, as we had become very close to her. She planned a trip back to Holland to visit her family, so we left after her plane took off.

We received word from other traveling yachts that Heinz was having a big gathering at Jau Island. Many of our ham contacts from around the world would be flying down to attend. We decided to sail over and meet the people we had talked with over the years: Dick, from Japan, Bogy, from Brunei, and Rowdy, who was coming down from Thailand. We arrived and anchored with many other yachts. There was a big French charter yacht with a full crew of young people aboard. Heinz was in his glory as he also had a ham radio station and had never met his many contacts either. He had no refrigeration in his resort and the food was placed out in the hot, humid weather on long tables. We were cautious about what we selected because we did not know how long this food had been on the island. I was just settling down to eat when a young French girl sitting at the table next to me jumped up and ran out of the building. She looked sick and I worried it may be food poisoning, so we decided to forego the meal and return to *Elysium*. As we motored by the French yacht, several people were hanging over the side, vomiting. We had only eaten a few bites, but we immediately climbed aboard and sipped some vinegar to hopefully calm down any problem our stomachs were facing. Neither Elmer nor I became sick, but the majority of the people that were there were very ill indeed. Heinz said that they all had the flu, but I was firm in my belief that all that food sitting in the hot sun had begun to spoil and they were suffering from food poisoning. It was great fun to meet all of our contacts and when they felt better, they came to visit us. In a few days we returned to Carmen to say goodbye to our friends there.

Sailing out from Carmen, we moved easily across the Visayan Sea, stopping each night to enjoy the beautiful islands circled with white sand along our route. At each stop we met friendly people who welcomed us into their homes and supplied us with several different kinds of bananas. We found the people in the Philippines very friendly and most of them spoke English fluently, so communication was very gratifying. We had to be extremely watchful and try to sail in the daytime, as the charts we had were not showing the extent of the reefs that plague the area. Nearly every day, Elmer climbed high up the ratlines and directed me through the perilous reefs in order to avoid going aground. We stopped at one uninhabited island just at dusk, where the water was filled with very large bright lights racing around under the boat. The lights darted swiftly back and forth for over an hour, never bumping into each other, before suddenly dimming and vanishing. We had seen many iridescent animals before, but nothing that would shine such a bright round spotlight like circle and move so rapidly. It remains a mystery to this day.

Our next destination was the island of Borocay. As we approached the island there were reefs all along the side we were trying to enter. We had been out overnight, were tired and eager to be laying at anchor, but each time we sailed in we encountered a reef that showed no passage through. It was extremely difficult to gauge the depth of the reefs with the crystal clear water magnifying the coral. We sailed in and then out again several times until we saw a small motorboat coming out toward us. A Philippino man was at the stern, waving for us to follow him. Rogelio led us through a channel to a place that was safe to anchor.

When we were well-anchored, he came aboard to invite us up to his little grass house for a plate of refreshing fruit. Borocay Island is a popular tourist vacation spot, so the beaches were lined with young people baking in the sun. Rogelio told us that the tourist season was now in full swing and while they were there, the prices of food became extremely expensive. He was fortunate to have his own papaya and banana trees and a small garden. A man from Germany hired him to be the caretaker for the large pyramid structure built as a quiet retreat from his busy life. He escorted us up to see this amazing house filled with crystals and many unusual esoteric works of art. He was well paid to look after the area and to keep it clean while the man was in Germany. We stayed several days to rest, and enjoyed the clean, white sand and snorkeled in the warm water.

We left Rogelio and his delightful family to sail on to the well-protected white sand anchorages on the numerous islands lining the coast. We were able to stop every night and occasionally we stayed a day or two on an uninhabited island to snorkel on the many reefs. On one island, we noticed heavy tracks coming ashore, like those made by a tractor. We didn't see any evidence of a boat or landing craft that would have allowed such a vehicle to embark. Finally, we discovered that huge sea turtles came up onto the shore at night to lay their eggs and they were responsible for the tracks. This was an incredible thing to witness as we sat quietly at night to watch the process in the half moonlight.

The next anchorage that looked safe was Port Culion on the north end of Palawan. It was designated a leper colony on the chart, but it was near nightfall so we stopped to anchor for the night. Soon after we anchored, a small boy came by sailing his little pram down wind. He stopped and came aboard for a cookie and told us about the island. His parents were caretakers for the lepers and he had lived on the island all his life. He loved to sail his little boat, but had a hard time sailing up wind to return to port. We brought out a basic sailing primer to give him and he was delighted to see pictures of ways to sail upwind. He learned to maneuver his little boat with wind on the beam. He then started tacking his boat back and forth to *Elysium*. He called out to invite us to come ashore and meet his parents. We put together a large sack of picture books for gifts and motored ashore to meet the people. As we arrived onshore, we were met by a group of people who were glad to have visitors. No other yacht had ever stopped in the anchorage, and they were very eager to hear about our trip and where we had come from.

They took us on a complete tour of the colony, a well-planned community with paths to each of the houses for the staff. There was a large hospital nearby for the patients and a house for their children, to keep them separated. As we moved on, a young man came out to tell us that Friar Javier Olazabal, who oversaw the island, requested that we come visit him. The Friar was the originator of the area and had come from Spain. We had to recall our very rusty Spanish to converse with him, but the conversation was lively and we had some help from his assistant who spoke English. Javier was very old and frail, but he was still very bright and alert and asked us many questions about *Elysium* and our trip. We invited him to come and visit and he readily accepted, telling us he would be out the next morning. When the sun was up, a boat arrived bringing the Friar with fifteen other visitors. Everyone was very excited to be onboard a yacht and examined every station eagerly. When they left, they invited us to come ashore for a meal with them.

We visited Friar Olazabal every day and found him to be an inspiring person. He felt that his work with the lepers had changed their lives from the living dead to a community of people. He had made many trips to Spain to plead for funding for his work on the island and was able to complete buildings using the meager tools at hand. After several days, we felt we needed to move on and sadly left this very friendly group. We had a large group of people waving from the dock as we sailed out of the bay.

It was mid-February, 1988, when we sailed south to Puerto Princessa, to stop and clean the bottom of the boat and to stock up on diesel and kerosene for our lamps. We were able to provision with plenty of food before sailing south to visit some of the tiny uninhabited islands before leaving for Borneo. We planned to sail from Urusurla Island, off southern Palawan, to Borneo, but a severe storm forced us into the very port that we had wanted to avoid, Clarendon Bay on Balabac, where Pier Tangvald had encountered pirates. We were alone in the big bay, hanging on while the storm raged outside, bringing a large swell into our anchorage and making the boat roll back and forth uncomfortably. After two days we desperately wanted to get off the rolling boat and walk along the shore. We had seen no one so we took a chance and motored in the dingy to the rocky beach. As we walked inland we found evidence that people lived nearby, but still saw no one.

That evening, in the very black of night, we had visitors come to the boat. Several grizzled looking Muslim men with grey beards and turbans on their heads were there in a dugout. We invited them aboard and I made some cookies and gave them tea as they struggled to tell us what it was that they needed. Finally, with gestures and pictures, they explained they had not been able to get supplies because of the storm and had no kerosene to light their lamps that were used to shine on the water to draw fish. This was their main source of food and they were in dire need. We were very relieved and gladly handed them two gallons of kerosene. We also gave them many tins of tuna fish and other food supplies that we could spare. They responded with immense relief and gratitude, each one bowing to us as they left.

We were very thankful that our encounter with the people who were famed as pirates had been so pleased with such a small gift. Several of them came out again the next morning with a stalk of bananas for us and asked if we needed anything else. We assured them that we would be leaving for Borneo as soon as the weather allowed. In the afternoon a very strange boat arrived. It was a round-bottomed lap-strake that had a full house covering the entire top. On the roof there were chickens walking around. We were just pulling up our anchor, so we did not have a chance to meet the inhabitants, but the lifestyle of these people looked unique.

As we sailed out into the Balabac Strait we looked back at the heavily forested island. The tall cliffs along the upper part of the island and the rocky shore gave no hint that there were people living on the island. Later, when we were able to find out more about the island, we learned that Chinese Islam traders who moved from Borneo and Balabac had settled there and used this area as a base to continue trading. The coastline of Palawan has one thousand seven hundred islands with atoll reefs and a high density of marine species that provided ample food and shells for trading. Their sparse living conditions allowed independence not found by many people and we felt fortunate that we were able to observe and enjoy this unusual tribe of people.

We left the last part of Balabac Island and were soon across the strait and on the coast of Borneo. We had not been able to find any information that told us what to expect when we arrived, but we had assurance from Bogy, our ham radio friend who was stationed in the neighboring country of Brunei, that there was a good anchorage in Kota Kinabalu, so we were confident that we would find adventures when we arrived in this new country of Malaysia.

Borneo, Malaysia

There is suffering in life, and there are defeats. No one can avoid them.
But it's better to lose some of the battles in the struggles for your dreams than
to be defeated without ever knowing what you're fighting for.

– Paulo Coelho

IN THE EARLY morning we sailed with a comfortable light wind and a calming sea. We decided to try a different light air sail and were pleased as it pushed us along extremely well in the gentle wind. As dusk neared an erratic, gusty wind suddenly arose and tugged violently at the sail. *Elysium* heeled over quickly and we rushed to the mast to take the sail down. The halyard was securely wedged between the sheave and the mast. "One of us has to go up to the top and free that halyard or we're in trouble," Elmer said. Glancing up the sixty feet to the top of the mast, I watched the top jerking back and forth as the boat rolled in the heavy sea. I wondered if I had the fortitude to go up there. The situation was urgent and I did not have the strength to crank Elmer up the mast fast enough. "Take me up," I declared, surprising myself as much as it did Elmer. I was uncomfortable with heights and did not enjoy going as high as the ratlines. I climbed into the bosun's chair and he took me to the top of the mast at the high speed of the winch. Looking up was not a problem for me and reaching the top, it was easy to see what had fouled the sheave, so I hastily released the line and the sail descended easily back to the deck. Now I had time to look out and realize how high I was. I clung to the top of the mast with all of my strength as the boat rolled back and forth without a sail raised to stabilize her. "Like being at the end of the tail of a dog," I thought, now becoming really frightened. With the sail down I could hear Elmer yelling, "Let go of the mast and start coming down. I'll let you down slow and easy." I began to release my grip and start down, my arms still circled around the slick varnish on the wood. When I finally got to the deck the sudden storm was nearly over and we were stable on the sea again. I was trembling and had to sit down on the deck to regain my composure. Elmer joked later that he found fingernail scratches all the way down the mast.

Relieved, we sailed with fair winds into the beautiful night beneath a full moon, grateful that the squall had passed completely. The gentle wind stroked the waves, bringing the slightest roll of foam curling to break, reflecting the moonlight as *Elysium* moved on toward Borneo. As the morning sun touched the sky, a strange cloud with a bright crimson halo appeared. We were headed toward the bay at Kota Kinabalu when Elmer said, "There's got to be a mountain up there in that cloud because it's wider at the base." We sighted the island of Borneo and as we drew closer, the mountain stayed in sight all day long. Mt. Kinabalu rises thirteen thousand, three hundred and forty-five feet above the shore and it was a magical vision rising high up into the fluffy clouds wrapped around its peak.

That night we both stayed awake trying to understand why the navigation lights weren't where they appeared on the chart. While on watch at midnight I saw a strange array of colored lights coming towards us. This conglomeration of lights didn't look like a stationary oil rig in the sea. There are many oil rigs marked on the chart and most of them are brightly lit to protect themselves from ocean traffic. I finally roused a sleepy Elmer to see what he thought. He looked out and said "That's an oil rig; it has no navigation lights." As we moved on, we both saw that this bizarre cluster of lights was now approaching us at a good speed. We moved out to sea just as it passed by, never signaling in any way that they saw us.

As we were about twelve miles from the bay we could now really feel the presence of Mt. Kinabalu. We called on the radio and a man named Errol, who was anchored in Borneo, offered to meet us and sail with us to the Tanjung Aru Beach Hotel where he had his yacht. We sailed in and anchored in the wide, protected bay, greeted by a welcoming warm breeze. Looking up, we saw that the cloud had drifted away from the peak of mountain and we could see the road that traversed diagonally back and forth up through the forested area and on to the base of the mountain. It looked so inviting we decided we would explore it when we were settled. We tied up to the small wharf where we found customs and immigration. When Errol arrived, we motored fourteen miles around Gaya Island to the bay where a large luxurious tourist area was. The well-appointed hotel was in the center and just on shore was a huge swimming pool. Errol and his wife, Prue, took us ashore to meet the manager who presented us with guest privileges, the use of the pool, showers and towels. He liked having international yachts anchored outside so his guests could meet people who had sailed from foreign countries. There were seven restaurants, with all different types of cuisine, a health spa, and several other amenities.

We asked Errol about the mountain that we could still see clearly from our anchorage. He told us that he and his wife had climbed it and that it was a great experience. They had also flown to Kuching and visited the Iban people on the Skrang River. They suggested that these things would be valuable experiences for us. We took a bus to town, exchanged our money and stopped at the post office where we had asked our daughter, LeAnn, to forward our mail. Going through mail from home was always a big treat and we answered each letter immediately. The market was filled with a wonderful selection of food, so we filled our packs with fruit and vegetables, eggs, and meat. We were able to catch a bus that dropped us near the hotel, so the walk back was easy.

As we rested aboard, we looked out at the peak of the mountain that commanded the skyline over the bay. We decided to find out more about this mountain that beckoned to us each day. We were inhabitants of the sea and although we had trekked many places, we had never been drawn to explore a mountain. We learned that it was a two-day trip to the top and that we needed to hire a guide, as no one could go beyond the base without one. The height of the mountain could cause altitude sickness and we were told that it could be deadly and to head back if we had headaches or nausea. We decided to join a group of five soldiers from the neighboring country of Brunei who had hired a guide for the trip. They were happy to share the expense with us and our only worry was that we would not be able to keep up with the fit young men after nearly a month at sea. We took the time to saturate our bodies with vitamin C to keep our muscles from becoming stiff after the climb.

A bus took us up the road that we had seen from *Elysium* and we arrived at the starting point of five thousand, one hundred and twenty-eight feet. The lush forest we rode through was filled with more biodiversity of flora and fauna than we had ever witnessed. Orchids and huge ferns were tucked inside the massive trunks of hardwood trees. Colorful birds flew from branches, frightened by the noise of the bus that invaded the sanctuary of the park.

We found accommodations and planned to ascend the mountain after a short nights sleep. Early the next morning we met our Malay guide, a stout young man that spoke very few words of English. We gathered at the bottom and the guide started up. We climbed, negotiating the steps that were made by placing small poles in front of an expanse of gravel. These steps were too wide and too tall for me to take as one step so instead, I would take two steps to manage a step-hop step on the next. As we continued up the very steep grade, our guide motioned to us to follow him off the path. There was a huge flower, at least three feet in diameter that exuded an amazing odor of rotten flesh. We found later when we looked up this anomaly that it was the largest flower in the world and only blooms a certain time each century. This parasitic flower is called Red Rafflesia and is only found in this locale where so many unusual species survive. Further up the trail we encountered a pitcher plant, which looks like a giant rust red urn. The Nepenthes Raja lives on the seeping ground water that is always prevalent on the mountain. This carnivorous plant can hold over a quart of water in its large lower appendage and specializes in attracting and capturing prey to hold and digest there. We learned that even mammals and invertebrates were of-

Helen descending Mt. Kinabalu

ten trapped inside the liquid.

We continued along, moving up more rapidly after we left the difficult steps behind. At this point Lee, one of the soldiers with us, began to complain of a headache. We were concerned because this was a sign of altitude sickness. The guide let us know that we would soon reach Rata Hut, our first rest stop, at ten thousand eight hundred feet, where we would spend the night, and he could decide in the morning if he wanted to continue. Porters bring all of the supplies for people staying at Rata Hut and we saw one carrying a fifty-five gallon drum on his back. I was having trouble just carrying my light pack. These porters exhibited remarkable stamina and strength and did not seem tired at all as they returned to descend the mountain. We gratefully took advantage of the delicious meals, hot showers, and very comfortable beds that Rata Hut provided. We were both a bit lightheaded and very tired and were glad to have a time to relax.

At 2:00 a.m. we were aroused from our sleep and served breakfast. We then continued to climb beneath a bright full moon that shone down on the smooth granite, reflecting beautifully on its surface, polished to a fine sheen by glaciers from the past. We climbed on naked granite for another two thousand six hundred feet to reach the high peak that pierced the sky above us. For the climber's convenience there were ropes that had been fastened by pitons for us to belay ourselves up the steep, slippery rock. As we neared the top we found water in the small dips left in the granite and in many places where small plants had gained a foothold to reach out with flowers in the warm breezes. When we arrived at the summit, the sun was just rising to meet the descending full moon. The South China Sea reflected a soft, pink blush that spread over the entire sky. The vision was enhanced by the rigorous climb and appreciation we felt after accomplishing this feat of endurance.

The descent was easier as we could hang on to the rope and make certain that we had good foothold in the granite that was now warming in the sunlight. We arrived at the base in time to catch a bus back to *Elysium*. As we parted, we invited our new climbing friends from Brunei to come visit us on *Elysium* the next day. We truly bonded with these young men as we all tackled and succeeded in climbing the mountain.

The next day we welcomed the warm water in the swimming pool to ease the muscle stiffness from the rigorous climb. We looked up from our swim and greeted a few of our climbing friends. They told us that the muscles in their legs were so stiff from the climb that they were barely able to walk and that some of them could not even get out of bed. These were young men in the army and were used to training, so we were very pleased that we experienced less of a problem. We took our visitors out to *Elysium* and cooked a small meal as they explored every part of our living quarters. They had never been onboard a yacht before and were amazed by the convenience and comforts onboard.

The next few weeks passed very quickly as we enjoyed the warm weather and daily swims in the pool. We ate in the restaurants and enjoyed conversations with people staying at the hotel. We met Americans who were stationed in areas nearby using the hotel as a getaway and groups that were from companies holding meetings for their employees. The pool was a place for us to enjoy watching how people from other countries interacted. We often invited the international visitors aboard to visit and see what our living space was like and to answer questions about our sailing experiences. This anchorage was easy living for us, as we had never had access to this much comfort and luxury before.

Our next trip was to visit the Skrang River and the Iban people, so we looked up the Interworld Travel Service located in Kuching, the capital of Sarawak. We made reservations and hired a guide named Yung Chin. We would board a plane March 14, 1988, and stay until March 25. We planned to spend a week with the Iban people in the Murat, Sungei Pinang, and Balaee longhouses and we would be taken upriver in a longboat. We were to take a jungle hike and see a pepper and cocoa plantation, and where the rubber was cut and harvested. Errol and Prue offered to watch *Elysium* while we were gone, so we had our passports stamped and caught a bus to the airport.

We embarked on a Fokker airplane that had a high wing, allowing us to clearly see the coastline. The entire coast was a mass of rivers, creating a muddy brown smear pouring from each flow, extending far out into the sparkling blue water of the South China Sea. There were no roads visible on the land, just rivers winding and doubling back on themselves. We landed first at Sibu, on the Rajong River, surprised to see seven ships loading huge hardwood logs onto their decks. We took a bus to our inexpensive hotel in a dilapidated part of town and settled in for the night. The young Chinese man, Yung Chin, who asked us to call him Ching, met us at the hotel in the morning and drove us south toward the Kalimantan boarder to the Pias Jetty at Sri Aman. There we met our longboat guide and began our trip up the Skrang River to the Murat Longhouse. We saw the building from the river as we rounded a very sharp bend. The longhouse was situated high on the bank, allowing the inhabitants a complete survey of the river, which was the only way to approach the area.

We climbed up the steep ladder entering the longhouse and viewed the large screened dorm with showers and accommodations that were being built for future guests. Ching told us that the people would set up a place for us to sleep inside the veranda area and proceeded to fix us an excellent dinner with food he had prepared ahead of time. The native people ate wild pig that was preserved in salt because they didn't have refrigeration. The meat was black and thick on their fingers as they dipped it and mixed it with a handful of cooked rice. The acrid, pungent smell of fermented pork filled the area as they chewed the mixture with delight. We were content that we were not expected to eat their food and that Ching had brought more familiar food for us.

A longhouse consists of a structure built high above the ground that holds individual rooms that are thirty by twenty-four feet, housing each family. There was also a toilet area, as the people had discovered long ago that the disposal of this waste kept everyone healthy. The toilets had a water catchment built into the roof for storage and the outlet flowed down a pipe into the lower area where the waste was washed into the river. All told, there were about twenty-seven families living in the longhouse. The porch or veranda-like area in front of the individual rooms is used for drying pepper in the morning sun, as a play area for the children, and as social area for the families. There was one communal cooking area where the residents gathered when it was time to use the continuous fire that burned with hot coals from the Borneo hardwood. The structure of the longhouse was expertly built from heavy planks and bamboo. The aroma of the pepper drying in the sun combined with the smell of smoke from the fire and was like fine incense filling the moist air. The gentle swirling of the river made a musical sound that combined with the call of the birds in the jungle.

In the evening, the Iban people performed a traditional dance to the sound of gongs. They even asked me to join in, which I did to their amusement. We gave them the sweets and biscuits that we had brought for gifts, which were a special treat in this remote place. We became sleepy as the dancing continued, so they showed us where we were to sleep on mats on the floor near the dancing area. The people continued to dance and talk as we slept. We would wake occasionally to see someone looking down at us and smiling. Above the area where we were sleeping hung a group of human skulls. The British had put a bounty on Japanese soldiers during WWII and the Iban had used their blowguns to kill them. They had shown us the heads with pride, telling us how they used the smoke of their fires to keep the spirits alive. This was the only sign of their violent past that we encountered, as they were very friendly, happy people. They had a good community, no theft or disagreements.

If someone did break the rules they had to leave. I wondered where they would go in this remote area!

We awoke at 4:45 a.m. when the rooster was crowing. There were many pigs and chickens living under the porch part of the longhouse. The combination was a perfect system to keep the flies and mosquitoes away from the inhabitants. People were already up and going about their chores for the day. Some were weaving the beautiful mats that lined the floor, and others were carving intricate designs on long hardwood poles. The kitchen fires were burning and some sweet smelling smoke filtered through the area. We had arrived during the rice-harvest, so some people were busily winnowing the rice and moving it onto the mats. Others were carrying hardwood branches in the flexible baskets on their backs. These baskets were made of some strong material and stretched as large as necessary to carry anything and leave their hands free.

We said goodbye to our hosts in the longhouse, boarded the long-boat and moved swiftly down the river for the Balaee Longhouse. The sun shone brightly, reflecting on the brilliant colors of the butterflies that were flitting in and out of the emerald-green foliage. We saw several giant blue-heron fishing on the river's edge, where small fish were abundant in the shallows. Suddenly, a Kingfisher's wings flashed bright blues and greens as it swooped down from the overhanging canopy of trees above us. The breeze gave the flowing water a dappled look as the sunlight peered through the large leaves of the hardwood trees. The air carried the scent of the river mosses and lush growth of sweet smelling flowers that lined the bank.

We stopped at a beautiful spot beside the river and the boatman and his wife made tea from water boiled inside a piece of bamboo set into the fire. We ate the traditional Nasi Goring that Ching had made that morning. In the early afternoon, we arrived at the Balaee Longhouse where we observed another night of dancing after all their hard work during the day. The chief brought out many beautiful, ancient pieces of hand-carved hardwood objects they desired to sell us. There were many valuable pieces, but we told them that we had no room for such treasures. They reluctantly put everything away and poured the rice wine for the celebration of the evening.

The next morning we moved to where a representative of all the long-houses lived. There was a school and medical facilities here at Pngurun. We spoke with the health worker and learned that their single medical problem was that only fifty percent of newborns lived. We ate the last of our vegetables grated in a soup served with rice and the chief ate dinner with us. A man brought in a wild boar that he had killed so we were able to watch the cutting and salting of the meat that was their staple food. They smoked the meat, put lots of rock salt on it and sealed it in big crock jars. That night we again slept as they continued dancing and drinking rice wine. It is such a strange sensation to wake up right in the midst of an evening gathering and dance.

In the morning as we started out on the river toward the Sungei Pinang Longhouse, we were aware of a strange light above us. Elmer and I thought that the light coming through the trees had dimmed, like a dark cloud had formed above. Finally the chief laughed and said "eclipse," to remind us that there would be a total eclipse of the sun at this time. After becoming very dark, the light was becoming stronger and we were nearing the next stop. Here we visited a less populated rustic longhouse but the ritual was the same; we bathed in the river and ate a good meal. Then we took a walk in the jungle where we saw rubber trees and watched how the black acrid smelling rubber was cut and shipped. In the evening everyone danced and we again drifted off to sleep.

We had a fantastic last trip back up the river to where Ching had left his car. There was shallow water at times, so we had to get out to lighten the load and push the boat along. We asked the chief if we could buy his prang (machete). It was well worn and we liked the fact that he had fashioned it himself and had used it many times on the trip, cutting bamboo and brush as we walked on-shore. He was pleased when we gave him thirty dollars Malay for it.

Arriving in Sri Aman, Ching told us that he had been born in this town and that the Chinese had not been treated well in Sarawak in the recent past. They had to carry an ID card with their race printed on it and had to be back in their homes by dark. When we said goodbye to Ching, he gave us a big hug and kiss. This was his first guided tour and he was pleased with the whole experience.

We had a bit of time before we were due at the airport to board the plane back to Kotakinabalu so we did some sightseeing. When we retuned to the airport, we learned that our tickets were unconfirmed and that we would have to wait until the next day. We had to find a place to stay for the night. Our clothes were dirty and we only had our grubby shorts and backpacks with us. We went to the big Holiday Inn near the airport to inquire about the price of a room. Outside there was a sign that said eighty dollars a night. Inside, everyone was dressed in suits and ties. We asked at the counter about the price of a room for the night. The clerk said, "Just go up," and gave us a key. We kept asking for a price and he finally whispered, "Eleven dollars." What a bargain that was for us! We were so dirty and disreputable looking that he just wanted us out of the lobby. We swam in the large pool, took long, long showers, and slept deeply in clean white sheets. The next day we flew back to *Elysium* filled with excitement about our adventure.

Back on *Elysium* we were ready to move on, but were finding it difficult to leave the luxury and convenience of the bay. We had to clean the bottom of the boat again, provision for the trip, and fill our tanks with water. The interior also had to be cleaned with Clorox as the blush of mold was making its appearance again. Finally on March 27, 1988, we left Tanjung Aru and sailed out in clear, calm weather. We had to motor, beating into a slight wind, until we reached the Island of Tega. As we looked back at Kota Kinabalu, the mountain looked larger than ever. We went ashore and met the Ranger who watches over the park on Tega. We walked around the park and saw hornbills, monkeys, huge lizards, and a great variety of butterflies. We visited the research station and spoke with the men working there.

As we started across the South China Sea, the water was completely flat with no breeze. I called on the ham radio asking for someone to give us a weather report. I found Ed Smith, whose call sign was KAI GV, a Portland, Oregon call sign. He was on a seven hundred and thirty-five foot bulk carrier filled with wheat headed from Portland to Singapore, then on to Karachi, Pakistan. He told us that he would be glad to give us weather reports every day so we would be aware of any sudden storms. We had a long chat and luckily there was plenty of sun to keep the batteries charged with the solar panels. They had been on a long trip and had experienced very rough weather around the Aleutian Islands and everyone was eager to hear about our journey from Oregon. They had never spoken to anyone on a yacht before and because we were both from Oregon it was even more interesting for them.

Earlier I had tried to sprout the wheat we had purchased in the Philippines. For our staple diet while sailing, we used the bright green sprouts for fresh vegetables and dried the rest for the nutritious sprouted wheat bread. Unfortunately, the wheat we purchased did not sprout and smelled of pesticides, so I sadly threw it overboard and watched the little buds drift down into the deep water, feeling a great loss. When Ed told me that they were carrying fresh Oregon wheat, I told him about the problem we had with our sprouts. He suggested that they could leave a bag at the Singapore embassy for us. We would arrive in Singapore in a few days where we could pick up all the wheat we needed for the next year.

Since there was no wind and we could not move without motoring, we eagerly looked forward to our conversations with our new friends on *Altair*. One morning Ed had some exciting news for us. The captain said that they could stop and off-load one hundred pounds of wheat for us. The big ship was nearing our position and we still had no wind so they figured they would catch up with us in twelve hours. It was hard to believe they could make sixty miles in that short of time. That distance would have taken us several days when we had good wind.

Speaking to Ed, we learned that each member of the crew had decided to make up a special box for us. They were filling the boxes with items they thought they would need if they were going to spend months at sea in a small sailboat. At about four o'clock in the afternoon we were able to see a small white dot on the horizon, which turned quickly into the brilliant ship cabin shining in the sunlight. Just as quickly, they were right next to us with the crew hanging over the side, hollering greetings and waving. They put over big ropes and bumpers so we could move alongside and raft to them. For a full fifteen minutes we attempted to motor alongside. Finally, with a heavily revved up motor we were able to swing close enough so I could grab a rope and with help from the crew, we could tie *Elysium* to the side of *Altair*. Now we could see our friends on deck just fifteen feet above us.

It was getting late and the captain wanted the exchange to be completed by nightfall, so they first lowered a giant bag of ice, a wonderful gift in this sweltering environment. The container was so large I could have made it into a small wading pool. Next they lowered one hundred pounds of beautiful golden, plump wheat berries that carried the aroma of fresh grain. After this, each man in the crew lowered his personal gift in a large box, containing very practical things such as toilet paper, floating flashlights with batteries, tie wire, duct tape, bug spray, sun block, and an array of screws and nails. There was also a big jug of protein supplement, a bottle of vitamins, bar soap, and a giant box of Tide. They gave us current newspapers, many well-read paperback books, and magazines so we could catch up on the happenings from back home.

Then came the very best of all as they carefully lowered big boxes of fresh food we had not seen or bought for a long time. There were carrots, celery, potatoes, oranges, apples, and pears. In another box they had packed canned meat, big jars of coffee, strawberry preserves, and raspberry jam. Next they sent the frozen foods in a box filled with banana-cream pie, Sarah Lee cakes, a gallon of rocky-road ice cream, two pounds of butter, a large, yellow brick of Tillamook cheddar cheese and dried fruit. They knew that we could not possibly keep all this produce but they would be in Singapore in a few days, where they would receive new supplies. "Just throw what you can't eat overboard," they told us.

They lowered the barbecue that Dwight, a crew member from *Altair*, had welded from a five-gallon drum. It looked just like a home barbecue painted black with a cooking grate covering the top. Alongside was a box of briquettes and a large Styrofoam container of frozen steaks, plus a carrier of Rainier beer. Dwight actually jumped with joy when Elmer admired the job he had done and told him how welcome the steak would be.

Daylight was fading so we had to say goodbye to our benefactors and motor away. To our amazement, they did not leave the area for at least a half an hour. When we spoke with Ed the next day, we learned that their reverse gear had not been working. That explained why we had so much trouble rafting to them. Ed had the motor repaired and was grateful that they had not entered the huge moorage with that problem. "We could have wiped out another boat if we had not been able to stop," he told us.

It was very dark and we needed to begin the night watch and get back to the reality of our trip. The six-knot wind gently pushed us along and we sailed slowly the entire night, warmed by our experience of the meeting at sea. We enjoyed a feast of steak barbecued on the grill and ice cream that was melting quickly. We were so filled with the rich food that we left the rest for the next day.

We were able to contact Ed at five in morning. They were in Singapore, had provisioned *Altair*, and were already moving up the Malacca Strait headed for Pakistan with the remaining sixty-four thousand tons of wheat. No one would ever miss our one hundred pounds! We wished them a safe journey and expressed our appreciation for all they had done for us. Ed said he would contact us when they returned to Singapore, where we expected to be within the next five days. We wondered what we would find in this busy country where industry is paramount. Would there be anyone anchored there that we knew and would we be able to find a place for *Elysium*?

We are travelers in the wilderness of this world, and the best we can find in our travels is an honest friend.

— *Robert Louis Stevenson*

EACH DAY WE were able and locate a bit more wind so we could give Luther, our trusty motor, a rest. Calling on the ham radio we were able to reach Tom and Bobbie on *Tomba*, who were now anchored in Singapore. We had not seen or heard from them since they left our home moorage at Sauvie Island nine years earlier. In Singapore, we would finally catch up with them and hear about their journey. We sailed along beneath a full moon and a light southwest wind moving us ever so slowly. Each morning when we turned on our ham radio we welcomed Ed's voice calling from *Altair*. The big ship was navigating up the very shallow Malacca Strait where traffic is confined to a narrow channel. We told them how much we enjoyed the food and gifts that they had given us. They, in turn, related the problems navigating the channel in a ship with such a deep draft. "A fishing boat cut right in front of us," Ed said with exasperation. "We can't avoid a collision by turning away and we're certainly not able to slow down. These fishermen don't realize what a risk they're taking." We told Ed we would be in Singapore either that day or the next. "If you're there in a few weeks when we return, you can come visit us," he said. "That is an invitation we'll take you up on," we replied.

Sailing on, the sea was dotted with big tankers and ships from every part of the world also headed to Singapore. Now that we had met the crew of *Altair*, we felt a kinship with these monster ships. We knew we were close—the air filled with smoke and we had only about five miles of visibility. As the evening approached we sailed ever so slowly, creeping along to avoid any confrontation with another boat or ship. We finally turned on the motor to free ourselves from the crowded water and to avoid being the smallest boat in the ocean of ships and big trawlers.

We were also battling a very strong current, so when the earliest strands of light lit the sky and we were in shallow water, we dropped our anchor. Both of us had been awake now for nearly twenty-four hours and required a bit of time to sleep without the constant sound of the motor. We were awakened a few times by fishing boats motoring near us and we had a very difficult time clearing our minds and remembering where we were. We were startled and fully awake when a huge thunderstorm hit us, bringing down buckets of rain. We decided it was time to call Tom and Bobbie and get directions for a safe anchorage in Changi. The sudden cold rain coming down so swiftly in the extreme heat of the morning fogged my glasses so I could barely see where to go as Elmer took the anchor up. It was a joyful sight to see Tom waiting for us as we rounded the bend into Changi. Just as we anchored, the powerful rain hit again and continued until four in the afternoon. When it stopped we were able to go ashore, stretch our legs, enjoy catching up with our friends, and join the group of yachties anchored in Singapore at the Changi Yacht Club.

We went ashore the next day to view the bustling, enormous city and to have our passports stamped, exchange our money for Singapore dollars, visit the port captain, and to retrieve our treasured mail. We walked for miles in the ninety-five degree heat and were suddenly plunged into the extreme contrast of air-conditioned buildings that were kept at a constant sixty-seven degrees. Being in a city of this magnitude, with its noise and traffic, was exhausting for us. We hurried to back to *Elysium*, glad to feel the cool sea breeze flowing through her ports.

We found Ed on the radio the next morning and learned that Altair was returning to Singapore. He said he would make arrangements for a launch to bring us out to visit them. We found a bus to Clifford Pier and met an agent for Borneo Shipping who showed us where our ride was. We were on the launch for a full hour, moving along at top speed, to reach *Altair*. When we arrived we did not recognize it at all, as the deck was fifty feet above the water and we had to board up a long ramp that they lowered for us. It was great to meet all of the crew and thank them for all that they had done for us.

They told us about Pakistan, where the people had removed the entire shipment of wheat in sacks over their shoulders. They had set up cooking pots and brought their goats aboard, living simply on deck while they toiled with the heavy load. It took several weeks for the entire evacuation from the hull. We toured the ship and Ed offered to pick up *Elysium* with their huge cranes and put her in the hold plus give us free passage back to Portland. We imagined how everyone would react if we showed up in Portland in a few weeks time, but we had already made plans to sail on to Africa, so we turned down the offer. After we ate lunch together, we said sad goodbyes and wished them a safe and easy trip back to the United States.

It was necessary for us to complete all the work *Elysium* needed in Singapore because we would not be near a boatyard for countless miles ahead. In the past, yachts had been able to stop in Sri Lanka where there was an excellent boatyard in Colombo. The recent wars ended any possibility of stopping there and we would not be able to find another boatyard until we got to South Africa. We were talking about our need to pull the boat out and work on the hull in the Yacht Club when someone mentioned Bala Tan's yard in Singapore. We planned to visit the yard the next day to get a bid for repairing *Elysium*.

Bala Tan himself came out to the boat a few days later and wrote down all the things we needed to have done. We had always done our own work on *Elysium* and we had no idea what labor and material would cost. There was a great deal of work that needed to be done. We needed to have new toe rails built and installed because our walnut had taken such a beating the last few years in the tropics that it was rotting, and the mild steel underneath it needed to be replaced with stainless steel. We needed to pull the masts and put on new varnish and epoxy, and rebuild some upper spreaders. The hull needed to be sandblasted and repainted and something had to be done about our bowsprit, but we hadn't fully decided what that would be.

The same day we received the bid we met Oliver. Oliver was from France and worked in a shipyard that was now empty. He told us that the yard was completely vacant because they had just completed a huge yacht for the Prince of Abu Dhabi. He showed us pictures of the vessel and we were very impressed with it and the facilities that were available. The bid from Bala Tan's boatyard was extremely high; at the same time Oliver told us we could do all of our own work and use their equipment. They had a crew that could pull the masts and we could use the gigantic building to refinish them inside, away from the constant downpour of rain. This seemed like the answer we were looking for.

We had to move from Changi within the week and Oliver said the dock in Jurong was available right away. We sailed *Elysium* over and found a completely empty structure about one hundred yards from the dock. Inside, there was a complete shop with immense space and protection from the weather.

We made arrangements to pull the masts first. This was a totally new experience for us. The men and equipment who arrived were Chinese and did not speak a word of English. They bustled around, preparing to pull the mast with a very antiquated crane while we frantically began marking where the halyards and stays would need to be repositioned. We had expected Oliver to at least visit, but we never saw him again after the arrangements were made. Once the masts were down and inside the building, we were able to begin work.

At the entrance of the yard was an Indian family, Mr. and Mrs. Ramish, who were the keepers of the gate. They gave us a key to the office and told us we could use the refrigerator and were welcome to make ice there. It was a long walk from the gate to the yard, but it was wonderful to have access to a refrigerator in the extreme humid heat of Singapore.

We made arrangements to have the hull pulled out, sand blasted, and painted while we made a quick trip back to the states to see the family. Our plan was to go for a few weeks and see the family and then come back to work on the exterior and topsides of *Elysium*. It was necessary to clear the boat work with Customs and the Port Captain. When everything was complete we left *Elysium* in the care of Oliver and a woman named Mrs. Tan.

Our visit to the states passed very quickly. Elmer's mother was not doing well and was in a nursing home. My mother was now in her nineties, so the time with them was very valuable. We did not know when it would be possible to visit again. One day as we were all sitting with the family, we noticed that Steve had lost some of his usual enthusiasm for what he was doing. Steve had been working as an engineer for the same company for several years and was feeling restless and thinking about traveling. I asked him what he would rather be doing and he replied, "I'd always dreamed of doing what you're doing, sailing the world." Without a lot of thought, I said "Why don't you quit your job and you and Anjali and the boys take *Elysium* for a year and we can do some of the land traveling we want to do." Not too much more was said until about a week later when we were planning to return to Singapore. Steve asked me "did you really mean what you said about us taking *Elysium* for a year?" Elmer and I agreed that Malaysia would be the very best place for them to try cruising, as the land and water system was safe. There were no more long passages and if they decided they wanted to, they could sail *Elysium* to India and we could meet them there after trekking in Nepal.

The next day, as we were ready to catch our flight, we made tentative arrangements to meet them in Thailand or Malaysia. They had decisions and arrangements to make about their house and schooling for the two boys: Raj, six, and Marco, nearly five. The big issue facing Steve was his employer, whether or not he could be granted a leave of absence for a year. We told them we would take care of any expense for *Elysium* that occurred while they were sailing. "What if something happens to her?" Steve asked. . We agreed we would continue to stay in contact with

George in Portland by ham radio, assuring him we had complete confidence in his ability.

Singapore is three degrees south of the Equator and extremely hot and humid. Three weeks after returning from Portland the heat there was exhausting. We caught a bus to the boatyard eager to see *Elysium* with her new bottom paint. Instead we found a gray, greasy topside. The boatyard scum had spread a thick layer over her white paint, making any view of the new paint impossible. We set to work immediately scouring her clean and getting ready to start the work on the masts that were lying on props inside the immense building. Since we could not see the bottom of the boat in the dark murky water, we hoped it had been done adequately. We began the long walks back and forth from the wharf to the building. I had to walk half a mile to catch the bus to shop for our fruit and vegetables. I took a taxi back from the market heavily laden with sacks of food to fill the refrigerator that Mrs. Ramish let us use in the office.

One day, as we were working on the topside of *Elysium*, a huge working ship drew near. A dark skinned man in bright white overalls called to us. "You're docked where we're supposed to be," he shouted. "Could we raft on the outside of you?" Elmer asked. "That would be fine," he replied. We started the engine, cast off the lines, and watched the big ship slide into our space. Once they were there, they put out big bumpers and we came alongside.

The man who had called out to us introduced himself as Samy Elangoevan. He shook hands with Elmer and jumped off the ship onto *Elysium*. He told us that he was an engineer for a big shipping company and that the ship we were rafted to had been carrying oil sludge that they were dumping on a small island in Malaysia. When the crew was discharging the sludge, the hose had broken loose and splattered the black, sticky material all over the ship. The crew brought it in because it needed to be scraped and cleaned, and it would be there for a few weeks. We showed Samy around *Elysium* and we had tea and cookies together, listening to the fascinating story of his life. His father was a Rajput, the highest rank in the British Indian Army. He was raised very strictly in southern India. "My father used to whip my legs when I was young and I could not show any emotion" he told us. This upbringing had made Samy very sensitive to the suffering of the people in Sri Lanka. He had visited there and found a young man who had been wounded in the Tamil wars and had given him a job on the ship in his jurisdiction. No wonder the crew of the ship we rafted to showed such affection for him! "If you need anything at all, let me know," he said as he left.

We found the crew of the ship most amiable. They smiled and called us Mama and Papa when we crossed over to work in the shipyard. The crew consisted of people from all over the world. There were men from Burma (now Myanmar), Sri Lanka, India, and Malaysia. When we crossed over, we had to go through the galley of the ship to reach the shore. Every day I left some gift that we had received from *Altair* such as a giant jar of strawberry preserves, coffee, or a giant bag of candy. These gifts were gratefully received and we were happy to make friends with this diverse group of men.

We continued to work on the mast every day, stripping the huge timber down to its original wood and applying epoxy to preserve the wood. Elmer built all new spreaders out of a hard, light colored, flexible wood and strips of the original spruce we had in the storage under the bunk. In the vacant spots between, he mixed cornstarch with epoxy and filled them in, covering it all with fiberglass. We needed to paint the entire exterior as we had scrubbed and sanded the surface. We were told that we could obtain excellent epoxy paint at Kim Seah Boat Builders Ltd. so we boarded a bus to town.

The paint was expensive by Singapore standards but the man behind the counter told us it was the very best for our job. We bought several gallons, loaded our backpacks and headed for the bus. After we had walked several blocks the young man who sold us the paint caught up with us. "I am Colin Lim," he explained breathlessly. I had to find out what enabled people your age to be able to walk so fast with such a heavy load. You must have many health secrets to allow you to be so strong and vigorous," he explained. As we walked along, he quizzed us about *Elysium* and our journey of now nearly ten years. "I have a small car and I will come out and visit you tomorrow" he told us as he turned back. "If you need anything for the boat, I can drive you and help you procure what you need." This was the beginning of an amazing friendship that lasted for many years. Working for a boat builder enabled Colin to buy things at the very best price and because he had a car, which is extremely rare in Singapore, it enabled us to reach the manufacturing plant and obtain just what we needed.

Samy was another frequent visitor. "Do you need anything at all?" He would ask as he left. Elmer had been trying to obtain diesel filters for our engine without any luck. These filters were the life's blood of the diesel system and we could not do without them. Elmer told Samy that we were not able to find them anywhere. Samy wrote down all the numbers and studied the system that we had built into *Elysium's* diesel engine protection. He was very impressed with the engine room and the care that Luther, out trusty Isuzu engine, had received. The next morning he arrived with a case of the filters. Elmer's eyes lit up as he asked "what do I owe you for these?" "Nothing, it is a gift," Samy replied.

Samy invited us to come to town and have lunch with him. We met at a very expensive Indian restaurant in the midst of Little India, a charming place with hand-carved, hardwood doors and the enticing aroma of spicy South-Indian food. Samy was welcomed with lots of warm affection, indicating that he was a well-respected guest who dined there often. The food and company were superb. After dinner, Samy took us to his office and pointed to the telephone. "Call your family and talk as long as you like," he offered. We made two calls and enjoyed the clear telephone contact, which seemed to please him very much.

The next day the big ship was cleaned and ready to depart. We told our friends goodbye and moved *Elysium* back into her slip. We finished the paint job and were now ready to tackle the toe rail. Mrs. Tan had promised us that she could get the rare Chengal hardwood that is called Malaysian Teak. When we called her asking for the time of its arrival she replied angrily, "That wood is impossible to get now!" At this point we were facing two big problems. We had removed the entire toe rail because the mild steel that held the wood in place had rusted very badly and we needed wood to complete the job. We also needed to have a welder near the dockside area because bringing it from the shop was nearly impossible.

At one time Steve had brought his good friend Gawain to our house to visit. Gawain was now a busy entrepreneur with a large business in Singapore. We had never had time to contact him, but now completely stymied in our progress, we decided it would be good to do something different. Gawain came out the next day and took us to his house for dinner. He was extremely interested in *Elysium* and the fine work that Elmer had accomplished building her. We had pictures of the building process, so he asked us to bring them to show his father, who would also be most interested. A sumptuous dinner was served in the great house where Gawain and his parents lived. The furniture was all carved teak and the sunlit room smelled of lemon oil and incense.

Gawain's father asked Elmer if he was able to find all the materials he needed for the repair we were doing. We told him how exasperated we were with Mrs. Tan. She had promised us the Chengal and Elmer had spent three weeks removing the toe rail and grinding off all the steel. "Maybe I can help you," he said in his soft easy way. We were not prepared for the immediate help he supplied. He came out the next day and told us that his friend had the wood we needed and asked if Elmer could go with him to see it. Elmer was delighted to get into the chauffeur driven Mercedes and even more pleased to find a big stack of green Chengal piled in the friends back yard. "How much do you charge for eighteen of these boards?" he asked. The two friends chattered in Chinese for several minutes and the man said, "we will give you a good price. When do you want it?" Elmer wanted it right away but was reluctant to appear too anxious. "At your convenience" he replied. We both were a bit concerned about agreeing to buy a large stack of extremely valuable lumber that was very much in demand, without finding out the price. We had to have the wood, and we decided we would just have to pay what he asked and leave it at that.

The next problem resolved itself in a very unusual way. Mr. Ramish told us another ship, the *Mary Livingston*, needed to be in our space, but that they would be agreeable to our rafting outside of them. The *Mary Livingston* was smaller than we had expected, but had enlisted their crew from many countries, a practice commonly found on these ships. The best thing about our new neighbor was that they planned to do some welding on the ship and they had a giant welder aboard. We almost were afraid to ask if we could use it, but when we gathered our courage, the captain replied, "Of course. If it doesn't take too long. We'll let you know when it is available."

Colin came down that very day and Elmer asked him if he could get some stainless steel pieces and welding rod. "Of course, that is very easy," Colin told him. "I could take you there right now." Everything was coming together just as we needed it to. The man bringing the Chengal arrived the next day. His price was, indeed, very good: much less than we expected.

Our next job was to carry the Chengal over to the building where Elmer could saw and fashion the strips. Then we carried them back to *Elysium* and fastened each one in place. This had to be done as quickly as possible because the wood that was now green and pliable would quickly turn very hard and into a beautiful lustrous brown as it dried. It had all of the red and yellow tones of the walnut but was so hard that smashing it against a dock would not even leave a small dent. It was a much better color than the teak we had seen. We assured Gawain and his father that we would take them sailing as soon as we had the mast back on and everything in working order.

The next month was a busy one. We finished all of the woodwork booms, spreaders, dingy and toe rails. The crane operator returned at the appointed time to bring the masts back and put them up while we frantically matched each stay to its proper place. We had three men chattering at us in Chinese, trying to help. The stays have to be in the proper place or we would not be able to tighten them and the purpose of their strength would fail. Finally, everything was complete. *Elysium* had new toe rails, varnish, repaired masts, new paint, and *Limbo*, our dingy, also shone like new. It seemed to us that everything was in tiptop shape.

Colin brought back the Sat-Nav that had been repaired and helped us obtain five heavy new batteries. That would have been nearly impossible for us to manage without a car. We were not unhappy to be leaving this noisy industrial-ship area, but were sad to say goodbye to the friendly family who guarded the entrance. They had been daily visitors, watching our progress and had been very helpful to us.

Trying to start the motor we found that the propeller was badly fouled. The color of the water was dark swamp-green, but from the dingy Elmer could see the long, spindly, white shell growth. "I have to go into the water and clean it or we can't use the engine," he said grimly "It's so dirty I wouldn't see a snake in there." I didn't want him go into dirty oily water, but we could not move at all so we had no choice. Elmer took a sharp trowel and put on his mask and snorkel to keep the sludge out of his eyes. He quickly scraped the largest part of the growth off. When he came up he said, "We'll have to clean the hull as soon as we get into clear water because there is a entire, living reef attached to it.

We motored slowly out of the bay and around to the Johor-Singapore causeway where the swift current leaves the water clear and clean. When we dove overboard, we wondered how *Elysium* had moved at all. There were giant white crustaceans and large green barnacles that had established a complex ecosystem covering the entire bottom of the boat. We even found green-lipped muscles attached inside the safety of the massive growth. We swam the length of the boat with a trowel, peeling off the heavy growth with each pass. As it dislodged and moved lazily down into the turquoise water, fish came from everywhere to partake of a meal. What a joy it was to be back in the clear, warm, tropical water again after three months in the boat-repair yard. Unfortunately the antifouling paint was not well affixed to the bottom and much had also peeled off. The entire bottom of the boat would have to be completely refinished soon.

With only a month left on our visa, we took boatloads of friends sailing in the light winds surrounding the island. The heavy downpour of rain every afternoon in Singapore usually ended our sail. We were finally free from boat work so we could enjoy Singapore's national identity, its world famous cuisine. We enjoyed fresh fruit of every description blended into cool, delicious smoothies. The bird park was our favorite place to visit. Tropical birds of every description from many parts of the world were beautifully housed in enclosures that emulated their home environment. After several days of sightseeing we were ready to sail into Malaysia.

As we entered Malaysia, we sailed north and enjoyed the protected anchorages in small islands along the way. We did not see another boat until we got to the port of Lumut. In Lumut Bay there was a local yacht club that provided floats to tie up to. For a small fee we could leave *Elysium* safely and take the train to Bangkok, where we would meet Steve and his family. At the yacht club there was an old man from England who had been living on his boat for many years. He was very pleasant and agreed to keep an eye on *Elysium* for us while we were gone. With that taken care of, we boarded a Malayan railway train for Bangkok, Thailand.

The train moved slowly through Malaysia and up into Thailand. Our seats changed easily into comfortable sleeping berths at night. As we looked out the train window, the early morning sun caught glints of the small village temples that were elegantly upswept with golden spires along the roofline. The people were just beginning their morning activities, filling water jars as chickens ran along the paths. As we neared Bangkok, the land became heavily populated with crowded huts bordering the track.

When we arrived in Bangkok we found two rooms in a hotel and then took a bus to the airport. Taking a bus in Thailand is an extraordinary experience. No matter how full the bus is, it always stops to pick up the crowds of people waiting at the bus stop. Eventually people are hanging out the front and back ends to let waiting passengers see that there is literally not an inch of room inside.

At the airport we met Steve and his family and decided to take a taxi back to the hotel. They had just arrived from Oregon and we thought that experiencing the crowded bus would be too much for the tired family. Bangkok is very hot in April and a tremendously different climate from the cool, rainy spring in Oregon. We enjoyed our hotel room very much because we had a ceiling fan. Over the next few days we visited the golden Buddha and the Watts (Buddhist temples) while we waited for train tickets back to Lumut. Bangkok is an extremely crowded, busy city so we were glad to be headed back to *Elysium*.

New crew: Raj, Marco, Anjali, and Steve

When we arrived she was waiting for us and we all enjoyed being on the water, where the cool breezes fanned away our fatigue. Everyone was eager to start sailing again. We also received a note from our British friend, Terry, who we sailed with in French Polynesia, saying that she was joining us for the sail north. When she arrived we all set off with a good, strong breeze that lifted the sails and pulled us along gently across the protected water of the Strait of Malacca, heading for the island of Phuket. We stopped at several islands along the way so we never had to be out all night. The Island of Pei Pei was exceptionally welcoming for all of us. The sun shone into the clear, blue-green water, revealing the design the current left on the white sand ocean floor. Brilliant azure blue, black and yellow fish swam around the rocky limestone promontories that surrounded the island.

We donned our snorkels and masks to explore the many caves and accessible rock formations below the water. Further on, I discovered that if I dove down under a rocky ledge, the sun shone in from an opening above, revealing thousands of small fish that had found sanctuary there. As the sun shone on their bodies, they flashed all of the colors of the rainbow. I swam out to bring Raj and Marco inside to see this place of wonder. Raj was frightened to dive down so deeply, as neither of the boys could swim, but Marco was without fear. He had on a mask and snorkel and I warned him to hold his breath until we were inside to see the dance of the fishes.

When we arrived in Phuket we anchored at Patong beach along with many other yachts. All of our crew felt that they were well acquainted with the sailing of *Elysium* and ready to explore the islands to the north on their own. As we left, we made arrangements to meet again Phuket in thirty-five days. Elmer and I returned to Bangkok again to fly to Katmandu, Nepal, where we planned to have a Himalayan adventure.

Nepal, and finally leaving *Elysium*

Let the world change you and you can change the world.

– The Motorcycle Diaries

ARRIVING IN NEPAL, we received our month-long touring visa and found an inexpensive room at the Kathmandu Guest House. In order to prepare ourselves for the altitude we planned to stay in the city for a week and run daily up the one hundred steps to what we called the monkey temple, because it was inundated with monkeys.

We met a young Nepalese man, Madhad, who claimed to be an excellent guide for trekking in the mountains of Nepal. His credentials looked credible so we agreed to have him guide us starting the next week. We spent the remaining week exploring the busy city, particularly appreciating the antique woodcarvings that were the face of each building. The delicate, wood-lace on the window grills and tiny pieces of wood set into place like an inlay adorned even the smallest abode. There was a large public square set aside for activities and we often found jugglers and other people performing with puppets, much to the enjoyment of the local population.

Every day huge carts of cauliflower, peas, and other vegetables arrived in the large, outdoor market. One day we offered a vendor an American dollar to buy peas; he filled a giant bag to the top. Elmer loves raw peas and these were a fresh, bright green and each pod was packed full. As we sat down to stuff ourselves with our prize, a small boy came by and held out his hands begging for a few peas. We had such a large sack-full that Elmer readily handed out a handful. Soon there was a line of small boys several yards back, each waiting for their portion. When they were all fed we only had a few handfuls left for ourselves but we enjoyed the contact with each of the handsome, dark-eyed children. "Imagine children begging for vegetables in the United States," Elmer exclaimed.

We felt ready for the trek as we had built "mountain legs" and learned everything about the deadly aspects of altitude sickness. We were to trek with four young couples that had also hired our guide. The journey began with a bus ride to Pokhara, where we left the bus. After this we walked all day, every day. Our porters easily carried food, water, pots, pans, and tents, while I was feeling the burden of the weight just carrying a camera and a water container.

The last day in Pokhara a small boy had offered me a tasty treat of fried peas, cooked rice, and lentils. I had snacked on it, never thinking about the health warning "never eat or drink anything that you do not see cooking or boiling." Nepal is noted for the gastrointestinal illness that strikes tourists because of the country's abysmal sanitation. We had been warned to be very cautious to avoid what is lightly called the "Kathmandu quickstep." On the second day of the steep climb, my head began to ache and I noticed that my face felt very hot. When it was bedtime, just as we were preparing to sleep, my fever raged to nearly one hundred and four and I felt extremely ill. The porters were outside by the fire singing and beating rhythmically on a drum. Elmer sat down on the floor next to me and said, "You are getting sleepy and going down a deep stairway, down, down, deeper, and deeper." I remember him telling me over and over, as I heard the beat of the drum, that I would feel better and better. As I listened to the rhythm of the song and dance, he said I was getting stronger and feeling really well. He also told me that the next day, when we had the longest climb of one thousand steps, I

Helen and Machapuchere

would become more energetic with each step as I reached the top. He repeated this hypnotic suggestion for several hours. When I awoke at midnight, my fever had broken and I was able to drop into a very deep sleep.

Early the next morning, when I awoke, I felt refreshed and eager to start the climb. As we approached the stone slab steps, I ascended them easily the entire day. Whatever we did worked very well and I had no more problems on the entire trek. As we climbed, we viewed the stunning scenery of the towering snow-encrusted peaks and enjoyed the contact with the local people that lived in the completely isolated high mountain villages. The fishtail shape of Machapuchere followed us along, towering well above the others. In the evening, after climbing all day, our guide would point to another peak saying, "Tomorrow all downhill, the next day all uphill to there." We watched the small, sturdy Gurung men carrying immense, two-hundred pound loads of steel, climbing easily in front of us. When we stopped to rest Elmer went over to try to lift the load. When he gasped at the weight, the men all laughed heartily. Each morning as we emerged from our tents we were served a big breakfast. As we hiked on, we stopped twice again to enjoy

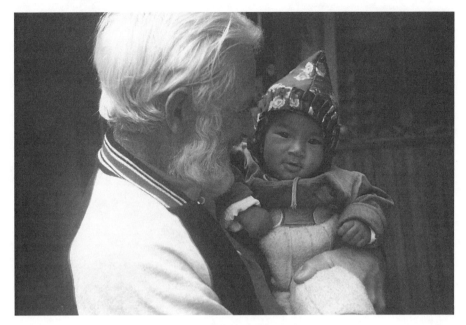

Elmer with Nepalese baby

the hot food and tea our porters served. They carried along all the food we needed to keep us strong and hydrated.

During the trek we were so tired at the end of each day, we were eager to climb into our tent to sleep. In the morning, when the brilliant sunshine lit the sky, we felt rested and the brisk mountain air gave us energy to tackle the next climb or descent. All through the trek to Ghorapani there were no roads, only paths passing by the whitewashed stone houses and terraced fields of growing rice and millet. We continued under dense growths of towering rhododendron whose brilliant red flowers topped the glossy, green leaves as they reached up into the sky. Large trees with white magnolia flowers peeked out from long, lustrous leaves. On our last days we could see the beautiful Annapurna, called the "abode of the Tibetan Goddess" reflected against the pure, deep-blue sky. As we moved through the area, every view was breathtaking. I used every one of the ten rolls of film I brought along. The people of the villages were warm and friendly and made the daily climb even more worthwhile. One night, after we had climbed all day, we sat by the fire in a village. A small boy came over to me and asked in broken English if I had one pencil. His eyes lit up when I pulled one out of my daypack and gave it to him. With only the glow of the fire to see by, he began to industriously write small letters on a piece of paper. It was a small gift to give but it made us all very happy.

After the ten-day climb we walked back to Pokhara where we boarded the bus to return to outskirts of Kathmandu. Unfortunately for our tired legs, there were no buses and we had to walk the four miles back to our guesthouse. Our plan for the rest of our stay in Kathmandu was to visit the Tibetan Buddhist stupa, Boudhanath, where a friend, Arlene Burns, had introduced us to the residing monk, Chokyi Nyima.

The stupa's brilliantly painted white dome is an imposing, three-hundred feet in diameter with all-seeing, painted eyes shining down in a disquieting stare. The clear blue sky was filled with thousands of brightly colored flags that radiated out, hanging on lines from the peak. The Buddhist people see the surge of the wind moving through the flags as prayers. Fortunately, Arlene had drawn a map for us to find the gompa that housed the Tibetan monk. When we arrived, we were directed upstairs to his receiving room. As we entered he called out a cheerful, "Hello," and motioned for us to sit by his side. We told him that Arlene had suggested that we look him up. He asked where we were from and about our travels. We told him that we had been sailing our boat for ten years to appear at this place and at this time. "What were you seeking to travel this far?" he asked. We told him that we had been seeking knowledge about other cultures and were interested in attaining spiritual growth. "I would like to have you come back often so I could teach you about the Buddhist way," he offered. We thanked him and told him we would be happy to come as often as he had time for. He gave us a list of books to read before our next visit. "The bookstore has them all, even one that I wrote," he said.

We had rented bicycles so we visited the bookstore and purchased all of the books he listed before returning to our snug little room at the guesthouse. Three days later we rode our bicycles back to visit him again. This time as we entered the gate, Chokyi Nyima was outside with many other monks. When he saw us he smiled and waved. We walked over to where they were and Chokyi Nyima put his hands on Elmer's

Chokyi Nyima blessing Elmer

head and said to the monks "Here is a great man who has traveled far to learn." Elmer was surprised to receive this admiration. We went inside and had our first audience with him. Some pilgrims who had just made the difficult journey from Tibet interrupted us; they lay flat at the floor and kissed his feet. We both felt uneasy about being in the presence of someone obviously worshipped. "Don't worry," he said, sensing our discomfort, "Each person follows his own belief. You do not need to do this."

We took a few days to use the tickets we had purchased to visit the Chitwan National Park south of Kathmandu near the border of India. We took a long bus ride and arrived in the afternoon. Our accommodations were in an inexpensive little hut built of native grasses. We were puzzled to find so few people staying in the large resort but we had arranged to have an elephant take us into the park. The park houses the last of the rare white rhinoceros and tigers found in Nepal and the safest way to view them is on top of the huge, shambling beasts. Mounting platforms helped us climb aboard and we sat just behind the Phanit, or elephant driver. As soon as we embarked, the Phanit began to drum a constant tattoo with his knees and feet behind the elephants' huge ears. The elephant began its slow, rolling movement and we were soon out in the area where the rhinoceros lived. We were able to get very close to several of them because they cannot see well and only sense that an elephant is going by. We saw one male with a huge rip in his skin from fighting making the skin look as thick as an inch, gaping away from the inner flesh. It was a thrilling experience to be so close to a wild animal in its own environment.

Returning, we were further mystified by the lack of tourists. We had enjoyed our ride so we thought it was best to leave early the next morning. When we got to the bus stop many people were waiting. We were told that there were problems with India and that they had closed their borders. The bus arrived and a man told us we could not board as it was full and there would not be another. Elmer and I pushed the man to one side, jumped onto the bus and hurried down the aisle. There was a huge tire lying on the floor so we both sat down on the rim. The driver looked back at us with exasperation, but finally gave up and started the bus. An hour later a few people left and we found a seat. I don't know what would have happened if we had not forced our way on, because there were no buses after this one. We learned later that native people were felling trees across the road to rob the passengers on buses in the area.

Back in our guesthouse we heard people talking about problems with India stopping all commerce entering Nepal. We did not pay a lot of attention until we rode our bicycles through town and saw policemen with guns and people who had been shot, bleeding lying on the ground. "We'd better get out of here right away" Elmer said. We went back to the guesthouse and called some friends we had met who were stationed in Nepal. "We don't even dare go to town. You should leave as soon as you can," she told us. We checked out of our guesthouse immediately and took a cab to the airport. There was pandemonium all through the building filled with tourists trying to depart. We were lucky to get a flight within two hours and were on our way back to Bangkok! After we left, things became more difficult as Nepal was unable to import gasoline or propane, which were the life's blood of tourism there. We had planned to stay three more weeks to spend time at Boudhanath with

Chokyi Nyima, and now that opportunity was gone forever. When we arrived in Thailand we went to the embassy and renewed our visas to stay another few months there.

We had time to visit Northern Thailand before we were to meet our crew on *Elysium*. Chaing Mai had a notable water festival called Song-kran. The Lonely Planet touring book listed some accommodations and we found that the Chaing Mai Garden Guest House offered exactly what we needed. Calling the number given, Chuckree Senthong answered in English. He told us he would meet the bus in his small, brown car and we should wait until he came and to not be persuaded to take any other vehicle. We assured him we would wait. When we arrived in Chaing Mai, we attracted many taxis with drivers who told us they were sup-posed to pick us up; we could see what Chuckree was talking about. Soon, the little brown car came by with Chuckree at the wheel. As we drove to the guesthouse we asked how he happened to speak such good English, because English is very rare in Thailand. Chuckree told us he and his wife had lived in Miami, Florida, where he earned a degree in agriculture at the University. His wife, Pessamore, had worked for a large hotel handling reservations. When they returned to Thailand he could not find a job in his field so they bought the guesthouse instead. With Pessamore's vast experience and contacts in the hotel field, they had enjoyed a thriving business.

When we arrived, we found the guesthouse was filled with young travelers from all over the world. Inside was a large chalkboard with the names of the guests, room number, and country of origin. Our name was placed on top with Papa and Mama written to the side. The tiny guesthouses with shared bathing facilities, did not appeal to older peo-ple. We particularly enjoyed communicating with the young people, listening to their travel experiences and sharing ours. One young man, Mark Gelband, was especially interesting. He was twenty-four and was a very gifted writer.

We all ventured out each day into the water festival where people splash water on everyone walking down the street. The good natured

Water festival in Chaing Mai

splashing continued all day and night. There was a warning to keep money and passports in plastic bags, because we were soaked just crossing the threshold of the guesthouse.

Mark told us about a special trek that he and some friends were getting together and we decided to join them. They had hired a man named Sonny to guide them up to the border to visit the hill tribe people. These tribes consisted of several distinct cultures of people who subsisted in a no-man's land on the Myanmar (Burma) border. We would be hiking on treacherous dirt trails and staying with people from four different tribes: the Akha, who were Tibetan in origin, the Hmong, from south China, the Karen, from the eastern boarder of Myanmar, and the Lisu people from China and Tibet. These people had all fled difficult conditions in their countries and had established villages, each retaining their own distinct language, dress, and culture. Thailand does not recognize these people as citizens so they had no passports or papers. Tourist facilities did not exist so we would be on our own, trusting Sonny to see us through the entire trip. There were eight young men going and we decided to take a chance and join them.

We took a bus of sorts to the mountain base. From there, we climbed for four miles through bamboo forests that were often on fire. The temperatures rose to one hundred and four degrees, and the fires on either side of us made it even more uncomfortable. The hill tribe's agricultural practice was to slash and burn everything to the ground. The hills where we were trekking would be their next village site when they replanted their crops. As we walked along we saw poppy fields covering a large area. We had heard that these people grew opium as it flourished at this altitude in the spring. After the opium is harvested, corn and oats grow in their place.

Looking ahead we saw some bamboo huts perched precariously on stilts clinging to side of a hill. Sonny told us this was a Karen village and we would stay overnight here. The owner of the hut required a small donation for cooking us a meal and allowing us to sleep on the veranda. After dinner Sonny went over to a mat and lay down. One of the men brought out a long pipe, placed it in his mouth and lit it. This was the first we knew that this trip was also an opium smoking experience for the young men on the trek with us. Elmer and I never liked the idea of taking any type of smoke into our lungs so we declined the offer to try it, as did a young Chinese man from Singapore, named Lee. "I would be hanged if I were to do that at home," he said. The thick blue smoke smelled nauseatingly sweet as it swirled around inside the small room. After several of the young men tried the pipe, we lay down to sleep on the bamboo floor of the veranda. We were given a thin blanket keep out the cool of the high mountain night air. The floor we slept on was made up of many bamboo slats placed a half an inch apart, giving us a view of the earth below. Soon shadowy figures, one after another, appeared below and began retching and vomiting noisily. Evidently, this is an expected aftermath of smoking the pipe!

The next day we journeyed on to observe the Lahu settlement that was further down the mountain. We were able to obtain elephants from our hosts, so we had an easy ride down the very rough terrain. My elephant had a small baby that ran alongside his mom trying for a suck of milk whenever she stopped. The elephant driver smacked him on his backside to keep us going along. The Lahu people had emigrated from

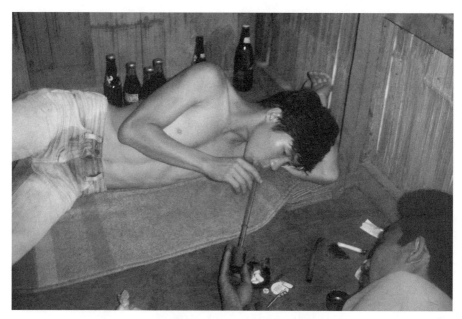

Our guide, Sonny, smoking opium

Tibet and wore brightly colored, hand-woven tunics.

We were now nearing the border where we saw many people emerging from the trees. Sonny did not know what was happening but it was apparent that something important was occurring. Only when we got back to the guesthouse did we find that there had been a major uprising in Myanmar (Burma). The military Junta that ruled the country opened fire on the people protesting the lack of freedom in the government. Thirty thousand people had been killed and many more were wounded. The crowds of people we observed were escaping across the border and running for their lives.

The last region we visited belonged to the Akha people whose colorful dress was made from black, hand-woven material, with shiny, round pieces of silver sewn onto their hats and around their waist. They were the most gregarious of the people and spoke some English so we were able to interact with them. They built their thatched roofed houses high on stilts and bordered them with fences. Under the houses were large crops of garlic hanging thickly from the floor joists. The Akha people also grew opium but used it mainly for medicinal purposes. Because they did not regularly smoke, the people were healthy-looking and actively interested in selling shirts and jewelry to us.

When we left the village, two Thai men came with us. They cut heavy bamboo trees down and wove them together to make two rafts. At a swiftly running river we boarded the rafts to make our way back down to the road home. The trip was very rough but the man guiding the big raft downriver was able to avoid the rocks as we moved swiftly along. We were a bit concerned to see the evidence of several rafts that had gone by the wayside, abandoned and broken beside the river. If we had not gotten to the road on the raft, finding our way through the heavy bush would have been extremely difficult. No one knew where we were and if we disappeared there would have been no trace of us. We were very relieved to arrive where the river pooled and there was some sign of civilization again. We gave our guide a good tip for our safe delivery and headed down a very dusty road to catch a ride back to the guesthouse.

Chuckree and Pessamore drove us around to see many more sights in Chaing Mai. We went to the Elephant Nature Park where elephants are trained to move the gigantic, heavy, teak log piles to load onto barges and be shipped out of the country. We visited a carver who reworked the teak into beautiful furniture inlaid with mother of pearl and precious stones. In the month of May, Chaing Mai becomes extremely warm and the fan in our room barely kept the room cool enough to sleep. We enjoyed the close communication with the group at the guesthouse, but our time was up and we sadly said goodbye to everyone. We exchanged addresses and invited them to come visit us on the boat.

After this adventure we took a bus back to meet with Steve and the family to find out how their sailing experiences had gone. *Elysium* looked beautiful sitting in Phuket. Steve and the family had adjusted easily to the sailing life. We sailed with them back to Lumut where we had mail and a ticket to visit the United States. When we opened our mail we found an invitation to visit Colorado Springs from a good friend who lived there. Colorado Springs sounded so cool and refreshing that we decided we would visit the states. We made a few trips on *Elysium*

with the family and planned to return when they wanted to end their adventure sometime within a year.

None of us realized we would never return, but we understood that through our experiences with the people that we had met, in some way we are connected to everyone. The love and assistance we received from everyone we met in the ten years we spent visiting twenty-five different countries gave us a faith in the future of the world. We discovered our ability to face adversity and achieve success. I particularly learned that there are few things that are unattainable; one needs the will and focus to accomplish what appears impossible.

Epilogue

When Elysium returned to the United States, we had purchased a small ranch in Colorado where we live to this day. We put her up for sale and soon another cruiser was inside, changing her to suit his lifestyle. We received letters from him for a while asking about different things on the boat, but soon lost contact completely. We have adapted to life in the high mountains and raise Hereford cattle and we finally have a big garden and raise our own food.

Looking back, we feel that we have benefited greatly from our experiences. We are happy we chose to sail the world while we were young and strong enough to rise to the challenge. Now we have the wonderful memories of the people we met who touched our hearts. Each individual we encountered broadened our understanding of our connection with each other. When we reached out to others on our travels we encountered the great generous and welcoming spirit people possess all over the world. The governmental policies often send a message of fear and distrust that does not come from people in small towns and villages. We received so much more from these people than we could possible replicate. Now the faces of all of these people stay with us and bring the memories of the love we all shared together.

We have adapted to the mountains and no longer wish to be on the sea. We often relate the story of a sailor that got tired of the sea so he put oars over his shoulders and traveled inland until someone asked him what they were. It took us fifteen hundred miles before we stopped. We are far from our home on the ocean but we have still found wonderful people here in the mountains who are willing to give love and friendship and who are there when we need help.

Walt Whitman spoke to us when he said "Now voyager, sail forth to seek and find."

Our new color drifter that Nan helped us move through customs
Chapter 12 - The Kingdom of Tonga

Elmer in front of Boudhanath stupa in Nepal
Chapter 20 - Nepal, and finally leaving Elysium

Bushman from interior village showing off his newly carved bow and arrow
Chapter 16 - Papua New Guinea

Western dress and ass-grass at the market in Mt. Hagen
Chapter 16 - Papua New Guinea

The caldera anchorage in Garove Island
Chapter 15 - The Solomon Island Chain

Helen and Martha at the Mt. Hagen market
Chapter 16 - Papua New Guinea

Helen doing laundry with the ladies at a fresh water river in the Solomon Islands
Chapter 15 - The Solomon Island Chain

Building the framework of Elysium's hull with bent waterpipe
Chapter 2 - Building Elysium

All the mesh and steel on the hull ready for plastering
Chapter 2 - Building Elysium

The steel pipe in place on top of the cabin
Chapter 2 - Building Elysium

Moving Elysium to water
Chapter 2 - Building Elysium

Helen using the gimbeled stove in the galley
Chapter 2 - Building Elysium

Relaxing in the back cabin while in anchored in Tahiti
Chapter 11 - Coral Reefs and Atolls

Fixing the big hole in Elysium's hull
Chapter 12 - The Kingdom of Tonga

Our Tongan family. Back row: Fuavai, John Tavaki, Beth, Ele, Elmer, Matoto
Front row: John Moa, Helen, Tanganoa, Fineola

Mending the sail in Santa Ana
Chapter 15 - The Solomon Island Chain

Street showers in Tahiti
Elmer with gifted lobster in Tonga

Antonio and family on Parida Island in Panama
Chapter 9 - The Lush Panama Coast

Truck on the road to Jaisalmer, Rajasthan
Chapter 17 - Palau, the Philippines, and India

The luscious fruit in Tonga - watermelon, pineapple, soursop, papaya, mango
Chapter 12 - The Kingdom of Tonga

Bushman and Elmer in Mt. Hagen, Papua New Guinea
Chapter 16 - Papua New Guinea

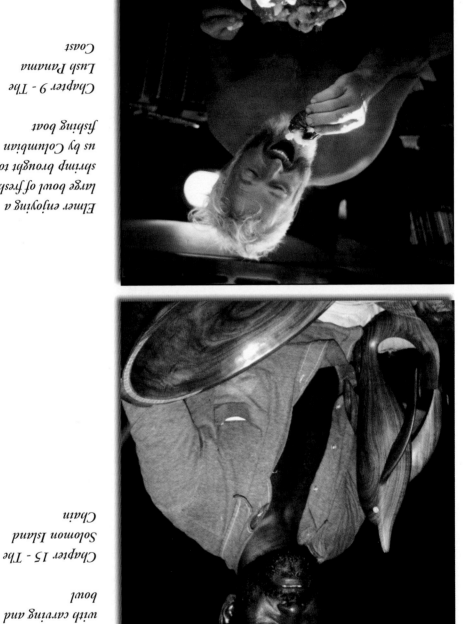

Elmer enjoying a
large bowl of fresh
shrimp brought to
us by Columbian
fishing boat

Chapter 9 - The
Lush Panama
Coast

Penne Sage Kalena
with carving and
bowl

Chapter 15 - The
Solomon Island
Chain

Trappy, the outback tracker who rescues lost people
Chapter 14 - The Tasman Sea to Australia

Our coast watcher friend in Guadalcanal
Chapter 15 - The Solomon Island Chain